LITERATURE AND
YOUNG CHILDREN

NCTE
Committee on Literary Experiences
for Preschool Children

Bernice E. Cullinan, chair
New York University, New York, New York

Carolyn W. Carmichael, associate chair
Kean College, Union, New Jersey

June Byers
Oakland Unified School District, Oakland, California

Joan Glazer
Rhode Island College, Providence, Rhode Island

Susan Hirschman
Greenwillow Books, New York, New York

Sara Lundsteen
University of California, Irvine, California

Ellen Raskin
Author, illustrator, New York, New York

Jessie A. Roderick
University of Maryland, College Park, Maryland

Rudine Sims
University of Massachusetts, Amherst, Massachusetts

Sandra Stroner Sivulich
Mercyhurst College, Erie, Pennsylvania

John Warren Stewig
University of Wisconsin, Milwaukee, Wisconsin

Dorothy S. Strickland
Kean College, Union, New Jersey

LITERATURE AND YOUNG CHILDREN

Bernice E. Cullinan and Carolyn W. Carmichael, editors

National Council of Teachers of English
1111 Kenyon Road, Urbana, Illinois 61801

For Jonathan, a boy who loved books

NCTE Editorial Board: Charles R. Cooper, Evelyn M. Copeland, Donald C. Stewart, Frank Zidonis, Robert F. Hogan, *ex officio*, Paul O'Dea, *ex officio*

Consultant readers: Charlotte S. Huck, Eileen Tway

Staff editor: William Ellet

Book design: Ronald W. Sterkel

NCTE stock number: 29722

Distributed jointly by the National Council of Teachers of English, Urbana, Illinois, and the American Library Association, Chicago, Illinois.

Library of Congress Cataloging in Publication Data

Main entry under title:

Literature and young children.

   Includes index.
   1.   Books and reading for children.   I.   Cullinan, Bernice E.   II.   Carmichael, Carolyn W.   III.   National Council of Teachers of English.
Z1037.A1L56   028.5   77-4870
ISBN 0-8141-2972-2

CONTENTS

Adults responsible for the education of young children differ in their statement of goals and in the approaches used to achieve them, but they share in common the resources with which they apply their differing methods. One resource unequaled in value for accomplishing goals in early childhood programs is literature. Research evidence shows us that experiences provided through literature add measurably to children's store of knowledge, enrich their use of language, and increase their ability to read. Knowledge gained from observation shows us that children who experience literature share a joy unknown to those who do not have literary experiences.

Literature then rightly belongs in early childhood education programs, which have multiplied as research has made clear how critical the learning stages of early childhood are to later development. Such programs include day care, head start, home centers, infant and toddler centers, nursery school, play groups, home-tutoring programs, kindergartens, and various clinic or school sponsored parent-child interaction programs.

"Literary experiences" may unfortunately sound a bit snobbish to some, but there is no other way to encompass the results that the forms and uses of literary materials can effect. The real problem here is the term *literature*. Books are only a part of this resource. Literature, in our understanding of the term, also includes the great oral tradition of the storyteller, whose art must be shared with the young. Films, recordings, slides, television, and other media likewise are literary materials that can each play a role in the enrichment of children's lives. Thus, whatever one wishes to call the resource, it offers many choices, and young children ought to share in all of them. Since young children are seldom able to read by themselves, it is important for adults to make literature a part of children's lives. While the primary assumption of this book is the value of literature for the young, it should be noted that sharing a book with a child not only enriches that child but rewards the adult.

The NCTE Committee on Literary Experiences for Preschool Children is made up of specialists in early childhood education: a reading and language arts consultant, an author and illustrator of children's books, an editor of children's books, a children's librarian, and, of course, teachers. In our professional careers we have seen the effects of good literature on children, and in this book we try to share that experience.

Please note that in the children's book reference lists and in the annotated bibliography of 100 best books for children, we have used the abbreviation *PB* to indicate books also available in paperback. In cases where the hardback and paperback publishers are not the same, the name of the paperback publisher follows the abbreviation.

ACKNOWLEDGMENTS

The editors and the committee gratefully acknowledge permission to reprint the following material:

Atheneum

"Bam, Bam, Bam" by Eve Merriam. Copyright ©1966 by Eve Merriam. From *Catch a Little Rhyme*. Used by permission of Atheneum Publishers and by permission of Eve Merriam c/o International Creative Management.

Thomas Y. Crowell

"Half Asleep" by Aileen Fisher from *My Cat Has Eyes of Sapphire Blue*. Copyright © 1973 by Aileen Fisher. Used by permission of Thomas Y. Crowell Company.

Farrar, Straus & Giroux

"frog" by Valerie Worth. Reprinted with the permission of Farrar, Straus & Giroux, Inc., from *Small Poems* by Valerie Worth, copyright ©1972 by Valerie Worth.

The Feminist Press

Excerpt from *A Train for Jane* by Norma Klein. © 1974, Norma Klein and Miriam Schottland. Reprinted by permission of The Feminist Press, Box 334, Old Westbury, New York.

Harper & Row

"Spring" from *In the Middle of the Trees* by Karla Kuskin. Copyright © 1958 by Karla Kuskin. Reprinted by permission of Harper & Row, Publishers, Inc.

Excerpt from *Chicken Soup with Rice* by Maurice Sendak. Copyright © 1962 by Maurice Sendak. Reprinted by permission of Harper & Row, Publishers, Inc., and by permission of William Collins Sons & Co. Ltd.

"What Is It?" from *A Pocketful of Poems* by Marie Louise Allen. Text copyright © 1957 by Marie Allen Howarth. Reprinted by permission of Harper & Row, Publishers, Inc.

Holt, Rinehart and Winston

"Sunday Morning Lonely" from *Some of the Days of Everett Anderson* by Lucille Clifton. Copyright © 1970 by Lucille Clifton. Reprinted by permission of Holt, Rinehart and Winston, Publishers.

Macmillan

"The Cow" from *The Pack Rat's Day and Other Poems* by Jack Prelutsky. Copyright © 1974 by Jack Prelutsky. Reprinted by permission of Macmillan Publishing Co., Inc.

G. P. Putnam's Sons

"Alike" by Dorothy Aldis. Reprinted by permission of G. P. Putnam's Sons from *Hop, Skip and Jump* by Dorothy Aldis. Copyright 1934, renewed 1961, by Dorothy Aldis.
"On a Snowy Day" by Dorothy Aldis. Reprinted by permission of G. P. Putnam's Sons from *All Together* by Dorothy Aldis. Copyright 1925, 1926, 1927, 1928, 1934, 1939, 1952; renewed.

Random House

"Poem" by Langston Hughes. From *The Dream Keeper and Other Poems* by Langston Hughes. Reprinted by permission of Alfred A. Knopf, Inc.

Simon & Schuster

"Mouse" and "Who Am I?" from *A Little Book of Little Beasts* by Mary Ann Hoberman. Copyright © 1973 by Mary Ann Hoberman. Reprinted by permission of Simon and Schuster, Children's Book Division.

Viking Press

Excerpt from "Home" from *In My Mother's House* by Ann Nolan Clark. Copyright 1941; copyright © renewed 1969 by Ann Nolan Clark. Reprinted by permission of The Viking Press, Inc.

We also thank Barbara S. Thuet for permission to reprint "The Music of Poetry," which first appeared in *Instructor*.

ILLUSTRATIONS

Bernice E. Cullinan

BOOKS IN THE LIFE
OF THE YOUNG CHILD

Books *can* play a significant role in the life of the young child, but the extent to which they do depends entirely upon adults. Adults are responsible for providing books and transmitting the literary heritage contained in nursery rhymes, traditional tales, and great novels. The responsibility lies first with parents but is shared by child care workers, early childhood teachers, pediatric nurses, librarians, television programmers, and all others whose work reaches young children. There is a great store of literature to share with the young, but the wealth could go unused if adults disregard their responsibilities. Adults must sing the songs, say the rhymes, tell the tales, and read the stories to children to make literature and all its benefits central to children's lives.

Literature enriches children's language. The complex process of acquiring language has not been fully explicated despite serious attempts to describe it. What *is* clear, however, is that children are affected by the language they hear and that they gradually learn to approximate the dialect spoken by those around them. Carol Chomsky (1972) examined children's language, specifically, knowledge of complex syntactic structures, in relation to the amount of reading done by them and the amount of reading aloud to them. She found, as others have, that children who are read to and who read more on their own have a greater knowledge of complex language structures than children who read less and are read to less.

Partial explanation for the effect of reading on language acquisition may be that language used in books differs in some ways from the language used in conversation and other kinds of oral discourse. Literary language is more provocative, more complex, and more highly structured; children who read it or hear it reflect the differences in their speech. Language in books also differs from the language children hear on television. Fasick (1973) found the language in children's books to be more complex and richer in syntactic

1

patterns than the language used in children's television programs. Furthermore, television engages the child in a passive way with language, whereas reading books and telling stories engage the child in an active way. Children actively *use* language as they look at books, repeat rhymes, and talk about the pictures. It has been clearly demonstrated (Cullinan, Jaggar, and Strickland, 1974) that active use of language has a far more powerful impact on language development than passive listening.

Children are word collectors. They play with language. They are fascinated by its sounds. When we read to them, we expose them to the beauty of literary language and a wider variety of language forms than they hear in other situations. Children pick up new words and phrases that sound interesting and are fun to say. In their play, they will use a familiar refrain they have heard from a good story, such as "No. No. No. Not by the hair on my chinny chin chin. I'll huff and I'll puff and I'll blow your house in." Children often memorize a particularly melodic word, phrase, or rhyme instantly. In *The Lore and Language of Schoolchildren*, Iona and Peter Opie explain:

> These rhymes are more than playthings to children. They seem to be one of their means of communication with each other. Language is still new to them, and they find difficulty in expressing themselves. When on their own they burst into rhyme, of no recognizable relevancy, as a cover in unexpected situations, to pass off an awkward meeting, to fill a silence, to hide a deeply felt emotion, or in a gasp of excitement. And through these quaint ready-made formulas the ridiculousness of life is underlined, the absurdity of the adult world and their teachers proclaimed, danger and death mocked, and the curiosity of language itself is savoured. (p. 18)

The cumulative impact of hearing stories, incorporating words and phrases into their language, and seeing reading as a desirable and pleasurable activity enriches children's language and leads them to independent reading.

Literature facilitates learning to read. Research findings have documented the commonsense notion that children who are read to learn to read earlier and more easily than children who are not read to. Durkin (1966) found that children who learned to read early had been read to and had had someone who answered their questions. Children who read along with parents or others from their earliest days through the primary school years seldom have difficulty with beginning reading. Children who see important people in their lives reading, who have their questions answered, who are encouraged in paper and pencil activities are not the ones assigned to remedial reading classes. Teaching children to read through a long, gradual induction more nearly parallels the way we teach children to speak. Continual reinforcement and motivation through daily reading and the pointing out of visual similarities in signs, labels, and words teaches children to break the code we use to represent speech. Books for children provide the substance for this teaching process, and they have the added advantage of making reading worth the effort. Any printed material used in this way might teach children to read, but good stories spur them on. Bettelheim (1976) cautions that "the acquisition of skills, including the ability to read, becomes devalued when what one has learned to read adds nothing of importance to one's life" (p. 4).

The very best situation for reading aloud is with the child on the adult's lap with the book in front of both. In learning to read, the child is learning the relationship between oral language and the letters of the alphabet. When children can see the words clearly and follow the story along in the lines of print, they are learning to read. Children who hear a story in a large group usually miss this opportunity. In the case of a large group, volunteer readers can be brought in so that each child can have this individual experience frequently. Cazden (1972) points out the reasons that the individual experience is so important.

> Reading to the young child may be a particularly potent form of language stimulation. As usually done, with the child sitting on the adult's lap, it brings a special relationship of close physical contact, easily shared visual focus, and adult speech about that focus spoken directly into the child's ear. Furthermore, reading aloud is likely to stimulate meaningful conversation about the pictures to which both adult and child are attending. (p. 107)

Literature nourishes the imagination. All aspects of growth in a child are related to one another. As children learn new concepts, their language expands; as they have new experiences, they express themselves in new ways. Developing an imagination and a sense of humor are important aspects of growth sometimes undervalued in the back-to-basics movement, although such areas of development enhance all other areas. Children who experience literature are provided a rich source of ideas for the imagination. Children learn through imaginative play: they pretend they are Mike Mulligan as they push their version of his steam shovel Mary Ann through a sandbox or dirt pile. They acquaint themselves with possibilities as they try out roles from literature.

In *The Uses of Enchantment*, Bettelheim discusses the child's need for magic. He proposes that fairy tales are especially good for young children, because they proceed in a manner which conforms to the way a child thinks and experiences the world. He further describes the way fairy tales offer new dimensions to the child's imagination by suggesting new images with which to structure daydreams. Through daydreams, a child seems to work out unconscious fears and anxieties using the magic of the fairy tale form.

> Like all great art, fairy tales both delight and instruct; their special genius is that they do so in terms which speak directly to children. (p. 53)

We need to nurture children's imagination. Literature provides a rich source for doing it.

Thus, the idea that experiences with literature have a profound effect on children's lives is widely accepted. Sebesta and Iverson (1975) discuss the importance of plain and simple picture books, books of objects to name, series of pictures, and the uncomplicated images of the nursery rhymes, and conclude:

> If you miss this stage with children, something is lost that can never be regained. The idea that pictures can convey reality, that books are windows to the world, must be introduced early and with care. (p. 134)

Young children can have valuable experiences with books if someone reads to them and encourages them to talk about the pictures. These are experiences that develop children's minds, excite their curiosity, and make them interested in reading on their own. Fisher (1962) explains, "What goes in one ear does *not* come out the other. It stays embedded in the memory" (p. 20). There are many reasons for making literature central to the young child's life. Knowledge, laughter, imagination, and understanding can grow from acquaintance with literature. More importantly, literature is part of children's rights.

Current trends in the education of young children. Research findings have established the critical nature of the early years for learning. Patterns begun in early childhood have a lasting influence on children's development. A visible result of the research is the increasing number of young children who are enrolled in a variety of early childhood programs. Many of these children are now introduced to prereading or reading skills for both justifiable and unjustifiable reasons. Encouraged by the fact that some children learn to read at an early age (Durkin, 1966), many have initiated the formal teaching of reading to very young children. Most often these programs focus on decoding skills. However, a major fallacy in basing programs on the early reading studies is that children who learned to read early did *not* do so from exposure to formal reading instruction. Findings show that children who learned to read early were the ones who were read to, who showed interest in paper and pencil activities, and who were interested in visual distinctions in signs and labels. Equally important was the behavior of the adults or older siblings around the children who learned to read early. In the case studies reported by Durkin, an adult or older child always read to the child and answered the child's questions. The children saw other people reading and their families valued reading as an activity. When the child pointed to a street sign or a cereal box label and asked, What does that say?, someone answered the question. Other case studies show that when someone writes down what a child says or the child attempts to write, the child learns that speech sounds can be represented in print. Later, children learn that messages encoded in writing can be decoded, or read, and that letters represent the sounds they use in speaking. The findings make it clear then that learning to read requires the child's involvement in a vast array of experiences with language, both oral and written. Beginning reading programs that provide children with lots of attractive books for looking and listening offer strong motivation for leading children into reading.

A BASIC COLLECTION OF BOOKS FOR YOUNG CHILDREN

A basic collection of good books which can be read to children, handled and looked through by them, and used as a stimulus for other activities is necessary in every early childhood classroom. The books recommended here and in the annotated list at the back of this book have proven to be continually useful in many early childhood programs. More titles should be added each year, but this basic group will provide a good beginning.

Mother Goose and Nursery Rhymes. The beloved old nursery rhymes are an indispensable part of a child's introduction to literature. Humorous incidents and characters are presented in verses with strong rhythm and rhyme to delight the ear. The best editions are sensitively illustrated to enrich children's understanding and appreciation of the old verses.

Favorite collections: de Angeli, *Book of Nursery and Mother Goose Rhymes*; Brooke, *Ring o' Roses*; Briggs, *The Mother Goose Treasury*; Rackham, *Mother Goose Nursery Rhymes*; Rojankovsky, *The Tall Book of Mother Goose*; Watson, *Father Fox's Pennyrhymes*; Wildsmith, *Brian Wildsmith's Mother Goose*. Favorite rhymes illustrated separately: Domanska, *If All the Seas Were One Sea;* Galdone, *The House That Jack Built;* Jeffers, *Three Jovial Huntsmen* (see Fig. 1); Spier, *London Bridge Is Falling Down.*

Fig. 1. Children will search for, and find, the animals the three jovial huntsmen do not see. (Original in color)
From Three Jovial Huntsmen, *adapted and illustrated by Susan Jeffers. Copyright © 1973 by Susan Jeffers. Reprinted by permission of Bradbury Press, Inc., and Hamish Hamilton Children's Books Ltd., London.*

Participation Books for Toddlers. The first books that children handle need to be sturdy so that they will withstand sticky fingers and a toddler's lack of dexterity in turning pages. Books made of cotton fabric, heavy plastic, canvas, or cardboard can provide good early experiences with books. Some books have pictures of single objects in bright colors, some use a game, some contain visual puzzles. The books can be used for pointing, labeling, stimulating language, and just learning how to handle books. Books which invite the active participation of the child while someone reads aloud delight both participants. Some books have flaps to lift up and peek under, soft furry patches to feel, rough sandpaper to touch, and holes to look through or stick a finger through.

Favorite editions: Lewis, *Zoo City*; Munari, *The Birthday Present, The Circus in the Mist*, and *Who's There? Open the Door*; Hoban, *Look Again*; Kunhardt, *Pat the Bunny*; Witte, *Who Lives Here?*; Carle, *The Secret Birthday Message.*

Folk and Fairy Tales. One of the best types of literature to use with young children is the old tale handed down from past generations. The simple plot and predictable ending appeal to children, who are reassured when things turn out right. Outstanding artists have illustrated many of the old favorites in single editions, and a large quantity of these belong on early childhood bookshelves.

Favorite editions: Marcia Brown, *The Three Billy Goats Gruff*; Galdone, *The Gingerbread Boy* and *Little Red Riding Hood*; Hogrogian, *One Fine Day.*

Award Books. Every early childhood center should contain many of the outstanding award books cited each year. One of the most prestigious, the Caldecott Award, is given to the illustrator of the most distinguished picture book for children published in the United States during the preceding year. Although appeal to children is not the basis for the selection, many of the books are favorites. The list below includes winners and honor books.

Favorite editions: Bemelmans, *Madeline*; McCloskey, *Make Way for Ducklings, Blueberries for Sal*, and *One Morning in Maine*; Krauss, *A Very Special House*; Yashima, *Crow Boy* and *Umbrella*; Keats, *The Snowy Day*; Lionni, *Inch by Inch* and *Swimmy*; de Regniers, *May I Bring a Friend?* (illustrated by Montresor); Emberley, *Drummer Hoff.*

ABC Books. Many of the best illustrators have used the alphabet to portray in various ways objects beginning with each letter. Strong, clear colors and familiar objects presented on uncluttered pages seem best to use with young children. Alphabet books have many uses beyond mere recognition of letters or learning the alphabet; they serve as excellent materials for pointing, identifying, categorizing, associating letters and sounds, and just talking.

Favorite editions: Anno, *Anno's Alphabet* (see Fig. 2); Baskin, *Hosie's Alphabet*; Brown, *All Butterflies*; Burningham, *John Burningham's ABC*; Feelings, *Jambo Means Hello*; Munari, *Bruno Munari's ABC*; Wildsmith, *Brian Wildsmith's ABC's.*

Fig. 2. Anno's alphabet looks as if it were carved from wood and the objects chosen to represent each letter are not the usual ones. (Original in color)
Reprinted by permission of Thomas Y. Crowell Company, Inc., from Anno's Alphabet *by Mitsumasa Anno. Copyright © 1974 by Fukuinkan-Shoten.*

Counting Books. Books that develop mathematical concepts, specifically, counting and size of sets, are available with vivid illustrations and photographs. Some present an increasing number of objects with a unifying theme or story, whereas others follow the counting sequence only. Bright, clear illustrations or photographs of easily discernible groups are best for conveying numerical concepts.

Favorite editions: Carle, *The Very Hungry Caterpillar* (see Fig. 3); Feelings, *Moja Means One*; Hoban, *Count and See*; Langstaff, *Over in the Meadow*; Tudor, *1 is One*; Wildsmith, *Brian Wildsmith's 1, 2, 3's.*

Wordless Picture Books. A new format which has become popular with many age groups is the wordless book—a story told entirely through illustrations. The first time through an adult and a child usually look at the book together, discovering the story and telling it to each other. Children "read" these books independently to themselves, to another child, to a scribe, or into a tape recorder many times after they know the story. Needless to say, such books contribute to oral language development, serve as a stimulus for creative storytelling, and develop a sense of story long before a child can read.

Favorite editions: Alexander, *Bobo's Dream*; Carle, *Do You Want to Be My Friend?*; Goodall, *Jacko, Naughty Nancy,* and *Shrewbettina's Birthday*;

Fig. 3. This ravenous caterpillar leaves behind a trail of holes in the food it eats and children will want to count every one. (Original in color) *Reprinted by permission of Wm. Collins+ World Publishing Co., Inc., from* The Very Hungry Caterpillar *by Eric Carle.*

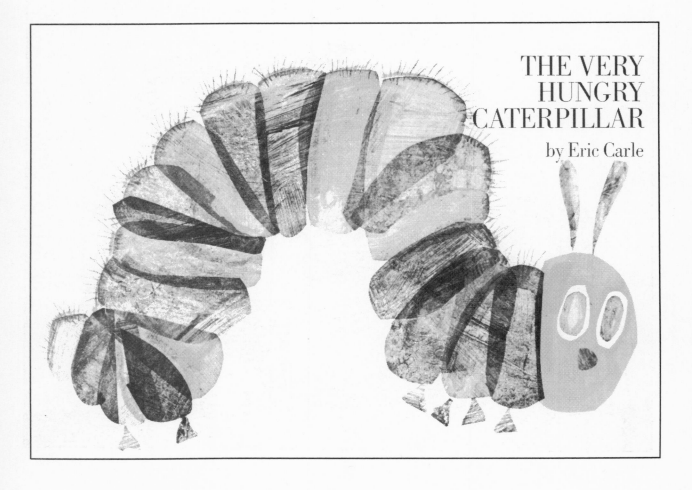

THE VERY HUNGRY CATERPILLAR
by Eric Carle

Hutchins, *Changes, Changes* (see Fig. 4); Mayer, *Frog, Where Are You?* and *Frog Goes to Dinner*; Wezel, *The Good Bird*.

Picture Books. A story told through both text and illustrations requires a reader for at least the first few times through. Children soon memorize the story and often fool observers, for they can recite verbatim what is printed on each page. Young children turn to picture books repeatedly during the pre-school and primary school years. Stories in picture books may be fanciful, realistic, traditional folktales, or ones told in verse.

Favorite editions: Lionni, *Frederick*; Brown, *Goodnight Moon*; Gág, *Millions of Cats*; Krauss, *The Carrot Seed*; Scott, *Sam*; Sendak, *Where the Wild Things Are*; Slobodkina, *Caps for Sale*; Steptoe, *Stevie*.

Concept Books. Some books help children develop concepts and the ability to generalize. Concept books for young children present the dimensions of an abstract idea, such as size or shape. They also include categories of objects, comparisons of words, and other creative ways to define a concept.

Fig. 4. The man and woman change their blocks into a new form each time disaster strikes. (Original in color)
From Changes, Changes *by Pat Hutchins. Copyright © 1971 Pat Hutchins. Reprinted by permission of Macmillan Publishing Co., Inc., and The Bodley Head.*

Favorite editions: Hoban, *Circles, Triangles and Squares*; *Dig, Drill, Dump, Fill*; *Over, Under and Through*; and *Big Ones, Little Ones* (see Fig.5); Pieńkowski, *Shapes*; Domanska, *Spring Is*; Spier, *Fast-Slow, High-Low*.

Informational Books. The best of these books present information on a specific topic which satisfies a child's need to know. Simply presented authentic information is best. Topics in science, math, social studies, and the arts are available.

Favorite editions: Brenner, *Bodies* (see Fig. 6); Cole, *My Puppy Is Born*; Goudey, *Houses from the Sea*; A. Rockwell, *The Toolbox*; H. Rockwell, *My Doctor*; Selsam, *How Kittens Grow*.

Poetry Books. A basic collection of books for young children should include as many books of poetry as the budget will allow. Young children respond to rhythm, rhyme, nonsense, and the sounds of language and will ask for rereading of their favorites often.

Favorite editions: Adoff, *Black is brown is tan*; Ciardi, *You Read to Me, I'll Read to You*; De la Mare, *Peacock Pie*; Fisher, *Cricket in a Thicket*; Kus-

Fig. 5. Concepts of big and little are reinforced by Tana Hoban's photographs of adult and baby animals. *Reprinted by permission of Greenwillow Books from* Big Ones, Little Ones *by Tana Hoban. Copyright © 1976 by Tana Hoban.*

Fig. 6. Children are interested in their own bodies. Barbara Brenner's informational book will help them develop a healthy respect for them.
From Bodies *by Barbara Brenner, with photos by George Ancona. Copyright © 1973 by Barbara Brenner and George Ancona. Reprinted by permission of the publishers, E. P. Dutton & Co., Inc.*

kin, *The Rose on My Cake*; McCord, *Far and Few: Rhymes of the Never Was and Always Is*; Milne, *When We Were Very Young*.

Song Books. Many favorite nursery rhymes and folk songs have been illustrated in single editions. There are also collections of familiar chants and songs that invite happy participation by young children.

Favorite editions: Aliki, *Go Tell Aunt Rhody*; Engvick, *Lullabies and Night Songs*; Larrick, *The Wheels of the Bus Go Round and Round*; Poston, *The Baby's Song Book*; Seeger, *American Folk Songs for Children*; Spier, *The Fox Went Out on a Chilly Night*.

Easy-to-Read or Read Alone Books. Many children will want to try reading on their own and they should have many easy-to-read books available. Authors have restricted the vocabulary, but not the imagination, so their books interest children.

Favorite editions: Lobel, *Frog and Toad Are Friends*, *Frog and Toad Together*, and *Mouse Tales*; Minarik, *Little Bear* and *Little Bear's Friend*; Rockwell, *No More Work*; Dauer, *Bullfrog Grows Up*; Schick, *Neighborhood Knight*; Schulman, *The Big Hello*.

CHILDREN'S BOOK REFERENCES

Mother Goose and Nursery Rhymes

Briggs, Raymond, ed. and illus. *The Mother Goose Treasury.* Coward, 1966.

Brooke, Leslie. *Ring o' Roses.* Warne, 1923.

de Angeli, Marguerite. *Book of Nursery and Mother Goose Rhymes.* Doubleday, 1954.

Domanska, Janina. *If All the Seas Were One Sea.* Macmillan, 1971.

Galdone, Paul. *The House That Jack Built.* McGraw, 1961.

Jeffers, Susan. *Three Jovial Huntsmen: A Mother Goose Rhyme.* Bradbury Press, 1973.

Rackham, Arthur. *Mother Goose Nursery Rhymes.* Viking, 1975.

Rojankovsky, Feodor. *The Tall Book of Mother Goose.* Harper, 1942.

Spier, Peter. *London Bridge Is Falling Down.* Doubleday, 1967. PB.

Watson, Clyde. *Father Fox's Pennyrhymes.* Illus. by Wendy Watson. Crowell, 1971. PB: Scholastic Book Services.

Wildsmith, Brian. *Brian Wildsmith's Mother Goose.* Watts, 1965.

Participation Books

Carle, Eric. *The Secret Birthday Message.* Crowell, 1972.

Cerf, Bennett. *Pop-Up Hide and Seek.* Random House, n.d.

Dunn, Judy. *Things.* Photographs by Phoebe and Tris Dunn. Doubleday, 1968.

Hoban, Tana. *Look Again.* Macmillan, 1971.

Kunhardt, Dorothy. *Pat the Bunny.* Western, 1940, 1962.

Lewis, Stephen. *Zoo City.* Greenwillow, 1976.

Matthiesen, Thomas. *Things to See: A Child's World of Familiar Objects.* Platt and Munk, 1966.

Munari, Bruno. *The Birthday Present.* World Publishing, 1959.

————. *The Circus in the Mist.* Collins-World, 1975.

————. *Who's There? Open the Door!* World Publishing, 1957.

Where's Timmy? A Real Cloth Book. A. Whitman, 1959.

Wildsmith, Brian. *Brian Wildsmith's Puzzles.* Watts, 1970.

Williams, Garth. *Baby's First Book.* Western, 1955.

Witte, Pat, and Eve Witte. *Who Lives Here?* Illus. by Aliki. Western, 1961, 1970.

Folk and Fairy Tales

Aardema, Verna. *Why Mosquitoes Buzz in People's Ears.* Illus. by Leo and Diane Dillon. Dial, 1975.

Asbjørnsen, P. C., and Jorgen E. Moe. *The Three Billy Goats Gruff.* Illus. by Marcia Brown. Harcourt, 1957.

Galdone, Paul, illus. *The Gingerbread Boy.* Seabury, 1975.

Grimm Brothers. *Hansel and Gretel.* Trans. by Charles Scribner, Jr. Illus. by Adrienne Adams. Scribner, 1975.

————. *Little Red Riding Hood.* Illus. by Paul Galdone. McGraw, 1974.

————. *Little Red Riding Hood.* Illus. by Bernadette. World Publishing, 1968.

————. *Rapunzel.* Illus. by Felix Hoffmann. Harcourt, 1961.

Hogrogian, Nonny. *One Fine Day.* Macmillan, 1971. PB.

Perrault, Charles. *Cinderella.* Illus. by Marcia Brown. Scribner, 1954.

Wildsmith, Brian. *Python's Party.* Watts, 1975.

Award Books

Bemelmans, Ludwig. *Madeline.* Viking, 1939. PB.

de Regniers, Beatrice Schenk. *May I Bring a Friend?* Illus. by Beni Montresor. Atheneum, 1964. PB.

Emberley, Barbara. *Drummer Hoff.* Illus. by Ed Emberley. Prentice-Hall, 1967. PB.

Keats, Ezra Jack. *The Snowy Day.* Viking, 1962. PB.

Krauss, Ruth. *A Very Special House.* Illus. by Maurice Sendak. Harper, 1953.

Lionni, Leo. *Inch by Inch.* Astor-Honor, 1962.

————. *Swimmy.* Pantheon, 1963.

McCloskey, Robert. *Blueberries for Sal.* Viking, 1948. PB.

————. *Make Way for Ducklings.* Viking, 1941. PB.

————. *One Morning in Maine.* Viking, 1952. PB.

Yashima, Taro. *Crow Boy.* Viking, 1955. PB.

————. *Umbrella.* Viking, 1958. PB.

ABC Books

Anno, Mitsumasa. *Anno's Alphabet: An Adventure in Imagination.* Crowell, 1975.

Baskin, Leonard, illus. *Hosie's Alphabet.* Words by Tobias Hosea and Lisa Baskin. Viking, 1972.

Brown, Marcia. *All Butterflies.* Scribner, 1974.

Burningham, John. *John Burningham's ABC.* Bobbs-Merrill, 1967.

Feelings, Muriel. *Jambo Means Hello: A Swahili Alphabet Book.* Illus. by Tom Feelings. Dial, 1974.

Munari, Bruno. *Bruno Munari's ABC.* World, 1960.

Wildsmith, Brian. *Brian Wildsmith's ABC's.* Watts, 1963.

Counting Books

Carle, Eric. *The Very Hungry Caterpillar.* Collins-World, 1970.

Feelings, Muriel. *Moja Means One: A Swahili Counting Book.* Illus. by Tom Feelings. Dial, 1971.

Hoban, Tana. *Count and See*. Macmillan, 1972. PB.

Langstaff, John. *Over in the Meadow*. Illus. by Feodor Rojankovsky. Harcourt, 1957. PB.

Pieńkowski, Jan. *Numbers*. Harvey House, 1975.

Tudor, Tasha. *1 is One*. Walck, 1956. PB: Rand McNally.

Wildsmith, Brian. *Brian Wildsmith's 1, 2, 3's*. Watts, 1965.

Wordless Picture Books

Alexander, Martha. *Bobo's Dream*. Dial, 1970. PB: Scholastic Book Services.

Carle, Eric. *Do You Want to Be My Friend?* Crowell, 1971.

Goodall, John S. *Jacko*. Harcourt, 1971.

_____. *Naughty Nancy*. Atheneum, 1975.

_____. *Shrewbettina's Birthday*. Harcourt, 1971.

Hutchins, Pat. *Changes, Changes*. Macmillan, 1971. PB.

Mayer, Mercer. *Frog Goes to Dinner*. Dial, 1974.

_____. *Frog, Where Are You?* Dial, 1969.

Wezel, Peter. *The Good Bird*. Harper, 1964.

Picture Books

Brown, Margaret Wise. *Goodnight Moon*. Illus. by Clement Hurd. Harper, 1947.

Gág, Wanda. *Millions of Cats*. Coward, 1928.

Keats, Ezra Jack. *Louie*. Greenwillow, 1975.

Krauss, Ruth. *The Carrot Seed*. Illus. by Crockett Johnson. Harper, 1945. PB: Scholastic Book Services.

Lionni, Leo. *Frederick*. Pantheon, 1966.

Scott, Ann Herbert. *Sam*. Illus. by Symeon Shimin. McGraw, 1967.

Sendak, Maurice. *Where the Wild Things Are*. Harper, 1963.

Slobodkina, Esphyr. *Caps for Sale*. Addison-Wesley, 1947.

Steptoe, John. *Stevie*. Harper, 1969.

Thomas, Ianthe. *My Street's a Morning Cool Street*. Illus. by Emily A. McCully. Harper, 1976.

Concept Books

Domanska, Janina. *Spring Is*. Greenwillow, 1976.

Hoban, Tana. *Big Ones, Little Ones*. Greenwillow, 1976.

_____. *Circles, Triangles and Squares*. Macmillan, 1974.

_____. *Dig, Drill, Dump, Fill*. Greenwillow, 1975.

_____. *Over, Under and Through*. Macmillan, 1973.

Pieńkowski, Jan. *Shapes*. Harvey House, 1975.

Spier, Peter. *Fast-Slow, High-Low: A Book of Opposites*. Doubleday, 1972.

————. *Gobble, Growl, Grunt*. Doubleday, 1971.

Informational Books

Brenner, Barbara. *Bodies*. Photographs by George Ancona. Dutton, 1973.

Cole, Joanna. *My Puppy Is Born*. Photographs by Jerome Wexler. Morrow, 1973.

Goudey, Alice E. *Houses from the Sea*. Illus. by Adrienne Adams. Scribner, 1959.

Rockwell, Anne. *The Toolbox*. Illus. by Harlow Rockwell. Macmillan, 1971.

Rockwell, Harlow. *My Doctor*. Macmillan, 1973.

————. *My Dentist*. Greenwillow, 1975.

Selsam, Millicent. *How Kittens Grow*. Photographs by Esther Bubley. Four Winds, 1973.

Poetry Books

Adoff, Arnold. *Black is brown is tan*. Illus. by Emily A. McCully. Harper, 1973.

Ciardi, John. *You Read to Me, I'll Read to You*. Illus. by Edward Gorey. Lippincott, 1962.

De la Mare, Walter. *Peacock Pie*. Illus. by Barbara Cooney. Knopf, 1913, 1961.

Fisher, Aileen. *Cricket in a Thicket*. Illus. by Feodor Rojankovsky. Scribner, 1963. PB.

Kuskin, Karla. *The Rose on My Cake*. Harper, 1964.

————. *Near the Window Tree*. Harper, 1975.

McCord, David. *Far and Few: Rhymes of the Never Was and Always Is*. Illus. by Henry B. Kane. Little, 1952. PB: Dell.

Milne, A. A. *When We Were Very Young*. Illus. by E. H. Shepard. Dutton, 1924. PB: Dell.

Song Books

Aliki. *Go Tell Aunt Rhody*. Macmillan, 1974.

Engvick, William, ed. *Lullabies and Night Songs*. Music by Alec Wilder. Illus. by Maurice Sendak. Harper, 1965.

Larrick, Nancy, compiler. *The Wheels of the Bus Go Round and Round: School Bus Songs and Chants*. Illus. by Gene Holtan. Childrens, 1972.

Poston, Elizabeth, compiler and arranger. *The Baby's Song Book*. Illus. by William Stobbs. Crowell, 1972.

Seeger, Ruth, ed. *American Folk Songs for Children*. Illus. by Barbara Cooney. Doubleday, 1948.

Spier, Peter, illus. *The Fox Went Out on a Chilly Night*. Doubleday, 1961. PB.

Easy-to-Read or Read Alone Books

Dauer, Rosamond. *Bullfrog Grows Up*. Illus. by Byron Barton. Greenwillow, 1976.

Hutchins, Pat. *Rosie's Walk*. Macmillan, 1968. PB.

Lobel, Arnold. *Frog and Toad Are Friends*. Harper, 1970.

_____. *Frog and Toad Together*. Harper, 1972.

_____. *Mouse Tales*. Harper, 1972.

Minarik, Else Holmelund. *Little Bear*. Illus. by Maurice Sendak. Harper, 1957.

_____. *Little Bear's Friend*. Illus. by Maurice Sendak. Harper, 1960.

Rockwell, Anne. *No More Work*. Greenwillow, 1976.

Schick, Eleanor. *Neighborhood Knight*. Greenwillow, 1976.

_____. *City Green*. Macmillan, 1974.

Schulman, Janet. *The Big Hello*. Illus. by Lillian Hoban. Greenwillow, 1976.

PROFESSIONAL REFERENCES

Bettelheim, Bruno. *The Uses of Enchantment: The Meaning and Importance of Fairy Tales*. New York: Alfred A. Knopf, 1976.

Cazden, Courtney B. *Child Language and Education*. New York: Holt, Rinehart and Winston, 1972.

Chomsky, Carol. "Stages in Language Development and Reading Exposure." *Harvard Educational Review* 42 (February 1972): 1-33.

Cohen, Dorothy. "The Effect of Literature on Vocabulary and Reading Achievement." *Elementary English* 45 (February 1968): 209-213, 217.

Cullinan, Bernice E., Angela Jaggar, and Dorothy Strickland. "Language Expansion for Black Children in the Primary Grades: A Research Report." *Young Children* 29 (January 1974): 98-112.

Durkin, Dolores. *Children Who Read Early: Two Longitudinal Studies*. New York: Teachers College Press, 1966.

Fasick, Adele M. "Television Language and Book Language." *Elementary English* 50 (January 1973): 125-131.

Fisher, Margery. *Intent Upon Reading: A Critical Appraisal of Modern Fiction for Children*. New York: Franklin Watts, 1962.

Opie, Iona, and Peter Opie. *The Lore and Language of Schoolchildren*. New York: Oxford University Press, 1959.

Sebesta, Sam Leaton, and William J. Iverson. *Literature for Thursday's Child*. Chicago: Science Research Associates, 1975.

John Warren Stewig

ENCOURAGING LANGUAGE GROWTH

Consider the utility of children's literature: it easily serves a variety of purposes. Pure pleasure is a primary purpose, as one author has pointed out (Huck, 1976, pp. 708-711). Understanding of literary form can result when children encounter books (Kingston, 1974). Children's literature can be used to enrich study of academic subjects (Chambers, 1971). It can be used to help children gain understanding of themselves, of others, and of other cultures (Lickteig, 1975). It can even be used didactically to impart a desired value system (Rudman, 1976).

Another purpose, well worth considering, is the impact books can have on children's language growth. Children come to school with an impressive command of language (Dale, 1976). Further development can be encouraged through a planned use of literature for the young. In this chapter we will consider the types of language growth which can occur as a teacher shares books and plans activities designed to enhance young children's speaking and writing abilities.*

No matter at what age boys and girls come to us, we begin with a rich input of oral reading. As we demonstrate our appreciation for books by reading to them, children's interest in participating will grow: oral language in a

---

* "Literature and Young Children: Classroom Approaches," a cassette by the author demonstrating classroom application of techniques discussed in this chapter, is available from NCTE (stock no., 72636).

This is the Cow with the crumpled horn,

That tossed the dog,

That worried the cat,

That killed the rat,

That ate the malt,

That lay in the house that Jack built.

Fig. 7. Discussion following the reading of this tale can help children understand the structure of the cumulative story, and then they can begin writing one of their own. (Original in color)
From The House That Jack Built *by Paul Galdone. Copyright © 1961 by Paul Galdone. Used with permission of McGraw-Hill Book Company.*

variety of forms will result. We read to children for the language input it provides. Whitehead (1968) has reminded us of the benefits of such sharing.

> Teachers who read to boys and girls . . . in the process expose them to the full beauty and flavor of the English language. . . . Indeed children often recognize immediately a particularly melodious, rhythmic, or emotional word or phrase . . . and thousands of such language elements have been memorized instantly by children. (pp. 81 ff.)

Exposure to such words or phrases entices children to say these with the teacher, to "talk-along," for example, with the "hundreds of cats,/Thousands of cats,/Millions and billions and trillions of cats" which Wanda Gág (1928) has given us.

To present these melodious, rhythmic, or emotional words to children most effectively, we need to think about the techniques of reading well. We read to a television generation, children who have absorbed verbal patterns presented by highly trained actors and actresses. The children may not ever have thought consciously about how these performers use the paralinguistic elements of pitch, stress, and juncture to create a character or capture and sustain a mood. Nonetheless, we have a fickle audience sitting in that circle around our feet—what we read must be well done, or we will lose their interest. How do we perfect our skills as readers of literature?

Oral Reading

First, we plan time in our curriculum for oral reading. We read every day and read widely, both from books for children and also from writing by children. Even five minutes a day can result in a vast quantity of literature being shared during the course of one year. For example, if you were to read just one poem a day for an entire school year, your children would encounter about 180 poems, more than most children encounter in the entire time they are in school. If you were to read prose for just five minutes a day, sharing on an average five or six pages each day, imagine how many books children could encounter in a year! Neither of these plans is recommended, for a program of reading must be carefully chosen to include a variety of forms. The figures are given simply to make the point that vast quantities of literature, of whatever form, can be shared with children if the teacher is disciplined enough to do this on a regular basis.

Having set aside time in the curriculum for reading, we then turn our attention to techniques. Of utmost importance is reading the material to ourselves before attempting to share it with children. We can't read *The House That Jack Built* unless we have said the incremental refrain to ourselves enough times so that we don't trip over our tongues. You might use the version of this tale which features Paul Galdone's (1961) appealing illustrations in black-ink line and watercolor wash (see Fig. 7). Another story that needs rehearsal for oral reading is *Drummer Hoff* by Barbara Emberley, with determined woodcut illustrations in intense color by Ed Emberley (see Fig. 8). The book features the rhyming of a gun part with the name of the person who brought it, and each new element is added at the beginning of the next verse. A follow-up activity is to compare and contrast this version with the one using different rhymes included in *The Annotated Mother Goose* (Baring-Gould, 1962, p. 173). Another story which needs a nimble tongue is Ellen Raskin's

Fig. 8. A strong linear quality, reinforced in the original by highly saturated color, dominates the complex illustrations by Ed Emberley for *Drummer Hoff*.
From the book Drummer Hoff *by Emberley and Emberley. © 1967 by Edward R. Emberley and Barbara Emberley. Published by Prentice-Hall, Inc., Englewood Cliffs, New Jersey.*

Ghost in a Four-Room Apartment. In both that book and *Who, Said Sue, Said Whoo?*, the author has created wonderfully wacky characters who deal with improbable situations in strongly written cumulative refrains.

You may wish to share *David He No Fear* or *Every Man Heart Lay Down*, both by Lorenz Graham, for the strong, idiomatic Liberian language they employ. These are retellings of the David and Goliath tale and the story of the birth of Jesus. Neither are easy to read aloud, and both need careful preparation. A different kind of regional language is explored in Edna Preston's *Pop Corn and Ma Goodness.* In it children are exposed to such quasi-archaic forms as *cotch* and *doon* and made-up rhyming words. Ma Goodness goes "a-skippitty, skoppetty" into the story from the first page until the last, tearing breathlessly toward the final recapitulation of all the rhymes presented earlier. Children will find the sound of the words appealing and will join in saying them with the teacher who has prepared the book carefully.

Distinctive language permeates *Black is brown is tan* by Arnold Adoff, a gentle lyric description of life in the Adoff household. Free verse of varying line lengths is characterized by a strong internal rhythm that will introduce children to the poet's theme of prizing differences in people.

We need to explore interesting ways to use our voices, incorporating pitch, stress, and juncture (or pause) to give added emphasis to our reading. The repeated words in *Jay Bird* (Ets, 1974) need variety to hold children's interest. Marie Hall Ets has given us her usual immediately identifiable illustrations, this time in brilliant blue watercolor. She writes about many animals, including:

> A hoptoad croaking
> in the swamp
> croaking, croaking, croaking.

In order to present this effectively, we need to think about ways to use pitch or emphasis to keep the repetitive text moving along.

Delightful humor abounds in *Shaggy Dogs and Spotty Dogs and Shaggy and Spotty Dogs* (Leichman, 1973). The verses, with all sorts of rhyming descriptions and illustrations, create a menagerie of dogs. This is not a tongue twister per se, but it does take rehearsal.

Leichman's book reminds us to make sure when reading to children that we include a sturdy segment of poetry. To prepare poetry for reading, give careful attention not only to pitch and stress, but most importantly to *juncture.* That is, where we make the breaks in poetry will make or break our presentation. The natural tendency is to break at the end of the printed line. In poetry this may lead to artificial segmenting not intended by the poet. For example, consider the following reading in which pauses have been inserted at ends of lines:

> On summer days a rustling tree/
> Could be the sighing of the sea,/
> And waves on any rocky shore/

> Sound like trees bowed down before/
> The wind, Oh, it is hard to say/
> Which is leaves and which is spray.//
> (Aldis, 1963, p. 216)

Such a reading of the poem "Alike" by Dorothy Aldis destroys the strength that poem had when it was written. Yet too frequently we tend to stop where the words do. Read it again, emphasizing the junctures at punctuation marks and ignoring the breaks at line ends.

> On summer days a rustling tree ⌣
> Could be the sighing of the sea,/
> And waves on any rocky shore ⌣
> Sound like trees bowed down before ⌣
> The wind,/Oh,/it is hard to say ⌣
> Which is leaves and which is spray.//

This interpretation evolved after I had spent about a week reading the poem to myself once a day to become familiar with it. Part of being able to read poetry effectively is living with a poem yourself long enough to understand how you want to read it before sharing it with children. Practice reading the poem several different ways, recording it so you can listen to your efforts and decide the best way to read it.

Another poem needing some study is "Godfrey, Gordon, Gustavus Gore" (Rands, 1954, p. 92). To read it well, notice that the breaks at the ends of the lines are the same in verses one, two, three, and five, but the juncture pattern is different in the other verses. The slamming of the door, the wind whistling and roaring, and the alliteration of all those *g*'s intrigue children.

Children As Oral Readers

The purpose of oral reading in the classroom is not only as a pleasurable activity for children in a passive role; with older children, it extends to involving them in reading to the group. This does not mean reading around the circle in reading class but, rather, more expressive creation which occurs when children choose something they like and want to share with others. To make this sharing more effective, the teacher does several things:

1. Brings to a conscious level what children have assimilated unconsciously about effective oral reading. Through discussion, the teacher can draw from children things an effective oral reader does. These may be simply discussed, or they can be formalized in a chart, which can be posted in the room.

2. Helps children select something to read, keeping in mind (a) the child's reading ability and (b) what has been read in class recently. We are trying to ensure as pleasant an experience as possible for all children in the room. If the child has chosen something too difficult, suggest something closer to the appropriate reading level.

3. Provides time for children to rehearse, because, like many of the oral arts, oral reading requires practice. A child needs time alone to

read what he or she has chosen: to manipulate pitch, stress, and juncture in different ways. Children need to experiment using their voices in a variety of sentence contours to bring life to the lifeless word.

4. Provides time for the child to evaluate his or her own work before reading to the group, perhaps by making available a cassette tape recorder. This, plus a quiet space, will result in some helpful evaluation of the reading. Children find listening to themselves as revealing as do adults; the child is sure to find different ways to read the material as a result of using the tape recorder.

Poetry is a logical resource for children to explore using their voices, especially an old favorite like "Over in the Meadow," which appeals to children in the version with lithographs by Feodor Rojankovsky (Langstaff, 1957). Reading to children continues throughout this program, but other components are equally important. As we read to young children, they will begin to say some of the repeated lines with us. The magic of the words draws children into participating; then is the time to begin choral reading.

Choral Reading

What is choral reading, and why should it be part of a literature-based oral language program? Whether it's called choral speaking or choral reading is unimportant. What is crucial is that children encounter the joys of interpreting poetry orally in a group. Both terms refer to children, either in unison or divided into some sort of grouping, saying together a piece of poetry they enjoy. A rich diet of poetry as part of the oral reading program is one of the best ways to establish interest in, and to continue developing enthusiasm for, the art of choral speaking.

The kindergarten teacher, in reading many poems to children, will discover them repeating some of the words or even a phrase or two. The teacher encourages this, but participation at this level remains simple. Groups may enjoy saying rhymes together, perhaps some from Mother Goose. Your children will enjoy the version by Brian Wildsmith (1964): sensuous color and bold design qualities make this a sophisticated treatment to delight the eye. In marked contrast is Tasha Tudor's (1944) version, which will appeal to children, for whom Tudor's introspective and intimate interpretaion seems just right. If it seems appropriate, the teacher may help nursery and kindergarten children learn to say poems chorally, but formal work in choral speaking is more logically a concern of the primary and intermediate grades.

May Hill Arbuthnot (1964, pp. 220-246; there is a newer edition of this book, but it does not include the chapter on choral speaking) has pointed out that older children may be divided into many types of groupings for choral reading: unison, refrain and chorus, dialogue or antiphonal, line-a-child, or solo voices with choir. Any teacher with a good poetry anthology will find poems of use, but some are suggested here in case you have never tried locating poetry for this purpose. For unison reading with any age child, try "Indian Summer" by Campbell (1968, p. 92). For refrain and chorus, the repeated

Fig. 9. Use these goblins to further visual sensitivity by comparing and contrasting them to those in Sendak's *Where the Wild Things Are* (see Fig. 30) and Mayer's *One Monster After Another.*
Illustration by Joel Schick from The Gobble-Uns'll Git You Ef You Don't Watch Out! *by James Whitcomb Riley. Illustrations copyright © 1975 by Pongid Productions. Reproduced by permission of J. B. Lippincott Company.*

line "Lawd, Lawd, Lawd" in the poem "Grey Goose" (1967, p. 122) can be especially effective. For dialogue or antiphonal reading, try "The Blind Man and the Elephant" by Saxe (1969, p. 73). For line-a-child reading, use the poem "Two Friends" by Ignatow (1961, p. 59). Finally, use the William Blake poem "Introduction" (1956, p. 38) for solo voice with choir. Have the choir read the descriptive material and one child read the dialogue.

As a composer decides which instrument will play a specific part in a musical score, so the teacher will need to decide—at least at the beginning—which children will say what lines. It is important to emphasize that the teacher will do this as children *begin*; soon children will have ideas about how the poem should be divided. The teacher ought to encourage these ideas and take time to try out the variety of ways children suggest.

Teacher and children alike may find it helpful to go through the poem and mark it so they will remember *how* they want to read it once a favorite way is agreed upon. A rudimentary system of marking can be developed to indicate a slight pause, a complete stop, a continuation of the voice so a thought is carried over to the next line, a heavy stress on a word, and a lighter stress on a word.

How do we begin choral speaking? Try reading "Five Little Pussy Cats," from *Mittens for Kittens* (Blegvad, 1974, p. 27). It's a bit of whimsy calculated to draw children into saying the short poems with you. Much alliteration, assonance, and repetition are found in poems included by Hoberman in *Nuts to You and Nuts to Me*, an alphabet of poems very useful for choral speaking. Kepes's book *Run Little Monkeys, Run, Run, Run* is also a helpful source of poems to speak chorally. This story of some tenacious leopards who pursue elusive monkeys is a favorite of children. The refrain in the title is repeated throughout the poem, and children will enjoy helping you tell the story by saying it with you.

With slightly older children, use poems in *Amelia Mixed the Mustard* (Ness, 1975). "The Adventures of Isabelle" (p. 22), the pugnacious girl who turns the tables on a bear and a witch, is well suited to saying in unison. "Jumping Joan" (p. 32) with its refrain, "One-ery, two-ery, ziccary, zac," is equally useful. With second and third grade children, try using *The Gobble-Uns'll Git You Ef You Don't Watch Out!* (Riley, 1975; see Fig. 9). This is a version of James Whitcomb Riley's well-known, but now largely neglected poem "Little Orphant Annie." The poem is one of several recommended by Hartley (1972) in an article containing valuable suggestions for ways to involve children with literature. Finally, don't miss an old favorite, *"I Can't" Said the Ant* by Cameron (see Fig. 10). This rhyming story of an accident in the kitchen entrances children, who like to say such lines as "'How bleak,' said the leak" and "'Give them time,' said the lime."

Adding Sounds to Words

Many poems which can be used for choral speaking lend themselves to the creation of verbal obbligatos. The term *obbligato*, borrowed from music, means a persistent background motif, usually a repeated theme played by an instrument against the major melody. In the case of choral reading, it means having some children in your group repeat at patterned intervals words or sounds that heighten the mood of the poem or evoke an image more clearly. For example, in "Trains" by James Tippett (1976, p. 51), part of the children may repeat the words *clickety-clack* in some rhythm they have created as the rest of the children say the poem. The teacher may have one group of children with high voices repeat the *clickety-clack* in one rhythm, while another group with lower-pitched voices repeats the same words in a different rhythm. This provides a background for a third group that says the poem. Another poem which lends itself readily to this technique is "The Cat's Tea Party" by Frederick Weatherly (1968, p. 119). Experimenting with *mew, meow,* and

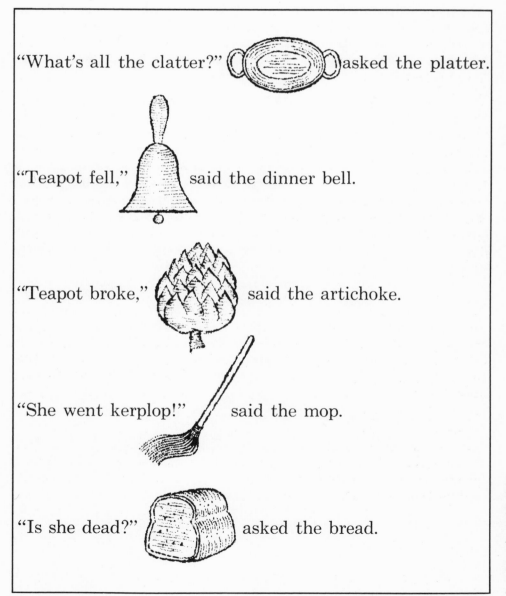

"What's all the clatter?"　　　asked the platter.

"Teapot fell,"　　　said the dinner bell.

"Teapot broke,"　　　said the artichoke.

"She went kerplop!"　　　said the mop.

"Is she dead?"　　　asked the bread.

Fig. 10. Clever use of rhyming words helps move along the rescue of Miss Teapot by the ant and his friends. (Original in color) *Reprinted by permission of Coward, McCann & Geoghegan, Inc., from "I Can't" Said the Ant by Polly Cameron. Copyright © 1961 by Polly Cameron.*

other cat sounds said in different pitches and rhythms can result in a very rich obbligato background.

A more involved background is necessary for Eleanor Farjeon's poem "Three Little Puffins" (1976, p. 74), which mentions panting, puffing, chewing, and chuffing, all in one poem. Children enter with enthusiasm into planning this intriguing collection of sounds as they vary rhythm and pitch to create an obbligato for the poem. A fine new opportunity is provided by Ed Emberley in *Klippity Klop.* It's a variation of the bear hunt plot used by so many preschool teachers as a participation story. The variety of possible background sounds includes *klippity klop, klippity klop; klumpity, klumpity; kwish, kwish; klick, klick;* and *kaarraaggaahh.*

No teacher interested in choral speaking with older children will want to miss the challenge in "Jabberwocky" by Lewis Carroll (1965, pp. 148-49). There are all manner of beasts: toves, mome raths, borogroves, jubjub birds, and, of course, the fearsome Jabberwocky. Children have created fantastic obbligatos of much complexity as they imagine rhythmic sounds for each of the animals included.

This kind of experience in sound emphasizes using a piece of poetry as a departure point for a complete creative expression. Certainly the same careful attention must be given to the basic reading of the poem as in simple choral speaking, but beyond that children are free to improvise as imaginative a group of sounds as they can. Mention should be made of the valuable uses a tape recorder can serve. As children create their obbligatos, the teacher captures the sounds on tape. After the children have done the poem one way, they may listen to it, reflect upon it, and discuss it. When they do this, new ways to do the piece will occur to them. Someone will suggest adding something, another person will suggest deleting something, and yet another may feel altering some part of the total poetry experience would help. As children reshape, listen, and reshape again, the piece moves from its tentative beginnings to a finished choral sound experience.

One of the most challenging oral-language experiences for children is putting together sounds or music and the spoken word in a poetry tape. A description of this activity is available in an article by Thuet (1971). This approach involves children in selecting a poem and preparing it as a finished product:

1. The child selects a poem he likes.
2. He plans the sound or music background for it. If using music, the goal is to get some piece which intensifies the mood of the poem. The thing to be avoided is the type of ubiquitous sounds which surround us in restaurants and elevators everywhere today.
3. The child records his sounds or music. Children can take cassette to the sound, if it is not present in the classroom. He might want a ticking clock, perhaps for use in the Eugene Field poem, "The Gingham Dog and the Callico Cat." If he uses records for background, he can dub the sound on the cassette tape.
4. The child practices the poem, varying the three paralinguistic elements of pitch, stress, and juncture, until he achieves an interpretation which satisfies him.

5. He makes the final tape, using a second recorder. As he plays the back-
    ground on one tape, the child reads the poem aloud and the two are recorded
    on the other tape.

(p. 83)

The procedure is within the capabilities of intermediate grade children. You
will need to demonstrate the procedure first and then supervise the actual
recording with children. Practice in reading the poems and recording the
background sounds can be on an independent basis as children have time. In
addition to recordings of music, the teacher may want to explore the possibility of obtaining some sound effects records. Many of these are available,
and the cost is no more than that of regular records. One would be a good
addition to the school library.

As the poems most frequently will be short, several can be put on one
tape. Children can listen to the poems when they have free time. Intermediate
grade children also enjoy having an opportunity to present their finished
poetry tapes to younger children. Such a session of sharing is rewarding for
both groups.

Words Set to Music

Related to choral reading is the involvement possible when you share the
fine participation songs available in book form. If you don't know the version
of *The Twelve Days of Christmas* illustrated by Ilonka Karasz, you would
find it worth locating. The simple pastel illustrations, done in a folk art style
with many repeated decorative patterns, are more appealing than flossier
commercial versions we've been subjected to recently. This particular verse-
song is now also available with pictures by Jack Kent (1973). Kent has
created a determined, pint-size suitor who doffs his hat to a tiny compatriot
before deluging her to the point of despair with gifts that threaten to push her
off the edge of the page.

Less seasonal, and therefore of greater usefulness, is the old song *Go
Tell Aunt Rhody*, with illustrations by Aliki. The rhyme and repetition can be
said or sung. Robert Quackenbush has done full-color illustrations contained
within intense black-ink line for two such songs, *Skip to My Lou* (1975) and
Clementine (1974). John Langstaff (1974) has dressed the old song *Oh,
A-Hunting We Will Go* in fresh crayon drawings arranged above the verses.
For a long time children have responded to the humor in such lines as "the
bear in his underwear"; "the whale in a pail"; "the snake in a cake"; and "the
pig in a wig." These are too funny to miss; do share them with your children.

Storytelling

Any description of a literature-based oral language curriculum for young
children must include attention to storytelling. The ultimate purpose in telling
stories is the same as that of oral reading: the teacher is trying to establish
in children's minds that oral activities are worth the time and concern of an
adult. The final goal is to motivate children so they will want to tell stories.

To accomplish this, the teacher provides a model, and in the case of story-telling this involves learning and telling stories to the children.

The first step is to choose a story which you like—one which captures your imagination. Read through several stories, and then set the project aside. After a while, one or two of them will come back to you. You should probably learn one of these.

There are three basic steps in preparing the story. The first is to divide the story into *units of action*. As you read any story, you will notice that most divide into an easily definable series of actions or episodes; these can be summarized in brief form, and then the sequence can be learned. This procedure will, for most people, prove a more efficient way of learning the story than simply trying to begin at the beginning and memorize to the end. The second task is to identify those sections which do need to be memorized verbatim. This may include some words, some repeated phrases, or perhaps some larger sections. A discerning storyteller learns verbatim these repeated sections, because the repetition encourages children to join in as the teller recites the lines. We retain these elements as they are in the story, because to eliminate them is to destroy some of the essence of the story.

These elements also offer insights into the variation possible in stories. For example, the mirror's response in *Snow White and the Seven Dwarfs* varies considerably. In the version translated by Paul Heins (Grimm Brothers, 1974), we find the mirror responds to the evil queen's question of who is the fairest in this way:

> Lady Queen, you are the most beautiful here,
> But Snow White beyond the mountains
> With the seven dwarfs
> Is still a thousand times more beautiful than you.

Children respond positively to the gothic illustrations by Trina Schart Hyman in this version. They also like Nancy Ekholm Burkert's formal paintings for the translation by Randall Jarrell (Grimm Brothers, 1972). In this version the mirror responds:

> Queen, thou art the fairest that I see,
> But over the hills, where the seven dwarfs dwell,
> Snow White is alive and well,
> And there is none so fair as she.

Finally, children should experience the version entitled "Snowdrop" (Rackham, 1973, pp. 7-16) with Arthur Rackham's original illustrations, recently reissued by Viking Press. Here, the mirror responds:

> Queen, thou art fairest here, I hold,
> But Snowdrop over the fells,
> Who with the seven Dwarfs dwells,
> Is fairer still a thousandfold.
>
> (p. 11)

Many traditional tales include such elements as these, necessary to the very essence of the story but usually brief and thus not difficult to learn.

The task of memorizing a story in its entirety is formidable, especially today when demands for more "practical" activities press upon us. The delightful thing about storytelling is that few stories need to be memorized. Most stories are more interesting to listener and teller alike if the teller learns the essence of the story and allows it to unfold in a slightly different way each time he or she tells it. Once units of action are identified, these can be learned in an easy conversational tone, using any words which come to you. It is simple enough to learn the units of action. Write them on index cards and carry them around with you. Then each time you have a few minutes, you can review the action and the sequence of the units. Using a procedure like this, I find it usually takes me about three or four days to learn a story.

An additional way to enhance the story is to use simple gestures when appropriate. Some authors recommend subordination of gestures because of their feeling that storytelling must not become drama. Despite this opinion, judicious use of some gestures can enhance a story. Such gestures must not obscure the story or become intrusive, but certainly each individual can use good judgment in this matter. Gestures can enhance a presentation, but they must be geared to the age group, probably being only a minimal part of storytelling for older children, who are apt to be self-conscious about body movement.

Children As Storytellers

While storytelling is a pleasant activity which serves the useful purpose of exposing children to a wealth of literature they might not otherwise encounter, regular storytelling serves another purpose. Children see the teacher as a storyteller and this demonstrates for them that storytelling is an acceptable and pleasurable activity for adults.

The teacher's goal is to encourage children to begin telling their own stories. As the kindergarten teacher fosters talk during share-and-tell periods, he or she is encouraging spontaneous oral composition. When children are allowed to tell short stories, which often will be only two to six sentences in length at the beginning, the groundwork for more formal storytelling activities is being prepared. An interesting way to begin is to use one of the many books with pictures but no printed story line. Those by Mercer Mayer are particularly helpful in eliciting stories. You might like to use *A Boy, a Dog, and a Frog* or *Frog, Where Are You?* (see Fig. 11). Another possibility is *The Elephant's Visit* (Barner, 1975). The book features large, blob-like characters and their responses to an elephant whose visit causes all sorts of problems. A unique feature of the book is the color combinations in the illustrations. *The Chicken's Child* (Hartelius, 1975) is equally useful as a stimulus for storytelling by children. What happens after the hen hatches an alligator who grows at a frighteningly rapid rate provokes interesting story creation by children. Another wordless book worth using is *Little Mops and the Butterfly* (Elzbieta, 1974). Against a very understated, precise black line background of mechanical evenness, Little Mops pursues a series of gentle encounters. Children enjoy retelling this story as they translate it from a visual to an oral mode.

In using such wordless picture books, the teacher shares the book with children, asking questions and drawing comments from the group as they look at it together. Later, the children create a group story, dictating it to the teacher, or the children may tell their individual stories into a cassette tape recorder. These cassette tapes can be added to the listening station so that they can be shared.

In addition to using wordless books to stimulate storytelling, try using modern fiction to stimulate story writing. After children hear *A Ghost Story* by Bill Martin, they can dictate or write their own version of this highly patterned story full of rhythm and repetition. Each verse of this story interlocks with the next one, and children can take the basic pattern and use it to make a new story. After hearing Martin's story, which involves dark doings in a frightening place, one child wrote:

> Over a bright, bright woods there is a bright, bright sun,
> Under a long, long bridge there is a long, long river,
> In a slippery, slippery fish there is a slippery, slippery minnow.

The child has used the pattern to create a new story of his own. Similar use may be made of Mayer's *One Monster After Another.* The circular tale begins with Sally Ann calmly writing to Lucy Jane and ends with her remaining calmly oblivious of the perils endangering her letter. In between, the author gives us repetition, e.g., "The official mailman opened the official mailbox,"

Fig. 11. Each picture in books by Mercer Mayer provides many objects for children to observe and describe.
Illustration excerpted from Frog, Where Are You? *by Mercer Mayer. Copyright © 1969 by Mercer Mayer. Reprinted by permission of The Dial Press.*

and lots of interesting names, e.g., the Letter-Eating Bombanat and the Paper-Munching Yallappappus.

Story Variations

The last two books mentioned are modern stories sure to appeal to the young child. But in sharing literature, we ought to be conscious of balance in the selections. Thus, folk literature must not be neglected. In kindergarten, children can understand that today stories are usually written down in books, while years ago stories were simply told, handed down from teller to teller. It is important to develop the idea that oral stories existed long before people could write and that each teller made slight changes. This insight helps children understand the process of story creation. Using a variety of folktales and discussing similarities and differences is therefore a useful experience.

One might use the story of the Gingerbread Boy. One version is "The Pancake," taken from a collection of Norse tales originally published in 1874 and included in *The Arbuthnot Anthology of Children's Literature* (1976, p. 238). An interesting feature is the rhyming names the pancake gives each animal it encounters, e.g., Henny Penny. These names form a cumulative refrain children enjoy saying with the teller. In *The Bun* by Marcia Brown much specific detail, like the hen wing sweeper and the sour cream in the bun, contribute to the Russian flavor of the story. Virginia Haviland includes another version, "The Wee Bannock," in *Favorite Fairy Tales Told in Scotland* (pp. 13-24). In this version the bannock (a flat oatmeal or barley cake usually baked on a griddle) encounters a human, in contrast to other versions featuring animals. Vocabulary in this version is particularly interesting; children hear such words as *breeks* (britches), *spindle, distaff, anvil*, and *peat*. Barbara Ireson's *The Gingerbread Man* is illustrated with bold, somewhat raffish pictures that make effective use of heavy black line. The repeated refrain is different than in other versions. Finally, Ruth Sawyer's *Journey Cake, Ho!* is an extended version by a master storyteller and includes monochromatic pictures full of rural details. The refrains are in rhyme, and the ending is quite different than in most versions.

Parallel Plot Construction

One kindergarten teacher devised an initial writing experience called parallel plot construction. To begin, this teacher uses several of these versions of the Gingerbread Boy. She reads these to children on successive days, initiating informal discussion about the stories. Children are helped to note similarities and differences and are encouraged to tell which version they like best and why. After this preparation, the children create their own version of the story. A class once decided to make the runaway a hamburger from a well-known national chain of drive-ins. The hamburger rolled out of the shop and eluded a policeman, a mailman, some shoppers, and a deliveryman before rolling into the school. There it avoided the principal, the secretary, and the janitor while rolling down the hall. Unfortunately, it rolled into the kindergarten and was there devoured by the children.

Second grade children who had listened to their teacher read "The Pancake" wrote the following stories. One follows quite closely the pattern in the original story; the other shows more variation. In both, there is rich detail and a commendable attempt at writing conversation. A boy wrote the following story:

> Once there was a peach that was growing on a tree. One day a man came along and said, "I want that peach." When the peach heard that, he got down and ran as fast as he could. Soon he met a man, and the man said, "Stop, stop!" But the peach rolled along. Soon it met a boy. The boy said, "Stop, stop!" But the peach rolled along. Soon it met a girl. The girl said, "Stop, stop!" But the peach rolled on and on. Soon it came to a pig. The pig said, "I'll get you away from them." So they ran away into the woods. Soon they came to a stream. The pig said, "I'll take you across. Hop on my nose." All of a sudden the peach was gone. He had been eaten. (Stewig, 1975, pp. 121-122)

A girl wrote this story:

> Once upon a time I bought a pack of football cards. The gum jumped out. I started to chase the gum. I ran out the door. I slipped on the edge of the door. He got away. He ran to a hen. The hen said, "Stop, I want to eat you." So the hen chased the gum. Then he ran to a cat. The cat said, "Stop, I want to eat you." "I didn't stop for the hen, and I won't stop for you." Then he ran to a cow. The cow said, "Stop, I want to eat you." The gum said, "Well, I didn't stop for the hen, and I won't stop for you." So the cow started to chase the gum. He ran to a dog. The dog said, "Stop, I want to eat you." The gum said, "Well, I didn't stop for the hen and the cow, so I won't stop for you." Then he ran to a farm. The farmer was feeding the horses outside. He ran to catch the gum. The horses ran away. The man said, "Stop. I won't eat you." The gum slipped, and the farmer caught him. He shared the gum with the others. (p. 122)

A third grade child wrote the following version in which the personified food didn't need to run away.

> Once there was a poor old lady. She said to herself, "Why shouldn't I have a little snack of oranges?" So she took out an orange. All of a sudden the orange said, "Why don't you eat another orange? How would you like to be eaten?" and with that the orange bit her nose, and that was that! From then on the lady knew better than to eat a smart orange. (p. 123)

Other possibilities for story dictating or writing include a version of Perrault's *Puss in Boots*, with illustrations by Barry Wilkinson (1969). Jewel-toned opulent colors evoke the setting of France in the 17th century in this story, which can be compared and contrasted with other versions. Harve Zemach has given us *Nail Soup*, a Swedish version of the stone soup tale, which can also be used for parallel plot construction. This version is useful for the contrast it provides with Willis Lindquist's retelling of *Stone Soup*. Any of these three would be useful for a session on parallel plot construction.

Children probably stay strictly with parallel plot construction very briefly. Before long they are experimenting, building upon the basic plot line. But they should be helped to see that there is nothing wrong in borrowing a kernel idea, or plot structure, from a story they have already heard. Rather, they should be encouraged to take an idea and make it uniquely their own. Great composers have for hundreds of years borrowed themes and motifs from earlier composers. The same is true of writers and of painters. If such is the case with mature, productive professionals in the arts and if such a technique facilitates the writing process, why should we be afraid to let children build on a plot they have already heard?

Plot Completion

Many teachers make use of the idea of *plot completion*, that is, reading a story but stopping before the end so children are motivated to finish it. The technique works with children at all age levels. Almost any story can be read to a crucial point in the action and stopped so children can finish the action in their own way. Old familiar folktales, as well as modern stories, can be used this way.

One teacher used *Little Red Riding Hood* with third grade children, reading it to the point at which Little Red discovers that the wolf, instead of Grandmother, is in the bedroom. To encourage her children in problem-solving abilities, the teacher asked the children: "How else could the story end?" Though the children knew the traditional ending, they had no difficulty in solving the problem other ways. Among the stories they wrote were these:

> Little Red Riding Hood came out of the cottage. Then she bumped into a fisherman going to a lake. Then the wolf began to run away. Grandmother could feel the wolf's heart go thump, thump. She could also feel the wolf's ribs, veins, and bones. The fisherman knew just what to do. He got his fishing pole, and threw it. The hook caught the wolf and stopped him. Grandmother walked out. And they had goodies for lunch. (Stewig, 1975, pp. 124-25)

> Little Red Riding Hood came screaming out of the cottage, yelling: "Wolf, wolf!" She met the forest ranger, and said, "Oh Mr. Forest Ranger, please help me." "O.K." he said. They went to the cottage and found the wolf lying on the floor. Two minutes later Grandmother popped out of the wolf's mouth. "How did you do it, Grandmother?" asked Red. "I took karate when I was nineteen, and just socked it to him," said Grandmother. (p. 125)

> Little Red Riding Hood ran out of the woods. She ran and ran. She ran about a mile. Then she jumped up in a tree. The wolf couldn't get her. She jumped to another tree, and then another. Her grandmother sure didn't feel well. Then right by the last tree was a little cliff. Little Red Riding Hood jumped on. The wolf climbed up after her. At the top of the cliff Little Red Riding Hood met a hunter. She asked him to kill the wolf, and he did. Then they went to the cottage. They cut open the wolf. The wolf had jumped so much that grandmother had jumped out a long time ago. She came in, and they all ate. And they gave the wolf skin to grandmother. (p. 125)

Another plot completion possibility is *Swimmy* by Leo Lionni, an engaging story of an adventuresome little fish. The story shows Swimmy's ability as a capable problem solver, despite his small size. Read the story to the point at which he declares something must be done about the marauding tuna. Then have children write their own solutions to this problem. Provide an opportunity when the writing is finished for children to share their stories orally, and then read Lionni's ending. When a group of third grade children heard the story, they wrote these solutions:

> Then Swimmy thought of an idea. They could find a huge clam shell and hide in it. They could keep it half open and peek. (Stewig, 1975, p. 126)

"I have it," said the youngest fish. "Let's go to the president of the fish. He is right over there at that boat." So they went. They held a fish conference. The president said, "We will build a sub that will have radar, and we'll go to the flying fish that will bomb the big fish with octopus fluids." It worked, so they had a party. (pp. 126-27)

Swimmy said, "I got it." Then he swam away. Meanwhile the red fish looked puzzled. Swimmy went to the eel and asked, "Will you come and protect us?" The eel answered, "Yes." Then he went to the lobster and asked, "Will you come and protect us?" The lobster answered, "Yes." Then Swimmy went back, and the fish started to swim. On the way they met the big red fish. All of a sudden, the eel came and hit the big fish with his tail. Then came the lobster and punched the big fish to death. And the little fish swam freely. (p. 127)

Becoming the Character

A teacher of first graders tried a plot rewriting technique. After reading a version of *Cinderella*, the teacher encouraged those who were interested to retell the story as though they were one of the characters. Children told their stories into a cassette recorder. These were transcribed by the teacher's aide into typed form and were used as the basis for many pleasant sharing sessions. One child told the story as if she were the main character:

I am Cinderella, dressed in rags. I live with my stepmother and stepsisters. I sleep on ashes by the fireplace. I have to clean the house every day.

The Prince was giving a ball. My mother wouldn't let me go to the ball. Then I had an idea. I asked my hazel tree. Of course it was magic, and so was the mourning dove.

First I had to curl up my hair in a bun. Then I asked for a pretty dress and some slippers. Then I was almost ready for the ball.

I danced with a handsome prince. He said he wouldn't let anyone else dance with me, so I danced with him until the clock struck midnight. Then I had to go, but I said to myself, "I'll see that prince again," and I did see him again.

One night I lost my slipper, and the prince found it. He searched and searched, and finally he came to the last house. He tried the slipper on both stepsisters, but it didn't fit. Finally he came to *me*. That slipper was mine, and then it happened. I was his bride. I lived with him in the castle, and the dove, and we lived happily ever after. (Stewig, 1975, pp. 75-76)

To motivate the retelling of this tale, you might use the version published by H. Z. Walck (Perrault, 1971). Very earthy-looking characters populate this version. Cinderella is pretty but not ravishing; she contrasts nicely with the corpulent, ugly sisters. Errol Le Cain (Perrault, 1973) has given us a beautiful, somewhat stylized Cinderella. Her sisters are wonderful *New Yorker*-esque caricatures who vie for our attention with the prince, who seems almost to disappear under his rich robes. For the language contrast it provides, use John Forbes's version (1974). The contemporary British idiom used may not appeal to you, but the book is a useful tool for thinking about language differences.

A teacher of third grade children tried the same plot rewriting technique using *Snow White and the Seven Dwarfs*. One child wrote her story as if she were the good queen.

One day I was sewing at the window, and I pricked my finger. It dripped three drops of blood. The snow was white, but then it was red. I was thinking of having a girl with black hair, rosy cheeks, and white skin. Then I did have a baby, and the baby had black hair, rosy cheeks and white skin. I love my baby. I think she's the loveliest girl in the world.

But now I am very sick. I think I'm going to die. I hope my baby is going to have a nice life. (p. 77)

Another child assumed the role of the huntsman.

I went to the forest, and Snowdrop was running about twelve feet ahead of me. We were entering the woods, and I took my knife in a hard grasp. Snowdrop was by a tree, and I threw my knife. I missed. I just couldn't do it. I told her to go off into the forest. She went. A fawn leaped into my path. This time I took my sword and stabbed the fawn. It was bloody murder. I brought back the lung and liver. The queen ordered me to take it to the cook to be pickled. I was glad that bloody mess was over. (p. 78)

These stories illustrate one of the strengths of first-person narration: it is more direct, because it is the character him or herself talking. Children find the challenge of thinking as one of the characters might to be a rewarding language experience.

Summary

This chapter is a summary, an outline, and a forecast. It is a summary of ideas that teachers have found work with children. It is an outline of a literature-based language program that puts a heavy emphasis on developing children's oral skills. Finally, it is a forecast of what you, a classroom teacher, can do with your group of children to expose them to the wealth of books which is their heritage. For many of the children with whom we work, the time they spend with us may well represent their only intense submersion in the excitement and challenge of literature. Such is the task—may some of these books and ideas help you begin.

CHILDREN'S BOOK REFERENCES

Adoff, Arnold. *Black is brown is tan.* Illus. by Emily A. McCully. Harper, 1973.

Aldis, Dorothy. "Alike" in *The Reading of Poetry.* Ed. by William Sheldon et al. Allyn and Bacon, 1963.

Aliki. *Go Tell Aunt Rhody.* Macmillan, 1974.

Baring-Gould, William S., and Ceil Baring-Gould, eds. *The Annotated Mother Goose.* Bramhall House, 1962. PB: New American Library.

Barner, Bob. *The Elephant's Visit.* Little, 1975.

Blake, William. "Introduction" in *This Way Delight.* Ed. by Sir Herbert Edward Read. Illus. by Juliet Kepes. Pantheon, 1956.

Blegvad, Lenore. *Mittens for Kittens.* Atheneum, 1974.

Brown, Marcia. *The Bun: A Tale from Russia.* Harcourt, 1972.

Cameron, Polly. *"I Can't" Said the Ant.* Coward, 1961.

Campbell, Wilfred. "Indian Summer" in *The Wind Has Wings*. Ed. by Mary A. Downie and Barbara Robertson. Illus. by Elizabeth Cleaver. Walck, 1968.

Carroll, Lewis. "Jabberwocky" in *The Golden Journey: Poems for Young People*. Ed. by Louise Bogan and William J. Smith. Illus. by Fritz Kredel. Reilly and Lee, 1965.

Elzbieta. *Little Mops and the Butterfly*. Doubleday, 1974.

Emberley, Barbara. *Drummer Hoff*. Illus. by Ed Emberley. Prentice-Hall, 1967. PB.

Emberley, Ed. *Klippity Klop*. Little, 1974.

Ets, Marie Hall. *Jay Bird*. Viking, 1974.

Farjeon, Eleanor. "Three Little Puffins" in *The Arbuthnot Anthology of Children's Literature*. 4th ed. Comp. by May Hill Arbuthnot. Lothrop, 1976.

Forbes, John. *Cinderella*. Jonathan Cape, 1974.

Gág, Wanda. *Millions of Cats*. Coward, 1928.

Galdone, Paul. *The House That Jack Built*. McGraw, 1961.

Graham, Lorenz. *David He No Fear*. Illus. by Ann Grifalconi. Crowell, 1971.

_____. *Every Man Heart Lay Down*. Illus. by Colleen Browning. Crowell, 1970.

"Grey Goose" in *Reflections on a Gift of Watermelon Pickle and Other Modern Verse*. Ed. by Stephen Dunning, Edward Lueders, and Hugh Smith. Lothrop, 1967.

Grimm Brothers. *Snow White*. Trans. by Paul Heins. Illus. by Trina Schart Hyman. Little, 1974.

_____. *Snow White and the Seven Dwarfs*. Trans. by Randall Jarrell. Illus. by Nancy Ekholm Burkert. Farrar, 1972.

Hartelius, Margaret A. *The Chicken's Child*. Doubleday, 1975.

Hoberman, Mary Ann. *Nuts to You and Nuts to Me: An Alphabet of Poems*. Illus. by Ronni Solbert. Knopf, 1974.

Ignatow, David. "Two Friends" in *Some Haystacks Don't Even Have Any Needle and Other Complete Modern Poems*. Ed. by Stephen Dunning, Edward Lueders, and Hugh Smith. Scott, Foresman, 1961.

Ireson, Barbara. *The Gingerbread Man*. Norton, 1963.

Karasz, Ilonka. *The Twelve Days of Christmas*. Harper, 1949.

Kent, Jack. *The Twelve Days of Christmas*. Parents, 1973.

Kepes, Juliet. *Run Little Monkeys, Run, Run, Run*. Pantheon, 1974.

Langstaff, John. *Oh, A-Hunting We Will Go*. Illus. by Nancy Winslow Parker. Atheneum, 1974.

_____. *Over in the Meadow*. Illus. by Feodor Rojankovsky. Harcourt, 1957. PB.

Leichman, Seymour. *Shaggy Dogs and Spotty Dogs and Shaggy and Spotty Dogs*. Harcourt, 1973.

Lindquist, Willis. *Stone Soup*. Western, 1970.

Lionni, Leo. *Swimmy*. Pantheon, 1963.

Martin, Bill. *A Ghost Story*. Holt, 1970.

Mayer, Mercer. *A Boy, a Dog, and a Frog*. Dial, 1967.

————. *Frog, Where Are You?* Dial, 1969.

————. *One Monster After Another.* Western, 1974.

Ness, Evaline. *Amelia Mixed the Mustard.* Scribner, 1975.

"The Pancake" in *The Arbuthnot Anthology of Children's Literature.* 4th ed. Comp. by May Hill Arbuthnot. Lothrop, 1976.

Perrault, Charles. *Cinderella.* Illus. by Errol Le Cain. Bradbury Press, 1973.

————. *Cinderella.* Illus. by Shirley Hughes. Walck, 1971.

Preston, Edna Mitchell. *Pop Corn and Ma Goodness.* Illus. by Robert Andrew Parker. Viking, 1969. PB.

Quackenbush, Robert. *Clementine.* Lippincott, 1974.

————. *Skip to My Lou.* Lippincott, 1975.

Rackham, Arthur, illus. "Snowdrop" in *Grimm's Fairy Tales: Twenty Stories.* Viking, 1973.

Rands, William. "Godfrey, Gordon, Gustavus Gore" in *First Book of Poetry.* Ed. by Isabel Peterson. Illus. by Kathleen Elgin. Watts, 1954.

Raskin, Ellen. *Ghost in a Four-Room Apartment.* Atheneum, 1969.

————. *Who, Said Sue, Said Whoo?* Atheneum, 1973.

Riley, James Whitcomb. *The Gobble-Uns'll Git You Ef You Don't Watch Out!* Illus. by Joel Schick. Lippincott, 1975.

Sawyer, Ruth. *Journey Cake, Ho!* Viking, 1953. PB.

Saxe, John G. "The Blind Man and the Elephant" in *Hold Fast to Dreams.* Ed. by Arna Bontemps. Follett, 1969.

Tippett, James. "Trains" in *The Arbuthnot Anthology of Children's Literature.* 4th ed. Comp. by May Hill Arbuthnot. Lothrop, 1976.

Tudor, Tasha. *Mother Goose.* Walck, 1944.

Weatherly, Frederick. "The Cat's Tea Party" in *Time for Poetry.* Rev. ed. Comp. by May Hill Arbuthnot and Shelton L. Root, Jr. Scott, Foresman, 1968.

"The Wee Bannock" in *Favorite Fairy Tales Told in Scotland.* Ed. by Virginia Haviland. Illus. by Adrienne Adams. Little, 1963.

Wildsmith, Brian. *Brian Wildsmith's Mother Goose.* Watts, 1964.

Wilkinson, Barry. *Puss in Boots.* World Publishing, 1969.

Zemach, Harve. *Nail Soup.* Illus. by Margot Zemach. Follett, 1964.

PROFESSIONAL REFERENCES

Arbuthnot, May Hill. *Children and Books.* Chicago: Scott, Foresman, 1964.

Chambers, Dewey W. *Children's Literature in the Curriculum.* Chicago: Rand McNally, 1971.

Dale, Phillip S. *Language Development.* New York: Holt, Rinehart and Winston, 1976.

Hartley, Ruth. "Poetry for Boys in the Primary Grades." *Elementary English* 49 (December 1972): 1153-1157.

Huck, Charlotte S. *Children's Literature in the Elementary School.* 3rd ed. New York: Holt, Rinehart and Winston, 1976.

Kingston, Carolyn T. *The Tragic Mode in Children's Literature.* New York: Teachers College Press, 1974.

Lickteig, Mary J. *An Introduction to Children's Literature.* Columbus, Ohio: Charles E. Merrill, 1975.

Rudman, Masha Kabakow. *Children's Literature: An Issues Approach.* Lexington, Mass.: D. C. Heath, 1976.

Stewig, John Warren. *Read to Write: Using Children's Literature as a Springboard to Writing.* New York: Hawthorn Books, 1975.

Thuet, Barbara S. "The Music of Poetry." *Instructor* 80 (April 1971): 83.

Whitehead, Robert. *Children's Literature: Strategies of Teaching.* Englewood Cliffs, N.J.: Prentice-Hall, 1968.

Dorothy S. Strickland

PROMOTING LANGUAGE AND CONCEPT DEVELOPMENT

Leland B. Jacobs's question, "Literature is beautiful language, and who among us does not want children to get the beauty of their mother tongue at its best?" (1966, p. 6), calls to mind the vast potential for helping children explore language through books. By exposing children to a rich variety of language models, we help them sense some of the infinite possibilities for experimenting with their own language. As we offer them books, we provide models and through experimentation children increase their ability to use language effectively.

It is only through the active *use* of language that its growth is fostered. Therefore, children must be given many opportunities to use language. Speech should be encouraged rather than discouraged, and planned activities for oral language development must be a part of every day. Books can be a tremendous asset in planning such language-learning experiences. Verbal activities which extend literary offerings provide excellent opportunities for children to use language. As young children listen to stories and poems and respond to them in a variety of ways, they are developing skill in both the receptive and expressive oral language processes. As they use literature as a resource for organizing and integrating information and for extending their imaginative powers, children develop in their ability to think. Finally, as children explore abstract ideas through books, they are helped to organize their world and expand their conceptual awareness.

Group discussion, creative dramatics, listening activities, storytelling, and puppetry can be stimulated through literature and can make the literary experience richer, as well as promote language development. It is the teacher's responsibility to make the most effective use of books as a natural means to the development of language and thought in the young child. This chapter offers a number of suggestions for achieving that goal.

Extending Language Awareness

As "beautiful language," literature can stimulate children to more imaginative uses of their own speech. A skillful teacher can help very young children explore the figurative language in picture storybooks and children's poetry without ever mentioning such terms as simile or metaphor. In the process, children begin to develop a sensitivity to language and the power of words to convey sensory images.

Obviously, the younger the child the less capable he or she is to deal with the abstractions in figurative language. For that reason young children respond to fewer and simpler figures of speech. It is probably true, however, that young children who are rarely exposed to figurative language will have considerable difficulty understanding it even when they have reached a sufficient level of maturity to do so. There is a need, then, for children to hear different forms of language, to play and experiment *with* language before they can be expected to talk *about* language.

As you read aloud to children, be alert to passages that are good examples of imaginative uses of language. At times you may wish to reread these and discuss them with the children. For example, in *White Snow, Bright Snow* Alvin Tresselt uses figurative language to delight the child's imagination.

> Automobiles looked like big fat raisins buried in snowdrifts. Houses crouched together, their windows peeking out under great white eyebrows. (p. 20)

By rereading such passages and pausing a moment to savor the words, teachers help to heighten the young child's sensitivity to the magic authors and poets perform with words.

After having had many experiences of this type, children can be expected to enjoy focusing on imaginative language and combining it with oral language and graphic expression in the following way. Children may close their eyes as you read a passage or poem that contains a considerable amount of visual imagery. A poem such as Dorothy Aldis's "Snow" is best used on a day when children have actually experienced walking and playing in the snow.

> The fenceposts wear marshmallow hats
> On a snowy day;
> Bushes in their nightgowns
> Are kneeling down to pray —
> And all the trees have silver skirts
> And want to dance away.

Read the poem a second or third time, asking the children to "paint" pictures in their minds of the things the words tell about. Ask questions such as: What kind of a day is it in your picture? How do the bushes look? Why are they "kneeling down"? How do the trees look in your picture? What makes them have "silver skirts"? After children open their eyes, have them tell about the pictures they painted in their minds. While children are sharing, they may wish to close their eyes again in order to help recall their mental images. Encourage the use of "describing words" related to color, shape, and size. Use questions to probe and extend the children's descriptions and to get at greater detail. As children talk about their mental images, any misconceptions related to the figurative language can be clarified. After the "pictures in their heads" have been shared, children may draw or paint their impressions of the poem or passage.

When planning activities such as the one just described, avoid selections that are outside of the children's experience. Asking children to paint mental pictures of a poem about snow would be unsuitable in a climate where it never snows. It is impossible to understand figurative language without a thorough knowledge of the referent the writer has in mind.

In the same way that writing can stimulate visual imagery in children, it can excite other senses through the use of interesting language. Young children delight in the sounds of the language found in picture storybooks. The sound of the rain drops as they fall on Momo's umbrella in Taro Yashima's story *Umbrella* is one passage that youngsters love to say and have read over and over again.

> Bon polo
> bon polo
> ponpolo ponpolo
> ponpolo ponpolo
> bolo bolo ponpolo
> bolo bolo ponpolo
> boto boto ponpolo
> boto boto ponpolo

Ann Grifalconi's book *City Rhythms* is full of exciting sounds that intrigue children. After listening to and discussing this book, children can be encouraged to think about the many words in our language that help describe the sounds we hear. Ask what words are used to describe the sound of a bell ringing, a glass breaking, a drummer drumming, a horn blowing, a dog barking, a cat meowing, and so on. Children will enjoy actually making various sounds with objects while others try to think of words to describe what they hear. As they engage in these activities, children increase their listening skills and extend their vocabularies. Equally important, they are learning more about how language is used to describe actual experience.

Repetition in stories and poems also appeals to the auditory sense and to the imaginations of young children. When reading books that contain repetition, encourage the children to join in on the repetitive verses or phrases. Repeat the selection as often as time and interest allow. In this way children can thoroughly enjoy active participation in the reading. Use Wanda Gág's *Millions of Cats* ("Hundreds of cats,/Thousands of cats,/Millions and billions and trillions of cats.") or Esphyr Slobodkina's *Caps for Sale* ("Caps for sale. Caps for sale. Fifty cents a cap.") or Arnold Adoff's *Black is brown is tan*

this is the way it is for us   this is the way we are

Fig. 12. Children like to repeat phrases after hearing them read aloud. (Original in color)
Illustration by Emily Arnold McCully from Black is brown is tan *by Arnold Adoff. Text copyright ©
1973 by Arnold Adoff. Pictures copyright © 1973 by Emily Arnold McCully. Reprinted by permission of
Harper & Row, Publishers, Inc.*

("Black is brown is tan/is girl is boy/is nose is face/is all the colors/of the race.").

Help children explore how language is used to describe the ways things taste, feel, and smell by pointing up examples where authors and poets do this so expertly. You can talk about Robert's feelings in *Stevie* (Steptoe, 1969) after Stevie has gone.

> We used to have some good times together. I think he liked my momma better than his own, cause he used to call his mother "Mother" and he called my momma "Mommy." Aw, no! I let my corn flakes get soggy thinkin' about him.

Or laugh together as you try to repeat Jack Prelutsky's "The Cow" in *The Pack Rat's Day*:

> The cow mainly moos as she chooses to moo
> and she chooses to moo as she chooses.
> She furthermore chews as she chooses to chew
> and she chooses to chew as she muses.
> If she chooses to moo she may moo to amuse
> or may moo just to moo as she chooses.
> If she chooses to chew she may moo as she chews
> or may chew just to chew as she muses.

In each case use the book as a catalyst for language development by providing opportunities for children to relate the language to their own experiences and by helping them to match those experiences with expressive words. Bring in items to taste, touch, and smell, encouraging children to verbalize the sensory experiences they are having. Later, specific vocabulary related to the sensory mode under discussion may be listed orally as well as on charts if this seems appropriate.

Developing Listening Skills*

Books can be used to help develop listening skills that range from perception of sound (acuity) and discrimination between sounds to comprehension of what the sounds mean. Much of the content of children's listening comes from nature (bird songs, thunder), from artificial objects (horns, drums, whistles), and from other people (family, acquaintances, and television or radio). Children have heard language used many ways: in the normal transactions of life, in self-expressive epithets (*ouch*—or worse), in scientific discourse ("the temperature will fall to a few degrees below zero tonight"), and in persuasive discourse ("Drink your milk. It's good for you."). But children may not have had much chance to listen to the literary use of language. Books are excellent vehicles for developing listening skills in addition to their many other values. But how? What are some teaching strategies and specific books that work?

Listening games are a natural outgrowth of reading some books, such as May Garelick's *Sounds of a Summer Night* or Paul Showers' *The Listening*

*The section on listening was prepared by Sara Lundsteen, University of California, Irvine.

Walk. Children listen for or make the sounds they hear in the stories. Listening for sequence is needed in Pat Hutchins' *The Surprise Party* and *Don't Forget the Bacon.* Cumulative tales are favorites with young children and develop some skills associated with learning sequence of events. Paul Galdone's *The House That Jack Built* is one of the most popular; Nonny Hogrogian's *One Fine Day* (see Fig. 13) and Galdone's *The Gingerbread Boy* are also favorites. The familiar telephone game amply illustrates how a message not listened to closely can be passed on and garbled with amusing or disastrous results. In Doris Orgel's *The Uproar,* for instance, a child thinks his mother said she was going to the uproar rather than the opera.

Discriminating between sounds is a spontaneous response to some books. Peter Spier's *Crash, Bang, Boom* and *Gobble, Growl, Grunt* use sounds as a means of identification. Both books lead children to join in noisily and to distinguish among the sounds they hear. Florence P. Heide's

Fig. 13. The fox, who wants his tail sewn back in place, repeats the sequence of events at each stop in this cumulative tale. (Original in color)
From One Fine Day *by Nonny Hogrogian. Reprinted by permission of Macmillan Publishing Co., Inc., and Hamish Hamilton Children's Books Ltd., London. Copyright © Nonny Hogrogian 1971.*

Sound of Sunshine, Sound of Rain portrays a blind boy using sound to find a friend. Margaret Wise Brown's Noisy Book series calls attention to the variety of sounds heard in different locales. Byrd Baylor's *Plink, Plink, Plink* speculates on what sounds seem like at night, and Helen Borten's *Do You Hear What I Hear?* increases attentiveness to various sounds.

Higher level skills of listening comprehension can also be enhanced through books. Charlotte Steiner's *Listen to My Seashell* explores the concept of sound. Lois Kaufman's *What's That Noise?* encourages children to think intelligently about new and frightening experiences. Roger Duvoisin's *Petunia, I Love You* builds on inferences and hypothesizing about outcomes: Raccoon tries to trap Petunia so he can eat her, and concerned listeners will want to warn her. Arnold Lobel's *Owl at Home*, an easy-to-read book, causes children to make inferences about the bumps in Owl's bed and why his tear-water tea tastes salty. Many listening skills are learned during story time without detracting from the primary objective of enjoying a good story.

Stimulating Group Discussion

Talking over a story read aloud is an opportunity for children to extend a shared experience. Because both children and teacher share the same reference, problems of confusion and misunderstanding can be handled with greater effectiveness than when a child shares ideas or events unknown to everyone else. Group discussion allows the teacher to help children relate the events in a story to their personal lives as they talk over the actual events of the story.

Discussion is most commonly used as a follow-up activity to reading aloud. Although this is a highly desirable way of eliciting oral language from children, teachers must not feel compelled to follow every reading with a discussion. Nor should planned follow-up discussion preclude very brief discussion at some points during the course of the reading when it is necessary to clarify or extend an idea.

Using Good Questions

Questions have always been a primary tool of the teacher. The careful framing of questions during discussion can help promote understanding and appreciation of a story and provide the basis for still other activities to follow. Through effective questioning, teachers can lead pupils into all kinds of thinking operations. Low quality questions center on isolated bits of knowledge and are usually designed to "test" what has been learned or remembered. High quality questions help turn the discussion into a problem-solving situation. Research indicates that the kinds of responses we get from children will depend in large measure upon the kinds of questions we ask of them. To put it simply, good questions evoke good answers.

The strong relationship between teacher questions and children's answers can be used to improve the quality of class discussion. For example, when framing questions, teachers might keep in mind the level of comprehension their questions are likely to produce. Three categories of reading comprehension that teacher questions lead to are literal comprehension, interpretation, and critical reading. Whether children are listening to the written word or reading for themselves, teachers can help expand children's understanding by asking for more than factual, or literal, comprehension. Interpretation, however, requires mental activities involved in supplying or anticipating meanings not stated directly in the text. Critical reading or listening goes farther, although it necessarily includes both: the reader or listener must evaluate and confer personal judgment on what is read.

A comparison of possible questions to be used following the story *Where the Wild Things Are* by Maurice Sendak illustrates the levels of questions. The story is about Max, who is sent to bed without supper for his unruly behavior and dreams of a fearless encounter with some marvelously comic, yet grotesque, creatures. Consider the following questions and the kinds of responses they would elicit from children.

Why was Max sent to bed? (literal)

What kinds of things do you think Max did to make his mother call him a wild thing? (interpretive)

The first question merely requires a two- or three-word response based on memory. The second requires the child to take known information and make inferences from it.

What kinds of things did the wild things do? (literal)

Pretend you are a wild thing. Show how you would look and how you would move about. (interpretive)

Ability to answer the first question depends totally on the child's capacity to recall information. Although the second question requires that same ability, it is extended and applied. In this case the child must apply his or her knowledge to another form of expression, that of movement and pantomime. More important, there is no one "right" way to move or look like a wild thing. Each child has an opportunity to share his or her unique impression of the events in the story. Divergent questions promote divergent responses.

How does the story end? (literal)

Think of another ending for this story. Which do you like best? Tell why. (critical)

The second question allows children to bring their own opinions and ideas to the discussion. It gives them an opportunity to thoughtfully recall and weigh various factors in the story and make a response based on their own judgment of the situation. Asking them to tell why elicits the criteria on which their judgment is based.

Group discussion is effective in helping children use books to deepen understanding of themselves and others. The use of higher level questions can assist children in relating characters and events to their own personal lives. Ann Herbert Scott's picture storybook *Sam* is excellent for this purpose. The story dramatizes the universal childhood experience of a youngster who seeks someone in his family to play with and finds himself a nuisance at every turn. A discussion might begin with the events of the story itself and gradually move toward helping children express their feelings of identification with Sam as they center more directly on their own personal experiences. Questions such as these may be used:

Characters and events in the story:

Do you think Sam's family meant to be mean to him? How can you tell?

Can you think of anything that Sam could have done to make himself feel better?

Can you think of anything else his family could have done to make him feel better?

Identification with characters and events in the story:

When have you ever felt the way Sam did in the story?

Did anyone help you to feel better? How?

What did you do to make yourself feel better?

How does it feel when someone takes something of yours that is very special to you (as Sam's sister and brother felt)?

Note that the final question requires the child to identify with the "other" person in the story and relate to *that* person's feelings in a given situation. As the discussion proceeds, encourage children to use the vocabulary associated with feelings and emotions. Such words as *angry, sad, mean, bad, terrible*, and *lonely* should be recognized as words that help tell others how we feel.

From Questioning to Creative Dramatics

After a discussion of this type, children can move into a more active mode of expression. Creative dramatics can further extend children's understanding of a story and help them to vent aroused feelings. In this instance literal questions can be very useful in laying the framework for the action. Without this framework, the dramatization is likely to be unsuccessful, since children must be thoroughly familiar with a story before they are asked to act it out.

Have the children recall the events of the story by asking if they remember what Sam did first, second, and so on. As they review the story in this way, children are helped to develop a sense of story line and sequence of events. At this point, you may wish to reread passages from the story to help children recall the dialogue; however, it is important to stress that they are to act out the story in their own words. Then select children to play the parts. Arrange them in order of sequence so that Sam can easily move from one to the other to play each scene. In the last scene they can all come together in the happy realization of how to make Sam happy again. Select new players and repeat the dramatization.

Promoting Creative Expression

Picture books without text are excellent stimulators of creative oral language expression. Wordless books that contain a story line invite children to infer meaning from pictures and engage in storytelling as they describe characters, settings, and events. Martha Alexander's *Bobo's Dream* and *Out, Out, Out,* Eleanor Schick's *Making Friends*, and Renate Meyer's *Hide and Seek* are all excellent examples of this type of picture book. Such books may be used both with individuals and with groups of children. In either case, at the outset, the children must be introduced to this new type of storybook format. This may be done simply by reading the title of the book to them and by using a few motivating questions to engage them in a brief discussion of the pictures on the book jacket and title page. After the children have been introduced to the story, explain that this book is unlike most other storybooks they know in that no words have been written on the pages. They must supply words to go with the pictures and tell the story. Assure the children that there are no "special" words that they must use.

Begin with a general question, such as, What is happening in the picture? Follow with probing and extending questions and statements, such as, Describe where the story is taking place. Describe the people or animals in the picture. Tell what they are doing. What do you think they are thinking and saying? Questions such as these make children more conscious of details as they focus on setting, characterization, and plot.

Allow several children to contribute to the storytelling of each page or two-page spread. You may wish to tape record the storytelling; if so, do this after the children have had a dry run. They will enjoy looking at the pictures again as they hear themselves telling the story on tape. Rather than record their stories on the tape recorder, you may decide to write down the children's

Fig. 14. Children become involved in solving the visual puzzles built into the format of Tana Hoban's book *Look Again*. Here children view the next page through a cutout and try to guess what is coming next. *Reprinted by permission of Macmillan Publishing Co., Inc., and Hamish Hamilton Children's Books Ltd., London. Copyright © Tana Hoban 1971.*

stories on chart paper to create a cooperative group story, or, after the discussion of each page in the story, you may have the children summarize their ideas by agreeing on one statement that best tells what that page is all about. Children delight in *Changes, Changes* by Hutchins where each time disaster strikes, a man and woman change a set of blocks to form a house, then a fire engine, next a boat, and finally a train to escape.

Some textless picture books do not contain a story line in the usual sense. However, these books also offer an excellent means for eliciting creative oral expression. Tana Hoban's *Look Again*, a good example of this kind of book, features intriguing black and white photographs that form visual puzzles which absorb children in an intense and lively discussion about what is coming next (see Fig. 14). Where no story line is present in a textless picture book, the emphasis should be on helping children to describe the pictures and then to discuss their reactions to them.

As noted before, creative dramatization is one of the most enjoyable ways to help children develop expressive language. In addition to acting out a story with dialogue, children can pantomime familiar stories as they are read aloud. Folktales that contain plenty of action and visual imagery are good for this purpose. *The Three Billy Goats Gruff* (Asbjørnsen and Moe, 1957; Galdone, 1973), *Stone Soup* (Marcia Brown, 1947), and *The Three Bears* (Galdone, 1972) are good examples of the type of story that will lend itself to pantomime by a group. When selecting stories, keep in mind the need for simple, yet action-filled plots with lively dialogue and a satisfactorily resolved conflict. As you read a story aloud for children to pantomime, you

may need to overdramatize your delivery a bit in order to produce the desired results and to help children capture the spirit of the characterization. Feel free to improvise when necessary by repeating certain portions of the story as you go along or by adding additional characters. Both of these techniques will enable a greater number of children to participate.

After children have had many successful experiences pantomiming a story read aloud, it is easy to move them into part-pantomime, part-acting-with-words. The story is read aloud for the children to pantomime, but the reader pauses long enough for the characters to fill in the appropriate dialogue. Cumulative tales are excellent for this purpose, since the repetition makes the dialogue easy to remember. *Henny Penny* (Galdone, 1968), *The Bun* (Marcia Brown, 1972), *Ask Mr. Bear* (Flack, 1932), and *One Fine Day* (Hogrogian, 1971) are good examples of this type of story. In each case, the child playing the main character moves from one lesser character to another,

Fig. 15. Prancing across a make-believe bridge is a natural response to the telling of this traditional tale. (Original in color) *Illustration by Marcia Brown. Reproduced from* The Three Billy Goats Gruff *written by P. C. Asbjørnsen and J. E. Moe, by permission of Harcourt Brace Jovanovich, Inc.; © 1957 by Marcia Brown.*

exchanging dialogue wherever the story indicates. Once involved in the action, each of the subordinate characters must listen and pantomime the remainder of the story. Role playing a particular character in a story is another good way to help children begin acting with words. Select scenes from stories where two characters are engaged in lively dialogue. Russell Hoban's series of books about Frances, an engaging little badger, are excellent for this purpose. Children identify easily with Frances's predicaments, and the language used is well within their frame of reference. It is not difficult for children to imagine themselves as Frances balking at her parents' urging to eat dinner in *Bread and Jam for Frances.* They are equally prepared to assume the roles of Frances's mother and father when they counter her maneuvers to postpone bedtime in *Bedtime for Frances.*

As children are exposed to longer stories with more intricate plots, they may approach dramatization by selecting certain scenes or parts of the story to act out. Favorite scenes may be listed on the chalkboard or simply discussed as possibilities for dramatization. Children may then be selected to play the various characters. In planning their dramatization, the children should be guided in visualizing the setting and planning the general scheme of movement. Once this is done, the words will come easily.

The entire group may participate in acting out different scenes from a story, or several small groups may take turns dramatizing the same scene. When several groups act out the same scene, it is important to note the value of having a variety of interpretations of a story. As children gain confidence in their ability to dramatize small parts of stories, entire selections become easy to do if they are thought of as a string of scenes put together. Most important, children should engage in creative dramatics frequently and with as little fanfare as possible. Props are not necessary and may even impede if too much emphasis is placed on them. Extended discussion and overpreparation prior to the dramatization may also render it stale and joyless.

Creating Experience Charts, Stories, and Books

Varied experiences with books starting from the very earliest years and continuing throughout school will enhance the child's ability to use written language effectively to express ideas. As pupils hear and read stories and poems, they grow in their awareness of the variety of ways in which written language can communicate. Authors create moods, they paint pictures and arouse other sensory impressions with words. They use both familiar and unfamiliar words in special ways that help develop and deepen an understanding of them.

The creative expression inspired by books may, of course, take both oral and written forms. Exposure to picture storybooks and poetry can serve as a motivation for the children's own creative writing. This may take the form of pupil-composed stories and poems, responses to works heard or read, or experience stories that extend concepts and ideas developed through books.

With young children unable to write for themselves, the teacher or some other adult may act as a scribe to get their ideas down on paper. Their efforts may be in the form of personal stories created by an individual child or cooperative charts developed by a group of children; they may be based on a spontaneous event or simply be one portion of a much broader activity that has been carefully planned in advance. In either case, the adult who is acting as the scribe will discuss with the children what took place. What the children say is recorded on chart paper, thus preserving the experience in the children's own language. The stories and charts are then displayed in the classroom and read as often as time and interest permit. Aside from the obvious value of preserving the important experiences in the child's life, experience stories help children gain an understanding of the relationship between speech and print. Just as important, they provide interesting, entertaining reading materials for the children to share. Mary Anne Hall (1970) lists the following advantages of using experience stories as materials for initial instruction in reading:

1. Experience stories permit the introduction of reading skills in a meaningful situation, since the materials are written in the children's language using their sentence patterns and vocabulary.
2. Experience stories provide a gradual and natural transition from the prereading state to the stage of beginning reading.
3. The material is easily comprehended, since it is a record of children's thoughts.
4. Experience stories can promote success and favorable attitudes in the beginning stages, since no pressure is exerted for mastery of a given number of words.
5. Experience stories demonstrate the relationship between spoken and written language. Children see that their speech can be recorded with print.
6. Experience stories involve the learner personally.

(p. 27)

There are numerous ways in which books may serve as a stimulus for children's own writing. Pupils can be encouraged to create their own stories about favorite characters. Curious George (Rey, 1941), Harry the Dirty Dog (Zion, 1956), Veronica (Duvoisin, 1961), and Petunia (Duvoisin, 1950) are well-loved characters that children will enjoy inventing new episodes about; or you may wish to have them create their own characters or group of characters to use as a basis for a series of stories. Story starters such as, What would happen if Curious George came to our classroom or Harry the Dirty Dog were my pet?, may be used to get pupils launched. Above all, an abundance of discussion should precede the writing down.

Children's responses to books also provide interesting content for experience charts. Children may wish to list their favorite storybooks or storybook people. They may retell their favorite part of a story and draw a picture to accompany it. An inferred story inspired by a textless picture book may also be written down by or for the children to create their own versions of a picture story.

An experience chart may be the outgrowth of a much broader experience, of which books are a part. For example, children may be inspired to make gingerbread after hearing *The Gingerbread Boy* (Galdone, 1975) or pancakes after a reading of *The Perfect Pancake* (Kahl, 1960). The teacher would then write the recipe on a chart and display it in a prominent place to be read before and during the cooking experience as a procedural check. Children thus learn the value of reading as a source of information. A reading of *The Hunting Trip* (Burch, 1971) or *A Walk in the Snow* (Busch, 1971) might precede a nature walk, from which individual and group stories can emerge. Indeed, a variety of stories and poems on any topic might precede the children's own writing about that topic. In this way, vocabulary, style, and general knowledge of the topic itself can be introduced in a pleasurable way.

Literature is at the heart of the language-learning program. It serves the child aesthetically and cognitively in fostering ability to listen, speak, read, and write.

FOSTERING CONCEPT DEVELOPMENT THROUGH LITERATURE

Ability to analyze problems, explore solutions, and see relationships in proper perspective is a necessary attribute for success both in and out of school. The development of basic concepts is directly related to this ability. Gray and her associates (1966) describe the relationship in the following manner:

> The child's ability to focus upon the relevant dimensions of the tasks he performs in school is related to his perceptual ability and his level of concept development. He must be able to distinguish a variety of forms, colors, numbers, and directions. School activities demand particular visual, auditory, and kinesthetic perceptual skills which must be learned. If he is to be successful in meeting these demands, the child must also have an adequate repertoire of concepts built on experience. (pp. 9-11)

Young children who have rich verbal and cognitive experiences with books are given a head start toward developing these abilities. "Too frequently we substitute the book for the experience, rather than enrich the experience with a book," states Huck (1976, p. 543). Experiences with books that are thoughtfully planned to promote active verbal exchanges of ideas will have lasting positive effects upon both the communicative mode and the cognitive structure of the child. Such experiences with books should not be considered a replacement for firsthand experience but should be used to make the experience more meaningful.

Large numbers of books for young children specifically designed to promote the development of basic concepts are available. Huck describes the "concept book" as "one that describes the various dimensions of an abstract idea through the use of many comparisons. In some respects, it is a young child's information book" (p. 133). Skilled questioning tied to such books helps the child relate the familiar to the unfamiliar.

Concept books are a relatively recent phenomenon in children's book publishing, the earliest examples having appeared in the mid-1950s. Books such as *Shapes and Things* (T. Hoban, 1970), *Colors* (Reiss, 1969), *Sparkle and Spin* (Rand, 1957), and *Fast-Slow, High-Low* (Spier, 1972) are considered concept books. Coupled with discussion and firsthand experiences, these books provide the teacher with an excellent tool for introducing, extending, or reinforcing the child's understanding of basic concepts. For example, *Are You Square?* by Ethel and Leonard Kessler may be used as an introduction to differences in shapes. It can lead to a variety of experiences that help children with their visual discrimination and identification of shapes. Children can follow the reading and discussion of Jan Pieńkowski's *Shapes* by finding various shapes in their environment, such as a round clock or square bulletin board (see Fig. 16). They can match cut-out shapes, building blocks, or pictures of shapes and can describe what is alike and what is different about them.

The books *How Big Is Big?* by Herman and Nina Schneider and *Big Ones, Little Ones* by Tana Hoban can extend and reinforce the concept of big and little by helping children to conceptualize that bigness is actually relative. The repeated use of the words *big, little, small*, and *large* in a variety of contexts, accompanied by explicit illustrations, helps the child to an understanding of size beyond the superficial level at which it is frequently treated. After the reading, the teacher may wish to display blocks of different sizes and ask which one is the biggest. Larger blocks can then be added and the same question asked, thus further extending the concept of relativity in size. A walk outside to observe relative differences in the bigness and smallness of houses, cars, trees, rocks, and other things in the environment can also reinforce the ideas in the books.

Fig. 16. Basic concepts are reinforced by words and illustrations in books for the very young child. (Original in color) *Reprinted by permission of Harvey House, Inc., Publishers, from* Shapes *by Jan Pieńkowski. Text and illustrations copyright © 1974 by Jan Pieńkowski.*

Using Books to Foster Thinking Skill

Probably of greater importance than the use of books specifically designed to teach certain concepts is what is consistently done to capitalize on

every opportunity to develop the child's ability to handle basic operations associated with thinking. Raths and his colleagues (1967, pp. 1-30) suggest that there are certain basic operations which relate to thinking: observing, comparing, classifying, hypothesizing, looking for assumptions, criticizing, imagining, collecting and organizing data, coding, problem solving, decision making, summarizing, and interpreting. It is their contention that it is the teacher's responsibility to provide daily opportunities for children to experience these operational skills and that in so doing they will be acquiring experience in thinking which will help them to mature. A variety of activities utilizing children's books can be designed to effectively engage children in the thinking operations. These activities need not be reserved for use only with concept books; on the contrary, these activities should be included whenever a suitable occasion arises.

Observing. Teachers help children develop skill in observing when they display a picture in a picture story and ask questions relating to various details in it.

Comparing. Children are engaged in comparing when they scrutinize pictures to compare changes that have taken place throughout the story or when they engage in a discussion comparing books on a similar theme or by the same author.

Classifying. Children can be helped to classify books according to content, e.g., funny stories, nature stories, stories about boys and girls, or simply stories they liked and didn't like. In using books as an introduction to the discussion of certain kinds of vocabulary, such as words that describe feelings, shapes, sizes, and colors, children are categorizing the words in their language.

Hypothesizing. When teachers ask, What do you suppose this story will be about?, or, What kind of a person do you think this character will be?, they are asking children to form a hypothesis—a good guess based upon certain given information, which might be a picture or the book jacket.

Organizing. When children review a story sequentially in order to prepare for creative dramatics, they are engaged in organizing information collected through reading aloud. In order to prepare for role playing a character, the teacher might ask what kind of character it is and what events occur in the story to let us know this.

Summarizing. Children can be asked to summarize, or tell in just a few words, what the story is about or to summarize the funniest part or the best part.

Applying. Although a particular concept or principle has been introduced through books, provision should always be made for firsthand experiences where children can actually apply the principle being developed.

Criticizing. Children should be encouraged to criticize the selections being offered. Their criticism should always be accompanied by reasons for the opinions given, however. Criticisms of characters in a story should be handled in the same manner.

The school day is filled with opportunities for child involvement in the kinds of thinking operations that have been discussed. As teachers, it is our responsibility to have a thorough understanding of these operations and to provide for planned, systematic approaches to them, while making maximum use of every chance opportunity for their development. Literature can certainly be a resource to that end.

CHILDREN'S BOOK REFERENCES

Adoff, Arnold. *Black is brown is tan.* Illus. by Emily A. McCully. Harper, 1973.

Aldis, Dorothy. "Snow" in *All Together.* Illus. by Marjorie Flack, Margaret Frieman, and Helen Jameson. Putnam, 1952.

Alexander, Martha. *Bobo's Dream.* Dial, 1970. PB: Scholastic Book Services.

———. *Out, Out, Out.* Dial, 1968.

Asbjørnsen, P. C., and Jorgen E. Moe. *The Three Billy Goats Gruff.* Illus. by Marcia Brown. Harcourt, 1957.

Baylor, Byrd. *Plink, Plink, Plink.* Houghton, 1971.

Borten, Helen. *Do You Hear What I Hear?* Abelard-Schuman, 1960.

Brown, Marcia. *The Bun: A Tale from Russia.* Harcourt, 1972.

———. *Stone Soup.* Scribner, 1947. PB.

Brown, Margaret Wise. *The City Noisy Book.* Illus. by Leonard Weisgard. Harper, 1939.

———. *The Country Noisy Book.* Illus. by Leonard Weisgard. Harper, 1940.

———. *The Indoor Noisy Book.* Illus. by Leonard Weisgard. Harper, 1942.

———. *The Noisy Book.* Illus. by Charles G. Shaw. Harper, 1947.

———. *The Winter Noisy Book.* Illus. by Charles G. Shaw. Harper, 1947.

Burch, Robert. *The Hunting Trip.* Scribner, 1971.

Busch, Phyllis S. *A Walk in the Snow.* Lippincott, 1971.

Duvoisin, Roger. *Petunia.* Knopf, 1950. PB.

———. *Petunia, I Love You.* Knopf, 1965.

———. *Veronica.* Knopf, 1961. PB.

Flack, Marjorie. *Ask Mr. Bear.* Macmillan, 1932. PB.

Gág, Wanda. *Millions of Cats.* Coward, 1928.

Galdone, Paul. *The Gingerbread Boy.* Seabury, 1975.

———. *Henny Penny.* Seabury, 1968.

———. *The House That Jack Built.* McGraw, 1961.

———. *The Three Bears.* Seabury, 1972. PB: Scholastic Book Services.

———. *The Three Billy Goats Gruff.* Seabury, 1973.

Garelick, May. *Sounds of a Summer Night.* Illus. by Beni Montresor. Addison-Wesley, 1963.

Grifalconi, Ann. *City Rhythms.* Bobbs-Merrill, 1965.

Heide, Florence P. *Sound of Sunshine, Sound of Rain.* Parents, 1970.

Hoban, Russell. *Bedtime for Frances.* Illus. by Garth Williams. Harper, 1960.

————. *A Birthday for Frances.* Illus. by Lillian Hoban. Harper, 1968.

————. *Bread and Jam for Frances.* Illus. by Lillian Hoban. Harper, 1964. PB: Scholastic Book Services.

Hoban, Tana. *Big Ones, Little Ones.* Greenwillow, 1976.

————. *Dig, Drill, Dump, Fill.* Greenwillow, 1975.

————. *Look Again.* Macmillan, 1971.

————. *Shapes and Things.* Macmillan, 1970.

Hogrogian, Nonny. *One Fine Day.* Macmillan, 1971. PB.

Hutchins, Pat. *Changes, Changes.* Macmillan, 1971. PB.

————. *Don't Forget the Bacon.* Greenwillow, 1976.

————. *The Surprise Party.* Macmillan, 1969. PB.

Kahl, Virginia. *The Perfect Pancake.* Scribner, 1960.

Kaufman, Lois. *What's That Noise?* Illus. by Allan Eitzen. Lothrop, 1965.

Kessler, Ethel, and Leonard Kessler. *Are You Square?* Doubleday, 1966.

Lobel, Arnold. *Owl at Home.* Harper, 1975.

Meyer, Renate. *Hide and Seek.* Bradbury Press, 1972.

Orgel, Doris. *The Uproar.* McGraw, 1970.

Pieńkowski, Jan. *Shapes.* Harvey House, 1975.

Prelutsky, Jack. *The Pack Rat's Day.* Illus. by Margaret Bloy Graham. Macmillan, 1974.

Rand, Ann. *Sparkle and Spin.* Illus. by Paul Rand. Harcourt, 1957.

Reiss, John J. *Colors.* Bradbury Press, 1969.

Rey, Hans Augusto. *Curious George.* Houghton, 1941. PB.

Schick, Eleanor. *Making Friends.* Macmillan, 1969.

Schneider, Herman, and Nina Schneider. *How Big Is Big? From Stars to Atoms.* Rev. ed. Illus. by Symeon Shimin. Addison-Wesley, 1950.

Scott, Ann Herbert. *Sam.* Illus. by Symeon Shimin. McGraw, 1967.

Sendak, Maurice. *Where the Wild Things Are.* Harper, 1963.

Showers, Paul. *The Listening Walk.* Illus. by Aliki. Crowell, 1961.

Slobodkina, Esphyr. *Caps for Sale.* Addison-Wesley, 1947.

Spier, Peter. *Crash, Bang, Boom.* Doubleday, 1972.

————. *Fast-Slow, High-Low: A Book of Opposites.* Doubleday, 1972.

————. *Gobble, Growl, Grunt.* Doubleday, 1971.

Steiner, Charlotte. *Listen to My Seashell.* Knopf, 1959.

Steptoe, John. *Stevie.* Harper, 1969.

Tresselt, Alvin. *White Snow, Bright Snow.* Illus. by Roger Duvoisin. Lothrop, 1947.

Yashima, Taro. *Umbrella.* Viking, 1958. PB.

Zion, Eugene. *Harry the Dirty Dog.* Illus. by Margaret Bloy Graham. Harper, 1956.

PROFESSIONAL REFERENCES

Gray, Susan, Rupert Klaus, James Miller, and Bettye Forrester. *Before First Grade: Training Project for Culturally Disadvantaged Children.* New York: Teachers College Press, 1966.

Hall, Mary Anne. *Teaching Reading as a Language Experience.* Columbus, Ohio: Charles E. Merrill, 1970.

Huck, Charlotte S. *Children's Literature in the Elementary School.* 3rd ed. New York: Holt, Rinehart and Winston, 1976.

Jacobs, Leland B. "Give Children Literature" in *Readings about Children's Literature.* Ed. by Evelyn R. Robinson. New York: David McKay, 1966.

Raths, Louis E., Selma Wassermann, Arthur Jonas, and Arnold M. Rothstein. *Teaching for Thinking: Theory and Application.* Columbus, Ohio: Charles E. Merrill, 1967.

Carolyn W. Carmichael

FOSTERING UNDERSTANDING
OF SELF AND OTHERS

The major concern of young children is their own being. Because they are at a stage of psychological growth that is totally egocentric, it is only the maturing process —of which books are, or should be, an important part—that can introduce children to the world beyond their own and that of their immediate family. Children should of course enjoy literature above all, and the other benefits made possible by the experience of books should be considered secondary. Yet, these secondary benefits are important and can be pursued without sacrificing or subordinating the primary end of pleasure.

As books open the doors to new knowledge, expand the imagination, and challenge children to reach beyond their known environment, they also offer children the opportunity to explore and understand their own feelings and the feelings of others. This kind of understanding is an essential aspect of the maturing process that can be pursued by the careful selection and use of books in the classroom and by appropriate follow-up activities. The purpose of this chapter is to identify some of the available imaginative books that elicit feelings, not merely describe them, and thus have the potential to become part of children's growth and maturing.

There is in fact an abundant supply of books written specifically for the younger child that are enjoyable to read and also encourage the child to identify with characters who feel sad, angry, lonely, shy, happy, and a multitude of other emotions, including perhaps the least complicated of emotions: the pure enjoyment of life. *Having Fun* (Dunn, 1971) uses photography to portray many experiences that are enjoyed by young children. The book's appeal is universal in its geographic settings and in the experiences portrayed, which range from helping a bucketful of ducklings take their morning bath to flying kites, swimming, and playing in the snow. As an interesting follow up, a class can put together a book of activities that they find especially appealing when they think of doing nothing but having fun.

Concerns, fears, and inhibitions inevitably cloud all of our lives on occasion, and many of these emotions felt as an adult are a result of an unpleasant, even traumatic, childhood experience. Some of these feelings have a cause that is easy to identify, while others are simply the result of "having a bad day." *The Wrong Side of the Bed* (Ardizzone, 1970) is a wordless book depicting just such a day. Everything seems to go wrong for the main character, a young boy trying to cheer up his mother by passing up candy for himself and buying her flowers. Wordless books may need some interpretation for younger children who have not had much exposure to books (e.g., the title *The Wrong Side of the Bed* may require an explanation to young listeners). However, many teachers have had great success in using wordless books to encourage and enlarge the verbal ability of withdrawn or nonverbal children.

Judith Viorst gives a delightful account of a terrible day in her humorous, yet realistic book *Alexander and the Terrible, Horrible, No Good, Very Bad Day.* From the outset, Viorst's style and humor amusingly bring across Alexander's account of his disastrous day (see Fig. 17). A simple question directed to your listeners, such as, What makes you have a bad day?, usually brings a flood of responses, since every young child is well acquainted with the causes of having a bad time. Other books that illustrate the feelings of a bad day are Joan M. Lexau's *I Should Have Stayed in Bed* and Edna Preston's *The Temper Tantrum Book.* The latter is a series of eight verses each portraying an animal having a temper tantrum. Each tantrum has a different cause—a lion, for instance, is enraged because his mother is combing his hair and an elephant hates getting soap in his eyes—and each has a surprise ending that appeals to young children.

Fig. 17. Alexander's day begins poorly and gets worse, an occurrence young listeners will laugh at, yet readily understand. *Text copyright © 1972 by Judith Viorst. Pictures copyright © 1972 by Ray Cruz. From Alexander and the Terrible, Horrible, No Good, Very Bad Day. Used by permission of Atheneum Publishers and Angus and Robertson, Ltd.*

I went to sleep with gum in my mouth and now there's gum in my hair and when I got out of bed this morning I tripped on the skateboard and by mistake I dropped my sweater in the sink while the water was running and I could tell it was going to be a terrible, horrible, no good, very bad day.

Feelings about Size

There are few individuals who have not, at one time or another, experienced some anxiety about their size in the course of their physical development. Concerns of this nature are specifically implied in many books designed for the younger child. In *The Best Thing to Be*, Julia Noonan describes the feeling of being small. In her book we meet Jonathan who, because of being small, finds himself often overlooked. He wants to be noticed and he imagines the advantages of being different kinds of animals, such as a lion, hippopotamus, eagle, seal, elephant, giraffe, pig, owl, and bear; but Jonathan comes up with reasons why it is best *not* to be any of these animals.

Titch (Hutchins, 1971) is the delicately illustrated story of a boy who is troubled by the consequences of being small: he must, for example, ride a tricycle rather than a bicycle and is given a pinwheel rather than a kite. Finally, a small seed that germinates and grows helps him put into perspective his present difficulties. Ruth Krauss also shows the final triumph of a boy who is small in stature in *The Carrot Seed* and portrays the wonderful feeling of growing up after having experienced smallness in *The Growing Story*, as does Barbara Borack in *Someone Small*. See also Robert Kraus's Night-Lite Library for a series of books on this subject.

The opposite of being small is discussed in *The Very Tall Little Girl* (Krasilovsky, 1969) in which an unnamed young girl reviews all the disadvantages and advantages of being tall and finds the advantages far outweigh the disadvantages.

> But best of all, being tall made her different from almost all the other little girls. It was fun to be special and special is exactly what most tall little girls always are!

Fear

Fear is a very real emotion in the life of a young child, and its causes are as varied as the individuals who feel it. Some of the common causes of fear in early childhood and, more importantly, the ability to overcome the feeling are dealt with in many children's books. Two of the best are Robert McCloskey's *One Morning in Maine*, where a storm is the all-consuming cause of fear, and Lexau's *Benjie*, where shyness is submerged by the desire to find the lost earring of a dearly loved grandmother. Shyness is also the central focus of *The Shy Little Girl* (Krasilovsky, 1970).

Accomplishment

With maturing come many different abilities. The thrill of first-time accomplishment is felt throughout one's life, but early accomplishments are very important to a child's positive self-concept. That first whistle for Willie in *Whistle for Willie* (Keats, 1964), Michael's ability to put aside his fear of the slide in *Michael Is Brave* (Buckley, 1971), and the thrill Rosa feels in

Fig. 18. James and John show young
audiences that even the best of friendships
is vulnerable to sudden shifts in feelings.
(Original in color)
Illustration by Maurice Sendak from Let's
Be Enemies *by Janice May Udry. Pictures
copyright © 1961 by Maurice Sendak.
Reprinted by permission of Harper & Row,
Publishers, Inc.*

first writing her name (Felt, 1950) are all well-executed examples of nearly universal childhood attainments.

Certain achievements, however, are expected of children, achievements which are sometimes frustratingly elusive. Kraus's *Leo the Late Bloomer*, brilliantly illustrated by Jose Aruego, speaks directly to first grade children who find the task of learning to read as overpowering as it is for Leo, reassuring them that it is not uncommon to have "adjustment problems" with the expectations of others.

Friends

As relationships outside the family become more and more important to children, problems intrude, especially when it is time for a child to enter school. For many children, the prospect of school may inspire the fear of not having any friends. Miriam Cohen's *Will I Have a Friend?* realistically begins with that lonely feeling and ends with Jim having a friend at the end of the day; in *The New Teacher* (Cohen, 1972) Jim experiences the same fears and concludes the day with those fears again left far behind. *Best Friends* (Cohen, 1971) takes a different tack, showing how friendship can grow through crisis.

An interesting book on the theme of wanting a friend is *Do You Want to Be My Friend?* (Carle, 1971). The only words in this book, "Do you want to be my friend?," are given but once so that the child must make up his or her own story based on the pictures presented. A small group, or even just one child, will find this a heartwarming book to "read" with the teacher while viewing the pictures. Another wordless book which is highly effective in stimulating discussion with a group is Eleanor Schick's *Making Friends*. Here a little boy is on his way to the park obviously wishing for a friend. At the park, he does find a girl to play with, just as his mother finds a friend with whom she can talk. The illustrations in this book are simple, and the young child will enjoy sharing this book with an adult.

Charlotte Zolotow has captured the security felt by individuals when they know all there is to know about a friend in her book *My Friend John.* A few lines neatly express the warmth of this book:

> John is my best friend
> and I'm his
> and everything that's
> important about each
> other we like.
>
> (p. 32)

It is also important for children to understand that being friends with someone doesn't exclude other emotions from the relationship and that only love is always felt between two friends. Children need to understand that the less positive emotional aspects of relationships should not make them feel guilty or threatened. Janice May Udry has tried to explain just this point in her book *Let's Be Enemies.* The sudden emotions that are so much a part of childhood are depicted in this book, with the final outcome for two boys being one of friendship after a time of obviously disliking each other (see Fig. 18).

The sadness of losing a friend is insightfully shown in *The New Friend* (Zolotow, 1968; see Fig. 19), the story of two girls who are friends, doing things together and enjoying each other, until one of the girls gets another friend, leaving her first friend alone and hurt. A decision is then made that

Fig. 19. *The New Friend* views friendship from a realistic perspective: the joy of doing things together and the pain in seeing a close friend drift away. (Original in color) *Reprinted by permission of Abelard-Schuman from* The New Friend *by Charlotte Zolotow, pictures by Arvis L. Stewart. Copyright © 1968 by Charlotte Zolotow.*

she, too, must get a friend. To be rebuffed by a friend is also demonstrated in another work by Zolotow, *The Hating Book*. When her friend apparently doesn't like her anymore, the main character has feelings of remorse. The book then deals with getting up the kind of courage needed to ask someone why they no longer like you and are treating you poorly. Other problems of friendship, including the absence of it, are often communicated by authors through animal characters like the lovable badger Frances in *Best Friends for Frances* (Hoban, 1969); the frog in *Frog and Toad Are Friends* (Lobel, 1970); and the bear in *Charles* (Skorpen, 1971). In the Skorpen book, the bear provides comfort and friendship for a boy who lacks human companions; the story thus can be a springboard for a discussion of how a young child can feel when there is no one around to do things with. Relationships

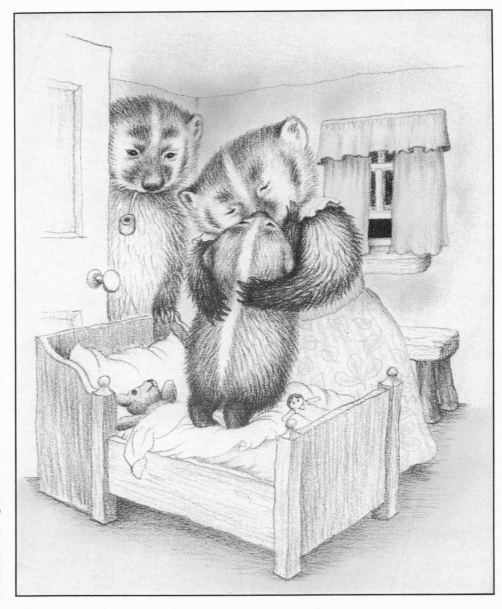

Fig. 20. Frances, an affectionate badger, is one of many animal characters skillfully used by authors to present universal childhood experiences. (Original in color) *Illustration by Garth Williams from* Bedtime for Frances *by Russell Hoban. Pictures copyright © 1960 by Garth Williams. Reprinted by permission of Harper & Row, Publishers, Inc., and Faber and Faber Ltd.*

can go wrong for a variety of reasons, but one would hope that a kiss, or lack of one, wouldn't have such a domino effect on lives as it does in Zolotow's *The Quarreling Book*: Mr. James forgets to kiss Mrs. James goodbye before leaving for work, setting off an unhappy chain reaction that affects one person after another until a reversal starts a happier reaction.

Sibling Rivalry

The emotions that can spring to the surface when a new child is introduced into a family are many and frequently less than benign. In some cases having a new sibling arrive in the home draws the very honest reaction of wanting to give the child away, as Oliver does in *Nobody Ever Asked Me If I Wanted a Baby Sister* (Alexander, 1971). Only when Oliver realizes how important he is to Bonnie, his new sister, does he decide he will keep her after all. A child often feels resentment for having to cope with a new sibling. Ezra Jack Keats discusses this in *Peter's Chair*. Peter takes offense when all his former possessions are being painted pink for his new sister. Finally, in a last act of frustration, Peter takes his dog, a picture of himself when he was small, his toy crocodile, and his favorite blue chair and leaves home. The discovery that he no longer fits in his chair leads him to change his mind about leaving home and to decide that perhaps he would like to paint the chair himself.

Rivalry is prevalent in many homes today because more and more mothers are caring for the children of parents who work outside the home. This is the case in John Steptoe's book *Stevie*. Stevie is dropped off at Robert's house and plays with his toys, climbs all over his bed with his dirty shoes, and is generally a real pest. Only when Stevie's mother and father come to take him away for good does Robert realize he will miss him.

Older brothers and sisters are usually given some sort of responsibilities for a younger child in the house. In Lexau's *Emily and the Klunky Baby and the Next Door Dog*, there is a fine description of how Emily feels about taking care of her baby brother while their mother, who is divorced, works on income taxes. Emily tries to run away to her father but returns home after experiencing much confusion in trying to find his house. Lexau thus reveals the frustrations that can come to both parent and child in a home where there is only one parent. The divorce situation is also the subject of Lexau's *Me Day*.

Rivalry continues in many homes long past the time when the younger sibling is an infant. An older brother's feelings of jealousy for his young brother are portrayed in *If It Weren't for You* (Zolotow, 1966), while in *Someday* (Zolotow, 1965) the main character expresses the hope that some time everything will go right:

> Someday . . .
> "I'm going to come home and my brother will introduce me to his friends and say, 'This is my sister.' Instead of—'Here's the family creep.'"

Lasting sibling rivalries generate powerful emotions and the desire to act on them. Contemporary children's authors do not shrink from dealing with these feelings for the sake of the sometimes saccharine picture of the proper child that has dominated books for children in the past. In *I'll Fix Anthony* (Viorst, 1969), for instance, a younger brother dreams of revenge and has a consuming desire to "fix Anthony," his older brother. What he plans and what actually happens are of course comically different.

Love

Zolotow has also written a sensitive dialogue between a mother and son whose father left before the son was born in *A Father Like That.* Love is likewise a powerful part of her book *Do You Know What I'll Do?* in which an older sister tenderly tells her little brother everything she wants to do for him. This is a good book to stimulate thoughts of kindness, rather than hatred and rivalry, in family situations.

Fortunately, there are many other quality books about love between family members that are neither trite nor simpleminded. *William's Doll* (Zolotow, 1972) involves an understanding grandmother who overrides the criticisms of other family members and buys William a doll "so that when he's a father he'll know how to care for his baby" (pp. 30-31). This book is of great value in helping to challenge preconceived sex-role stereotypes regarding objects of play. In *Runaway Bunny* (M. W. Brown, 1972) a bunny who threatens to run away is lovingly told that no matter where he goes, his mother will always find and love him. This book has not been out of print since 1942, and the 1972 edition cited contains redrawn illustrations by the original artist, Clement Hurd. *Little Bear* (Minarik, 1957) is also a book that rings of love at every reading. I would encourage readers to become acquainted with the complete series by Else Holmelund Minarik: *Father Bear Comes Home, A Kiss for Little Bear, Little Bear's Friend,* and *Little Bear's Visit.*

Love also permeates such books as Ruth Sonneborn's *I Love Gram* and *Friday Night Is Papa Night.* Sheer enjoyment of other members of the family is shown in the following books by Helen E. Buckley: *Grandfather and I, Grandmother and I, Michael Is Brave,* and *My Sister and I.*

Security

Just how attached we become not only to the people in our homes, but also to the objects there is illustrated by books such as Myra Berry Brown's *The First Night Away from Home.* Stevie embarks on his first overnight and finds he cannot sleep without his teddy bear, a need many children will be able to identify with. The need for a physical object for security is frequently satisfied with the familiar blanket. This is the subject of playwright Arthur Miller's only work for children, *Jane's Blanket.* It is a lengthy text, with the end result being that Jane realizes cherished objects can be taken away unintentionally but used for the happiness of others—in her case, a bird pulls the threads from the small remainder of Jane's security blanket to make a nest for her young.

Death

Of late, more attention is being given to the entire cycle of life in books for children. Not only is the process of living encountered, but also its termination. Some adults may hesitate to use such books, but if one is tempted to rule out for children any exposure to books dealing with death, one should carefully consider the following point made by Mary Q. Steele (1971): "The world has not spared children hunger, cold, sorrow, pain, fear, loneliness, disease, death, war, famine or madness. Why should we hesitate to make use of this knowledge when writing for them?" (p. 20).

The death of a pet is most frequently the initial encounter a child has with death. For this reason, Sandol Stoddard Warburg's *The Growing Time* is an important book for younger children. It depicts the death of King, an old Collie dog, and the despondency of his owner, a young boy named Jamie. A new puppy and its cries for love help Jamie get over the loss of King. The book is sensitively written and is a fine introduction to the subject of death which does not deny the pain of loss as it is felt by the child. *The Tenth Good Thing about Barney* (Viorst, 1971) also offers comfort, not condemnation, for feelings produced by the loss of a pet (see Fig. 21). A boy is asked to think of ten good things to say about Barney, his pet cat. He can only think of nine, but later the thought comes, "He'll help grow the flowers, and he'll help grow that tree and some grass. You know . . . that's a pretty nice job for a cat."

My cat Barney died last Friday.
I was very sad.

I cried, and I didn't watch television.
I cried, and I didn't eat my chicken or even
the chocolate pudding.
I went to bed, and I cried.

Fig. 21. Recent children's books give a more inclusive picture of a child's life, including the first encounter with death.
Text copyright © 1971 by Judith Viorst. Drawings copyright © 1971 by Erik Blegvad. From The Tenth Good Thing about Barney. *Used by permission of Atheneum Publishers and William Collins Sons & Co. Ltd.*

The Dead Bird (M. W. Brown, 1958) deals with children preparing for the funeral of a bird they have found. The realism may be shocking to some adults otherwise familiar with the ways of children, but showing the children returning to their play and forgetting about the bird is a true picture of how flexible children can be in both thoughts and actions.

The books mentioned in this chapter should not be taken as a comprehensive list for the topics discussed. Whatever books one selects, however, two points ought to be kept in mind. Some books must be used with a sense of restraint, because the problems and emotions they involve may be portrayed in such a manner that they become a source of amusement for the adult reader while at the same time placing the child—listener or reader—in a precarious state. Ivan Sherman's *I Do Not Like It When My Friend Comes to Visit* is a case in point. The adult may chuckle when the protagonist's possessions are left in a shambles, but parents will certainly sympathize with the frustrations felt by the child whose things are left in disarray. Another example is Schick's *Peggy's New Brother*. The discovery that her mother is pregnant and Peggy's wish that she could have a dog or cat instead of a new baby brother or sister may be a humorous, if unoriginal, tale to the adult, yet it may not be quite so amusing to the child. This caution is given briefly but not lightly, for every adult who works with children must constantly keep in mind the audience for whom these stories are intended and the life context on which the child will reflect as he or she listens to the narrative.

The second caution is that books of seeming simplicity are often overlooked by adults when considering selections for young children. Such books seem to contain so little of the elements like conflict and resolution that, to adults, are the signs of worthwhile stories and serious intentions. And yet the wonder of these books so often lies in the execution of the illustrations, the ability of the artist to take the ordinary and, almost magically, weave into it a sense of wonder and delight. I would hope that adults would always keep this in mind when reviewing any book for the younger child.

The children's books most appropriate for dealing with the child's affective domain are those in which problems are handled in a thematic fashion. A book is most effective when its emotional content is a valid part of the story context, instead of being a "message" which the story attempts to justify. Nevertheless, no matter how effectively we think a story will help children to understand themselves and others, we must recognize that it will take more than a book to get children through difficult, deeply rooted problems. Yet, children basically desire to please adults. When an adult shares a book with a child, the adult is, in effect, demonstrating to the child that emotions are accepted as natural and common. This in turn may ease the child's feelings and, in many cases, eliminate the need for discussing them.

CHILDREN'S BOOK REFERENCES

Alexander, Martha. *Nobody Ever Asked Me If I Wanted a Baby Sister*. Dial, 1971.

Ardizzone, Edward. *The Wrong Side of the Bed*. Doubleday, 1970.

Borack, Barbara. *Someone Small.* Illus. by Anita Lobel. Harper, 1969.

Brown, Margaret Wise. *The Dead Bird.* Illus. by Remy Charlip. Addison-Wesley, 1958.

———. *The Runaway Bunny.* Illus. by Clement Hurd. Harper, 1942, 1972.

Brown, Myra Berry. *The First Night Away from Home.* Illus. by Dorothy Marino. Watts, 1960.

Buckley, Helen E. *Grandfather and I.* Illus. by Paul Galdone. Lothrop, 1959.

———. *Grandmother and I.* Illus. by Paul Galdone. Lothrop, 1961.

———. *Michael Is Brave.* Illus. by Emily A. McCully. Lothrop, 1971.

———. *My Sister and I.* Illus. by Paul Galdone. Lothrop, 1963.

Carle, Eric. *Do You Want to Be My Friend?* Crowell, 1971.

Cohen, Miriam. *Best Friends.* Illus. by Lillian Hoban. Macmillan, 1971. PB.

———. *The New Teacher.* Illus. by Lillian Hoban. Macmillan, 1972. PB.

———. *Will I Have a Friend?* Illus. by Lillian Hoban. Macmillan, 1967. PB.

Dunn, Judy. *Having Fun.* Photographs by Phoebe and Tris Dunn. Creative Educational Society, 1971.

Felt, Sue. *Rosa-Too-Little.* Doubleday, 1950.

Freeman, Don. *Dandelion.* Viking, 1964. PB.

Hoban, Russell. *Best Friends for Frances.* Illus. by Lillian Hoban. Harper, 1969.

Hoffman, Phyllis. *Steffie and Me.* Illus. by Emily A. McCully. Harper, 1970.

Hutchins, Pat. *Titch.* Macmillan, 1971.

Keats, Ezra Jack. *Peter's Chair.* Harper, 1967.

———. *Whistle for Willie.* Viking, 1964. PB.

Krasilovsky, Phyllis. *The Shy Little Girl.* Illus. by Trina Schart Hyman. Houghton, 1970. PB.

———. *The Very Tall Little Girl.* Illus. by Olivia Cole. Doubleday, 1969.

Kraus, Robert. *Leo the Late Bloomer.* Illus. by Jose Aruego. Windmill, 1971. PB.

Krauss, Ruth. *The Carrot Seed.* Illus. by Crockett Johnson. Harper, 1945. PB: Scholastic Book Services.

———. *The Growing Story.* Illus. by Phyllis Rowand. Harper, 1947.

Lexau, Joan M. *Benjie.* Illus. by Don Bolognese. Dial, 1964.

———. *Emily and the Klunky Baby and the Next Door Dog.* Illus. by Martha Alexander. Dial, 1972.

———. *I Should Have Stayed in Bed.* Illus. by Syd Hoff. Harper, 1965.

———. *Me Day.* Illus. by Robert Weaver. Dial, 1971.

Lobel, Arnold. *Frog and Toad Are Friends.* Harper, 1970.

McCloskey, Robert. *One Morning in Maine.* Viking, 1952. PB.

Miller, Arthur. *Jane's Blanket.* Illus. by Emily A. McCully. Viking, 1972.

Minarik, Else Holmelund. *Father Bear Comes Home.* Illus. by Maurice Sendak. Harper, 1959.

———. *A Kiss for Little Bear*. Illus. by Maurice Sendak. Harper, 1968.

———. *Little Bear*. Illus. by Maurice Sendak. Harper, 1957.

———. *Little Bear's Friend*. Illus. by Maurice Sendak. Harper, 1960.

———. *Little Bear's Visit*. Illus. by Maurice Sendak. Harper, 1961.

Noonan, Julia. *The Best Thing to Be*. Doubleday, 1971. PB.

Preston, Edna. *The Temper Tantrum Book*. Illus. by Rainey Bennett. Viking, 1969. PB.

Schick, Eleanor. *Making Friends*. Macmillan, 1969.

———. *Peggy's New Brother*. Macmillan, 1970.

Sherman, Ivan. *I Do Not Like It When My Friend Comes to Visit*. Harcourt, 1973.

Skorpen, Liesel Moak. *Charles*. Illus. by Martha Alexander. Harper, 1971.

Sonneborn, Ruth. *Friday Night Is Papa Night*. Illus. by Emily A. McCully. Viking, 1970.

———. *I Love Gram*. Illus. by Leo Carty. Viking, 1971.

Steptoe, John. *Stevie*. Harper, 1969.

Udry, Janice May. *Let's Be Enemies*. Illus. by Maurice Sendak. Harper, 1961. PB: Scholastic Book Services.

Viorst, Judith. *Alexander and the Terrible, Horrible, No Good, Very Bad Day*. Illus. by Ray Cruz. Atheneum, 1972.

———. *I'll Fix Anthony*. Illus. by Arnold Lobel. Harper, 1969.

———. *The Tenth Good Thing about Barney*. Illus. by Erik Blegvad. Atheneum, 1971. PB.

Warburg, Sandol Stoddard. *The Growing Time*. Illus. by Leonard Weisgard. Houghton, 1969. PB.

Zolotow, Charlotte. *Do You Know What I'll Do?* Illus. by Garth Williams. Harper, 1958.

———. *A Father Like That*. Illus. by Ben Shecter. Harper, 1971.

———. *The Hating Book*. Illus. by Ben Shecter. Harper, 1969.

———. *If It Weren't for You*. Illus. by Ben Shecter. Harper, 1966.

———. *My Friend John*. Illus. by Ben Shecter. Harper, 1968.

———. *The New Friend*. Illus. by Arvis L. Stewart. Abelard-Schuman, 1968.

———. *The Quarreling Book*. Illus. by Arnold Lobel. Harper, 1963.

———. *Someday*. Illus. by Arnold Lobel. Harper, 1965.

———. *William's Doll*. Illus. by William Pène du Bois. Harper, 1972.

PROFESSIONAL REFERENCES

Cianciolo, Patricia, ed. *Picture Books for Children*. Chicago: American Library Association, 1973.

Coody, Betty. *Using Literature with Young Children*. Dubuque, Iowa: William C. Brown, 1973.

Egoff, Sheila, G. T. Stubbs, and L. F. Ashley, eds. *Only Connect: Readings on Children's Literature.* New York: Oxford University Press, 1969.

Hagman, Elmer R. "A Study of Fears of Children of Pre-School Age." *Journal of Experimental Education* 1 (1932): 110-30.

Huck, Charlotte S. *Children's Literature in the Elementary School.* 3rd ed. New York: Holt, Rinehart and Winston, 1976.

Landau, Elliott D., Sherrie Landau Epstein, and Ann Plaat Stone, eds. *Child Development through Literature.* Englewood Cliffs, N.J.: Prentice-Hall, 1972.

Larrick, Nancy. *A Parent's Guide to Children's Reading.* 4th rev. ed. New York: Doubleday, 1975.

Purves, Alan C., and Richard Beach. *Literature and the Reader: Research in Response to Literature, Reading Interests, and the Teaching of Literature.* Urbana, Ill.: National Council of Teachers of English, 1972.

Raths, Louis, Merrill Harmin, and Sidney B. Simon. *Values and Teaching: Working with Values in the Classroom.* Columbus, Ohio: Charles E. Merrill, 1966.

Reid, Virginia M., ed. *Reading Ladders for Human Relations.* 5th ed. Washington, D. C.: American Council of Education, 1972.

Rosenblatt, Louise M. *Literature as Exploration.* 3rd ed. New York: Noble and Noble, 1976.

Sebesta, Sam Leaton, and William J. Iverson. *Literature for Thursday's Child.* Chicago: Science Research Associates, 1975.

Steele, Mary Q. "Realism, Truth and Honesty." *Horn Book* 47 (February 1971): 17-27.

June Byers

PRESENTING POETRY

Young children respond easily and naturally to the language of poetry for two very good reasons. First, it usually is a shared experience with a loving adult, and, second, young children and poets are quite alike in their uses of language to express their observations. Listen to the figurative language used by small children: "I'm as wet as the rain"; "the Mountains look like lying down elephants"; "the waves spanked me"; "my toes ate a hole in my sock"; "your stomach is laughing." Such similes and personification are used by small children to render intelligible to themselves their perceptions of their environment. James Britton in *Language and Learning* explains clearly how children use language to structure their experiences. They use figurative language to incorporate new knowledge into their already established sense of reality. Poets do the same thing. Small children's use of the sounds of their language is also remarkable. "Milk, Albuquerque milk!" sung out by a three year old has an emphatic rhythm created by the contrast between the soft vowels and hard /k/'s. "Hyampon-Hoopa! Hyampon-Hoopa!" illustrates another child's delight in alliteration and meter. The chant evokes the 1 2 3 4, 1 2 3 4 beat of an Indian drum. Young children play with the sounds of language, as do poets. Young children speak of their perceptions in concrete terms, in images: "mothers water plants"; "fathers give you a piggy back ride"; "brothers are sticky"; "babies smell." Young children are very specific. They create images to explain how things seem to them. Again, poets do the same thing.

If at least these elements of poetry, figurative language, sound patterns, and imagery, are used spontaneously by very young children in their own speech, then it is not surprising that they respond quite naturally to poetry.

Fig. 22 (opposite). "Mary had a little lamb": Mother Goose rhymes should be among the first poetry selections read to young children. (Original in color)
From Book of Nursery and Mother Goose Rhymes *by Marguerite de Angeli. Copyright 1953, 1954 by Marguerite de Angeli. Used by permission of Doubleday & Company, Inc.*

Usually, Mother Goose rhymes provide the first experience. And how like their own language it is:

> Deedle, deedle dumpling, My Son John
> Went to bed with his stockings on.
> One shoe off and one shoe on.
> Deedle, deedle dumpling, My Son John.

The play with the sounds "Deedle, deedle dumpling," the repetition of the first and last lines, and the strong visual image of "Went to bed with his stockings on./ One shoe off and one shoe on" are so childlike that it is no wonder Mother Goose is an all-time favorite. Moreover, in this rhyme there is the "sense of nonsense" Kornei Chukovsky (1963) describes. As soon as a child becomes completely aware that shoes and stockings come off at bed-time, he or she is ready to laugh at My Son John's foolishness. Children verify their knowledge of things as they are when they see the reversal of the normal relationship of things. In *From Two to Five*, Chukovsky says, "We know that the child—and this is the main point—is amused by the reverse juxtaposition of things only when the real juxtaposition has become completely obvious to him" (p. 101).

Getting started. So start with Mother Goose rhymes. Although not always considered poetry, they provide the desirable sharing climate needed to introduce children to poetry. Children love to clap "Pease Porridge Hot," to go "Hippety Hop to the Barber Shop," to jump "Jack, Be Nimble," and to march "The Grand Old Duke of York" when the rhymes are available at an instant's notice, that is, when adults know them by heart. But sharing also happens over a book. Teachers and parents who read aloud rhymes and poems they themselves enjoy and who do not demand an immediate response create a sharing climate. Children often disclose their interpretation of a poem hours or even days after hearing it. Their response might be in the form of a painting, dance, song, or clay sculpture. Adults may not always recognize the response, but that is all right, too, because to quiz children about meaning or to demand identification of rhyming words or in any way to push for an interpretation probably short-circuits many children's need to respond on their own terms.

Beatrice Schenk de Regniers states succinctly in the introduction to *Poems Children Will Sit Still For* some hints for reading poetry to children.

> If you enjoy a poem yourself, you needn't be a theatrical star to read the poem so that children will enjoy it too. Just remember to:
> Read the poem aloud to yourself before you try it on the class.
> Read slowly enough so that children can absorb the images or the ideas.
> Read naturally, expressing whatever feelings you really feel. Do not adopt a special hushed poetry-reading voice.
> Have a good time. Your children will too.
>
> (p. 8)

Resources for teachers and other adults. Teachers and other adults often need ideas for enjoyable activities which deepen children's appreciation and understanding of poetry. *Find Time For Poetry: Kindergarten, First and*

Second Grade, developed under the leadership of Virginia Reid, lists suggested activities for more than 200 rhymes and poems, many appropriate for very young children. *Poetry and Verse for Urban Children*, edited by Donald J. Bissett, and *Poems Children Will Sit Still For*, compiled by de Regniers, are two very useful collections of poems as well as first-rate sources of activities which invite children to participate in the poetic experience. Gertrude A. Boyd's *Teaching Poetry in the Elementary School*, Betty Coody's *Using Literature with Young Children*, and Virginia Witucke's *Poetry in the Elementary School* are three small paperback books directed specifically to teachers and other adults which provide help on how to use poetry with children. The Children's Book Council has just completed *Prelude: Children's Book Council Mini-Seminars on Using Books Creatively*, a series of taped sessions which includes "Reading Poetry Aloud" by Sam Sebesta, who tells how to read to children effectively and provides follow-up activities. All these resources include suggestions for such physical or vocal engagement as pantomime, finger plays, expressive movement, clapping, marching, using rhythm instruments, dramatizing, echoing or joining in repetitive lines, and comparing events in the poems to personal experiences, as well as quiet listening and enjoying. The use of audio-visual equipment is discussed by some authors.

Acting out. Many poems elicit a physical response—stomping, leaping, prowling, or hopping—from small children, who like to be elephants, cats, rabbits, or frogs. Gather a small group of children around you sitting on the floor in an open space in the room. Choose a poem from *The Arbuthnot Anthology of Children's Literature* (Arbuthnot, 1971), such as "The Squirrel" (p. 60) or "Little Snail" by Hilda Conkling (p. 66) or "The Elephant's Trunk" by Alice Wilkins (p. 78), and read it aloud. If you choose "The Squirrel" because *you* like it, the children, having sensed your delight, will probably ask to hear it again. Then you might ask how many have seen a squirrel go "Whisky, frisky, Hippity, hop" and invite two or three to show how it moves. Others will want to join. Let them, as the excitement spreads, but never insist on complete participation. When all the children feel safe and are interested, all will want to take part in the fun.

Valerie Worth's "frog" (1972) offers an opportunity for a quiet group experience.

The spotted frog	His gold-circled eyes
Sits quite still	Stare hard
On a wet stone;	Like bright metal rings;
He is green	When he leaps
With a luster	He is like a stone
Of water on his skin;	Thrown into the pond;
His back is mossy	Water rings spread
With spots, and green	After him, bright circles
Like moss on a stone;	Of green, circles of gold.

(pp. 32-33)

After you read the entire poem, tell the children you will reread the first verse and they, staying right where they are around you on the floor, may become the spotted frog when they are ready. Read several times softly and slowly, "The spotted frog/Sits quite still/On a wet stone." Look thoughtfully around and say, "How still you are, James," or, "I can almost see your spots," or, "Can you feel how wet the stone is?" You might then invite the children to show, one after another, how a frog leaps.

Young children also like to be airplanes, boats, and steam shovels or to operate any kind of mechanical device. "Bam, Bam, Bam" by Eve Merriam (1966) excites some children to become demolition experts. If your children are city children, they may already know a great deal about the machinery used to knock down buildings.

> Pickaxes, pickaxes swinging today,
> Plaster clouds flying every which way.
>
> Workmen are covered with white dust like snow,
> Oh, come see the great demolition show!
>
> Slam, slam, slam,
> Goes the steel wrecking ball;
> Bam, bam, bam,
> Against a stone wall.
>
> It's raining bricks and wood
> In my neighborhood.
> Down go the houses,
> Down go the stores,
> Up goes a building
> With forty-seven floors.
> Crash goes a chimney,
> Pow goes a hall,
> Zowie goes a doorway,
> Zam goes a wall.
>
> Slam, slam, slam,
> Goes the steel wrecking ball;
> Bam, bam, bam,
> Changing it all.
>
> (pp. 12-13)

See if the children recognize the jump rope rhythm of these lines:

> Down go the houses,   (In comes the doctor,
> Down go the stores,   In comes the nurse,
> Up goes a building   In comes the lady
> With forty-seven floors.   With the alligator purse.)

Hardly a child can resist an opportunity to show how to be sassy or to tease. Shel Silverstein (1969) gives that opportunity in "Not Me." Before you read this poem, ask the children to be sassy in the way they sit, in the way they look at a neighbor, and in the way they stand. Then read:

> The Slithergadee has crawled out of the sea.
> He may catch all the others, but he won't catch me.

No, you won't catch me, old Slithergadee,
You may catch all the others, but you wo-
(p. 63)

Children always like this one very much and will, on the second or third read-ing, act out all kinds of sassy behavior. A few may realize the Slithergadee *did* catch the speaker, but some won't. With older children, a teacher may want to ask, "What happened?," and, "How do you know?," in an offhand manner, but probably not with very young children.

Dancing a poem. "Spring" by Karla Kuskin (from *In the Middle of the Trees)* provides an occasion to move with the rhythm of the lines. It is a good poem for dancing.

> I'm shouting
> I'm singing
> I'm swinging through the trees
> I'm winging sky high
> With the buzzing black bees.
> I'm the sun
> I'm the moon
> I'm the dew on the rose.
> I'm a rabbit
> Whose habit
> Is twitching his nose.
> I'm lively
> I'm lovely
> I'm kicking my heels
> I'm crying "Come dance"
> To the fresh water eels.
> I'm racing through meadows
> Without any coat.
> I'm a gamboling lamb
> I'm a light leaping goat.
> I'm a bud
> I'm a bloom
> I'm a dove on the wing.
> I'm running on rooftops
> And welcoming spring!
>
> (p. 10)

The most natural way to help children start dancing is to ask them to clap the rhythm as you read it. If you can remember the words without looking at the page, then you can more easily guide the rhythm and share the joy of the poem as you smile directly first at one child and then another. Then ask them to face a partner and hold hands. Repeat the words of the poem, this time swaying with the rhythm. They will swing hands and swing their bodies; some will even begin to move around the room. It is hard to resist, especially if you take a partner and join the dance. You will all get the feel of the poem in your bones.

Another poem with a very different rhythm is "Chant III" by David McCord (1952; see Fig. 23). Instead of a smooth, gliding dance evoked by "Spring," the children will produce a quick staccato set of movements. It is almost impossible for young children to listen to this poem and not tap their feet or clap their hands. With a partner in a large circle, children can experiment with the rhythm as you read or recite the words. Most of them will probably start with a march. Encourage them to improvise. If you need to, ask, "Can you skip to this?," or, "What else can you do?" The second or third time you do this poem, you will be pleased with the variations the children have discovered.

Choral speaking and joining in repetitive lines. Some poems invite a vocal response. Children naturally join in when the sounds of the language

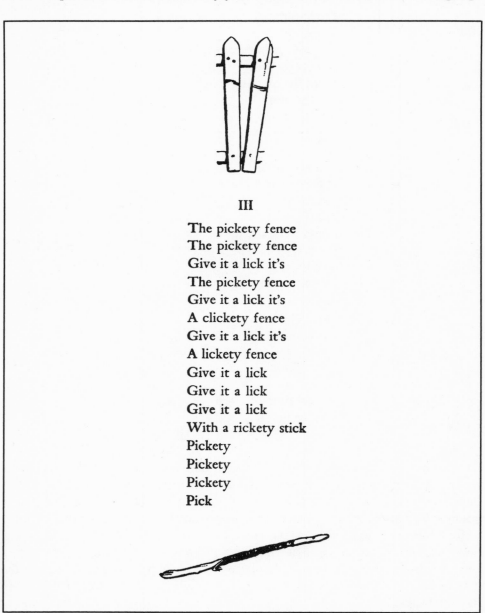

III

The pickety fence
The pickety fence
Give it a lick it's
The pickety fence
Give it a lick it's
A clickety fence
Give it a lick it's
A lickety fence
Give it a lick
Give it a lick
Give it a lick
With a rickety stick
Pickety
Pickety
Pickety
Pick

Fig. 23. Children catch the rhythm of this poem lickety split.
Copyright ©1952 by David McCord. From Far and Few: Rhymes of the Never Was and Always Is *by David McCord, by permission of Little, Brown and Co.*

give them pleasure. Try "Mouse" by Mary Ann Hoberman (in *A Little Book
of Little Beasts*):

Dear little
Mere little
Merry little
Meadow Mouse
    Where do you live? Where do you live?
In a mole's hole
Bird's nest
Hollow of a hickory
  That's where I live. That's where I live.

Dear little
Mere little
Merry little
Meadow Mouse
    What do you do? What do you do?
Hunt for food and care for my babies
  That's what I do. That's what I do.

Dear little
Mere little
Merry little
Meadow Mouse
    What do you eat? What do you eat?
Roots and
Seeds and
Nuts and
Insects
  That's what I eat. That's what I eat.

Dear little
Mere little
Merry little
Meadow Mouse
    What do you fear? What do you fear?
Every kind of stranger
Every kind of danger
  That's what I fear. That's what I fear.

Dear little
Mere little
Merry little
Meadow Mouse
    What do you love? What do you love?
Running and
Racing and
Chasing round in circles
  That's what I love. That's what I love.
                        (p. 29)

Before you finish the poem, many children will help you with the first four lines of each verse. By the second or third reading, they will join in the question, "Where do you live?," and the answer, "That's where I live." If it gives them pleasure, you might divide them into two groups, one to ask and one to answer each question in unison with you. But don't make it a chore.

Chicken Soup with Rice by Maurice Sendak has the same appeal for children.

> In January   In February
> it is so nice   it will be
> while slipping   my snowman's
> on the sliding ice   anniversary
> to sip hot chicken soup   with cake for him
> with rice.   and soup for me.
> Sipping once   Happy once
> sipping twice   happy twice
> sipping chicken soup   happy chicken soup
> with rice.   with rice.
>
> (pp. 6-7)

The poem continues on through all the months of the year. Children catch on to the pattern of the last four lines and sing them out with gusto. "Sipping once/sipping twice/sipping chicken soup/with rice" quickly becomes a great favorite. Children will pick up phrases from Ellen Raskin's comical rhymes in *Who, Said Sue, Said Whoo?*:

> The polka dot cow said moo.
> Then who, said Sue,
> Said chitter-chitter-chatter,
> And who said whoo?

Finding the animals, guessing who made the strange sounds, and repeating the rhymes quickly involves children in this book (see Fig. 24).

Rhymes and jingles to chant. Almost all young children love the old folk rhyme "Over in the Meadow." They love to chant first the number words; then, on a second or third hearing, entire lines become their own and they love to help read it, "'Buzz,' said the mother,/'We buzz,' said the five." The beautiful edition of the poem illustrated by Ezra Jack Keats (1972) will enrich any collection of picture poetry books for children. Poems, rhymes, and jingles which contain a "sense of nonsense" or just play with the sounds of language greatly attract young children to sing along. *It's Raining Said John Twaining,* Danish nursery rhymes collected by N. M. Bodecker, *Father Fox's Pennyrhymes* by Clyde Watson, and *Let's Marry Said the Cherry* by Bodecker will probably be around for a long time. Children like them.

Riddles. Poems read as riddles elicit another type of verbal response enjoyed by young children. Try "What Is It?" by Marie Louise Allen (in *A Pocketful of Poems*). Ask the children if they like riddles and then say, "I'm going to read you a riddle. Listen carefully and when I have finished, see if you know the answer to this riddle."

Tall ears
Twinkly nose
Tiny tail
And—hop, he goes.

His ears are long
His tail is small
And he doesn't make any
Noise at all.

What is he—
Can you guess?
I feed him carrots
And water cress.

Tall ears
Twinkly nose
Tiny tail
And—hop, he goes.

(pp. 8-9)

Fig. 24. Sue takes a ride and finds her car filled with animals and their sounds. Children enjoy repeating her question. (Original in color) *Copyright ©1973 by Ellen Raskin. From* Who, Said Sue, Said Whoo? *Used by permission of Atheneum Publishers.*

With older children, you might ask, "How did you know it was a rabbit?," but the teacher or parent has to decide whether or not the children are interested in this activity. Most very young children are not.

Another short riddle is "Who Am I?" by Mary Ann Hoberman (in *A Little Book of Little Beasts*).

> No matter where I travel,
> No matter where I roam,
> No matter where I find myself
> I always am at home.
>   (pp. 36-37)

After letting the children guess, show the elegant two-page answer to the riddle, a turtle drawn by Peter Parnall. Tucked down in the lower corner of the right-hand page, easy to miss, is a small snail, with this verse:

> Sniffed the snail
> In its shell
> "This fact is true
> Of me as well."

This is a lovely, low-key way of extending children's ability to note likenesses and differences.

Private responses. Not all poems elicit either physical or verbal participation. Many are for quiet listening, enjoying, wondering. Children's responses may be very private and they may not wish to share. So don't press for a discussion; just read the poem and sit quietly, being guided by the children's mood. Try "Sunday Morning Lonely" by Lucille Clifton (in *Some of the Days of Everett Anderson*).

> Daddy's back
> is broad and black
> and Everett Anderson loves to ride it.
>
> Daddy's side
> is black and wide
> and Everett Anderson sits beside it.
>
> Daddy's cheek
> is black and sleek
> and Everett Anderson kisses it.
>
> Daddy's space
> is a black empty place
> And Everett Anderson misses it.

Many parts of *In My Mother's House* by Ann Nolan Clark are ideal for quiet listening.

> This is my Mother's house;   He made it big;
> My father made it.   He made it high;
> He made it with adobe bricks; My Mother's house,
> He made it strong;   I live in it.
>   (p. 6)

The poem "Half Asleep" by Aileen Fisher (in *My Cat Has Eyes of Sapphire Blue*) amuses children. Although they may ask to hear it often, they may not want to talk about it. They often laugh and puzzle privately.

> To assume a cat's asleep
> is a grave mistake.
> He can close his eyes and keep
> both his ears awake.

(p. 9)

"Poem" by Langston Hughes (in *The Dream Keeper*) is well received by young children. They are susceptible to the tender feelings expressed.

> I loved my friend.
> He went away from me.
> There's nothing more to say.
> The poem ends,
> Soft as it began—
> I loved my friend.

(p. 12)

You will find other poems very young children like to hear, and you may not always know why they appeal to young listeners. Perhaps it is because poets possess the gift of immediacy which helps keep alive in children their native love of language. Gifted poets help them grow in their power to use language, to sort out their own experiences, and to discover for themselves the meaning of their own worlds. Children need many joyous experiences with poetry and with people who love poetry.

CHILDREN'S BOOK REFERENCES

Allen, Marie Louise. *A Pocketful of Poems.* Harper, 1957.

Arbuthnot, May Hill, comp. *The Arbuthnot Anthology of Children's Literature.* Rev. ed. Scott, Foresman, 1971.

Bissett, Donald J., ed. *Poetry and Verse for Urban Children.* 3 vols. Chandler Publishing, 1967.

Bodecker, N. M. *It's Raining Said John Twaining: Danish Nursery Rhymes.* Atheneum, 1973.

———. *Let's Marry Said the Cherry and Other Nonsense Poems.* Atheneum, 1974.

Clark, Ann Nolan. *In My Mother's House.* Illus. by Velino Herrera. Viking, 1941. PB.

Clifton, Lucille. *Some of the Days of Everett Anderson.* Illus. by Evaline Ness. Holt, 1970. PB.

de Regniers, Beatrice Schenk, et al., eds. *Poems Children Will Sit Still For: A Selection for the Primary Grades.* Citation, 1969. PB.

Fisher, Aileen. *My Cat Has Eyes of Sapphire Blue.* Illus. by Marie Angel. Crowell, 1973.

Hoberman, Mary Ann. *A Little Book of Little Beasts.* Illus. by Peter Parnall. Simon and Schuster, 1973.

Hughes, Langston. *The Dream Keeper.* Illus. by Helen Sewell. Knopf, 1932.

Keats, Ezra Jack, illus. *Over in the Meadow.* Four Winds, 1972.

Kuskin, Karla. *In the Middle of the Trees.* Harper, 1958.

McCord, David. *Far and Few: Rhymes of the Never Was and Always Is.* Illus. by Henry B. Kane. Little, 1952. PB: Dell.

Merriam, Eve. *Catch a Little Rhyme.* Illus. by Imero Gobbato. Atheneum, 1966.

Raskin, Ellen. *Who, Said Sue, Said Whoo?* Atheneum, 1973.

Sendak, Maurice. *Chicken Soup with Rice* in *The Nutshell Library.* Harper, 1962. PB: Scholastic Book Services.

Silverstein, Shel. "Not Me" in *Voices: An Anthology of Poems and Pictures.* Book 2. Ed. by Geoffrey Summerfield. Rand McNally, 1969. PB.

Watson, Clyde. *Father Fox's Pennyrhymes.* Illus. by Wendy Watson. Crowell, 1971. PB: Scholastic Book Services.

Worth, Valerie. *Small Poems.* Illus. by Natalie Babbitt. Farrar, 1972.

PROFESSIONAL REFERENCES

Boyd, Gertrude A. *Teaching Poetry in the Elementary School.* Columbus, Ohio: Charles E. Merrill, 1973.

Britton, James. *Language and Learning.* Coral Gables, Fla.: University of Miami Press, 1971.

Chukovsky, Kornei. *From Two to Five.* Ed. and trans. by Miriam Morton. Berkeley, Calif.: University of California Press, 1963.

Coody, Betty. *Using Literature with Young Children.* Dubuque, Iowa: William C. Brown, 1973.

Reid, Virginia, ed. *Find Time for Poetry: Kindergarten, First and Second Grade.* Hayward, Calif.: Alameda County Schools, 1963.

Sebesta, Sam. "Reading Poetry Aloud." *Prelude: Children's Book Council Mini-Seminars on Using Books Creatively.* New York: The Children's Book Council, 1975. Cassettes.

Witucke, Virginia. *Poetry in the Elementary School.* Literature for Children Series. Dubuque, Iowa: William C. Brown, 1970.

Bernice E. Cullinan

TRADITIONAL LITERATURE: CHILDREN'S LEGACY

There are strong connections between young children and traditional tales and nursery rhymes. Those who know children and folk literature have commented about children's natural affinity for that body of literature. Young children are drawn to the old tales as if by magnetic force, and many have conjectured about the causes.

Huck (1976, pp. 22-24) proposes that the developmental stages of children's thinking described by Piaget and the characteristics of folklore serve as partial explanation for this affinity. Children between the ages of two and seven are in the "preoperational stage." Their thoughts are largely based on perception; they may successively attend to particular aspects of an object or an experience, but they are usually unable to generalize or to deal simultaneously with more than one of these aspects at a time. Consequently, they are as yet unable to handle complex relationships or to deal with abstractions, e.g., young children have difficulty remembering a large cast of characters and a series of events in a story. Therefore, cumulative folktales which repeat each event from the beginning, such as *This Is the House That Jack Built* and *The Gingerbread Boy*, are especially appealing to children of this age. Cumulative tales bring all previous events into the present to build a scene with the past plainly visible.

Children who are trying to comprehend seriation, i.e., attempting to arrange things in sequence, are interested in stories which have characters of increasing size, such as *The Three Bears* (Baby Bear, Mama Bear, and Papa Bear) and *The Three Billy Goats Gruff* (the littlest goat, the middle size goat, and the great big goat). Many folktales have three characters and three events in which the gradations in size are made explicit in the presentation of the story.

Children's thinking during the preoperational stage is animistic and parallels that of the prescientific peoples who created the fairy tales. Explanations, often involving magical powers, were created for those things that were

85

not understood. The world of the fairy tale, peopled with dragons, witches, trolls, and elves, is very believable to the young child. The mythical quality of the language of the old tales reinforces, in fact, creates, the magic. Children alter their beliefs and behavior as interactions between their inner schemata and the outer world demand it, but during this stage, they see great appeal in a body of literature geared to their level of thought.

While folk literature embodies the superstitions, feelings, and dreams of simple people, thus providing basic fare for young children, who share the tales' uncomplicated view of the world, folk literature is nonetheless the foundation of all literature. In it, the wit and wisdom of the ages are captured and preserved to be passed on to each new generation. As the special province of young children, the old tales serve as the basis for understanding all other literature and can provide children with their initial experience in the magic good literature can weave.

Bettelheim (1976) supports the use of folk and fairy tales for yet another reason. He believes they are crucial for the psychological development of the child. He makes a convincing case that folklore helps children overcome psychological and emotional insecurities by suggesting images for their fantasies. He describes the tales as a magic mirror which reflects the inner fears and fantasies that children have. The old tales reassure the child because good always overcomes evil, the weak and small win through perseverance, and justice prevails. Since it is often the littlest child, the youngest son or daughter, or the smallest animal who succeeds in the tales, young children find comfort in knowing that in a world where it seems everyone is bigger and stronger, they can win in the end. They can expect hard work and trials of some kind, but the hope of future success sustains them. Thus, children are subtly reassured; moreover, their moral development is influenced because virtue pays off in these stories.

> Fairy tales, unlike any other form of literature, direct the child to discover his identity and calling, and they also suggest what experiences are needed to develop his character further. Fairy tales intimate that a rewarding, good life is within one's reach despite adversity—but only if one does not shy away from the hazardous struggles without which one can never achieve true identity. These stories promise that if a child dares to engage in this fearsome and taxing search, benevolent powers will come to his aid, and he will succeed. (Bettelheim, 1976, p. 24)

Young children have fears which they cannot express and do not really understand. Folklore gives body and form to their fears and treats those forms in a way that children can accept. The happy endings are a satisfying and comforting ingredient to young children, since they are encouraged to believe that things will be all right in their world, too. They accept the fact that a fairy godmother is looking out for them, and this provides a source of comfort. Children are hopeful and optimistic about their world, where they expect good things to happen. As Huck (1976) states, "When you close the door on hope, you have left the realm of childhood" (p. 6). The fairy tale form, with its happy ending, is as it should be in the child's mind. At the same time, just as virtue is rewarded, so is evil punished. The witch is destroyed and Hansel and Gretel return to their father, who welcomes them. The troll is pushed over the bridge into the raging waters below. This matches the uncompromising type of justice which the young child expects. The frightening parts in folk and fairy tales heighten the drama and add to the suspense, but children know that things will turn out right. They are sure that witches will be pushed into ovens, that trolls will be beaten, and that wolves will be caught. Children who are snuggled safely in an adult's lap while they hear such terrifying events are not really scared. They ask for such stories to be repeated time and time again, enjoying the shivers while they wait for the anticipated ending when all is well.

Beyond moral development, the tales encourage a sense of humor in young readers or listeners and the exercise of the imagination. Folktales make children laugh. There are Noodlehead stories where the child knows better than to do the ridiculous things that the silly hero does. Children are in on the joke. They know it is only an acorn that hits Henny Penny on the head and makes her think that the sky is falling. They realize that Hans is not in luck trading for less valuable things each time he has a problem with a newly acquired item. The sense of humor used in stories like *The Squire's Bride* (Asbjørnsen, 1976), *Hans Clodhopper* (Andersen, 1975), and *The Three Sillies* (Front, 1975) is exaggerated and overdone, so children know what is lampoon and what is straight.

Chukovsky (1963) believes that "fantasy is the most valuable attribute of the human mind and should be diligently nurtured from earliest childhood" (p. 119). The magic of words and pictures in folk and fairy tales creates new images and feeds children's insatiable curiosity. The old tales make visible to the inward eye things that the child wonders and fantasizes about; they encourage dreaming and fantasizing about the world that each child will conquer, allowing children to imagine what might be rather than leaving them in the realistic world of what is.

The potential rewards of traditional literature for the child are due in part to the tales' accessibility, that is, their clear-cut structure, characters, and language. The dramatic dilemmas of the tales, for example, are stated briefly and pointedly, with no confusing side issues. This simplistic view of the world is acceptable to young children and stories that embody this world view are comprehensible to them: the Gingerbread Boy must run as fast as he can to get away from the little old woman and the little old man; the queen must guess Rumpelstiltskin's name or he will take her child; Hansel and Gretel must get away from the old witch or she will eat them. The plots within which these dilemmas occur are short and direct. The three pigs seek their fortune and each builds his house of different material; the wolf tries to huff and puff and blow each house down, which he does until he comes to the third pig's house, and there he gets his comeuppance. The definitive conclusion of the tale appeals to children's sense of finality.

The characters in folktales are also clearly drawn. To the adult reader they are stereotypes, not fully developed characters. But folk characters embody the virtue or vice they represent as symbols for goodness, purity, greed, or wickedness, a function that excludes all ambiguities in the presentation of characters. Children can easily recognize who should be punished and who should be rewarded, e.g., the three Billy Goats Gruff are just going across the bridge to eat the green grass; it is the terrible troll who is at fault and it is a just reward when he is butted into the stream.

Finally, folktales have appealing language with an immediacy similar to the language a child uses. They are tempered to the tongue, because they have come from an oral tradition. The tales' language is direct and conversational, making the listener feel that the storyteller is speaking directly to him or her. All unnecessary descriptions, details, and lengthy sections have been pared away in the process of handing the stories down by word of mouth, and stilted prose has been deleted through repeated adaptations. Only the elements crucial to understanding remain.

The language contains phrases which are easily committed to memory and devices which aid the storyteller in remembering the tale. There are clues which serve to jog the storyteller's memory, and phrases, once started, almost repeat themselves: "First she tasted Papa Bear's porridge. It was too hot. Then she tasted Mama Bear's porridge. It was too cold. Then she tasted Baby Bear's porridge. And it was just right. So she ate it all up." The refrains intrigue children. They want to join in. They mimic the Gingerbread Boy who says, "Run, run, as fast as you can. You can't catch me. I'm the Gingerbread Man. I ran away from the little old woman. I ran away from the little old man. And I can run away from you. I can. I can." Children respond to the rhyme and the rhythm and can repeat the refrain after one hearing. The repetition of phrases and events is welcomed by the young child, who responds to language play.

EXPLORING TRADITIONAL LITERATURE WITH CHILDREN

Traditional literature can be used as basic content for early childhood programs. Some of the many ways in which it can be explored are presented here. Children rightfully deserve traditional literature; it is their legacy. Use it generously!

Comparisons of Different Versions of the Tales

Illustrations. Since the traditional tales have been interpreted by many different artists in single editions, there are several versions of many of the tales. Compare the way Marcia Brown (Asbjørnsen and Moe, 1957) portrays *The Three Billy Goats Gruff* with the way Paul Galdone (Asbjørnsen, 1973) and Susan Blair (Asbjørnsen, 1963) picture them. Since the illustrations are such an integral part of the experience for young children, they can be compared to see which version carries the most impact in its depiction of characters and events. *Hansel and Gretel* has been portrayed in very different ways—Adrienne Adams's version (Grimm Brothers, 1975) gives the dark, spooky feeling of the forest (see Fig. 25); Joan Walsh Anglund in *Nibble Nibble Mousekin* pictures cherubic children lost in a tangle of woods, vines, bats, and other scary things, while Arnold Lobel (Grimm Brothers, 1971)

Fig. 25 (opposite). Adrienne Adams's forest is dark and spooky. (Original in color) *Illustration by Adrienne Adams is reprinted by permission of Charles Scribner's Sons from* Hansel and Gretel. *Illustration copyright © 1975 Adrienne Adams.*

portrays them in a totally different way. Bernadette's Red Riding Hood (Grimm Brothers, 1968) wanders amid flower-filled pages, whereas Galdone's interpretation (Grimm Brothers, 1974) presents a very cocky wolf leaning against a tree talking with the spritely little girl (see Fig. 26). Both Trina Schart Hyman (Grimm Brothers, 1974) and Nancy Ekholm Burkert (Grimm Brothers, 1972) have produced lovely editions of *Snow White* in which medieval backgrounds provide the setting. *Rapunzel* has been portrayed very differently by Bernadette Watts (Grimm Brothers, 1974, 1975) and Felix Hoffmann (Grimm Brothers, 1961; see Fig. 27).

Characters in the Mother Goose rhymes are interpreted differently by Evaline Ness in her *Old Mother Hubbard and Her Dog* (Mother Goose, 1972) and by Ib Spang Olsen (Martin, 1975). Katrin Brandt's elves in *The Elves and the Shoemaker* (Grimm Brothers, 1967) prance nakedly across the page, while those pictured by Adams in *The Shoemaker and the Elves* (Grimm Brothers, 1960) are much more refined. *Cinderella* looks much different as envisioned by Sheilah Beckett (Perrault, 1974), Brown (Perrault, 1954), Errol Le Cain (Perrault, 1972), and Beni Montresor (Perrault, 1965).

Plot. Many of the same basic plot lines appear in folklore of different countries. *Duffy and the Devil* by Harve and Margot Zemach is a Cornish

Fig. 26. Galdone's version of the wolf and Little Red Riding Hood adds humor to the old tale. (Original in color)
From Little Red Riding Hood *by Paul Galdone. Copyright © 1974 by Paul Galdone. Used with permission of McGraw-Hill Book Company.*

Fig. 27 (opposite). The magic ambience of *Rapunzel* is intensified by Felix Hoffmann's illustrations. (Original in color)
Reproduced from Rapunzel *written by the Brothers Grimm by permission of Harcourt Brace Jovanovich, Inc., and Mrs. Felix Hoffmann; copyright 1949 by Amerbach-Verlag, Basle; © 1961 by Oxford University Press, London.*

version of the German *Rumpelstiltskin*. *Chicken Licken* by Kenneth McLeish is built upon the same sequence of events as Galdone and Veronica S. Hutchinson's treatments of *Henny Penny*. The name of the main character varies delightfully (Duck Luck, Cock Lock), but the same sad end comes in each. *The Gunniwolf* by Wilhelmina Harper is structured much like *Little Red Riding Hood*. There are several variations of *The Gingerbread Boy*, among them *Journey Cake, Ho!* by Ruth Sawyer and *The Bun* by Brown. All involve a cake, cookie, or bun that tries to escape, although the circumstances and the other characters differ. Variations on this theme are found in Cynthia Jameson's *The Clay Pot Boy* and Jack Kent's *The Fat Cat*. Both the boy and the cat eat everything in their paths as they make their way through these cumulative tales. The story of the man and wife who trade jobs for a day varies somewhat as told by David McKee in *The Man Who Was Going to Mind the House* and by William Wiesner in *Turnabout*. Barbara Walker has presented a variation of *Hansel and Gretel* in her *Teeny Tiny and the Witch Woman*, while Janina Domanska's *The Turnip* differs slightly from Alexei Tolstoy's *The Great Big Enormous Turnip*.

Language. Some children will want to compare the language of the tales. Only the English version of *Tom Tit Tot* (Jacobs, 1965) illustrated by Ness has the pleasing rhyme "Nimmy Nimmy Not, My name's Tom Tit Tot," while the German *Rumpelstiltskin* is less colorful. Edith Tarcov's retelling of the latter story (Grimm Brothers, 1973) includes common names of today — "Is it Tom? Is it Dick? Is it Harry?" — as the queen tries to guess the name.

Plotting the Sequence of a Folktale

Cumulative tales are good for plotting the trail of events. Long strips of paper or roller movies can be used to show the route and the characters along the way. *King Rooster, Queen Hen* by Anita Lobel, a variation of *The Bremen Town Musicians* (Grimm Brothers, 1968), is appropriate for this activity. As the rooster and hen make their way toward the city, many other animals offer their services to help them along. Each new addition can be plotted along their journey to the sudden climax at the fox's house. *One Fine Day* by Nonny Hogrogian, *Hans in Luck* (Grimm Brothers, 1975), illustrated by Hoffmann, and *The Old Woman and Her Pig* by Galdone are also good tales to plot.

Storytelling

By telling the tales themselves, children can have the experience of being the storyteller, using the dramatic voice, telling things in sequence, and entertaining their classmates. The younger the child, the simpler the tale; the older the child, the more variations on a theme.

Using the story framework as a basis for a new story is a popular activity which helps young children develop the concept of a beginning, a middle, and an end for a complete story. Stewig calls this activity parallel plot construction (see his chapter "Encouraging Language Growth"). The familiar tales which have three characters and three events serve well for the story framework, e.g., *The Frog Prince* (Grimm Brothers, 1975), illustrated by Galdone.

Although children in the egocentric stage seldom can assume and maintain a point of view different from their own, it is fun for them to try to tell a story from the point of view of one of the characters generally maligned in the original version. Ask children to pretend that they are one of Cinderella's stepsisters, the troll in *The Three Billy Goats Gruff*, or the giant in *Jack and the Beanstalk* and to tell the story as that character might.

Exploring Parodies and Modernized Versions of the Tales

Because the folktales are so well known, children can enjoy parodies of them. In order to appreciate a parody, one must know the original well. Stories such as *Jim and the Beanstalk* by Raymond Briggs, *King Grizzly Beard* (Grimm Brothers, 1973), illustrated by Maurice Sendak, and *The White Rat's Tale* by Barbara Schiller are fun to read. Children can write their own satiric tales with a group or by themselves.

An interesting dialect version of *Goldilocks* is found in *Old Tales* (Grimm Brothers, 1970); Galdone's *The History of Mother Twaddle and the Marvelous Achievements of Her Son Jack* is another interesting variation.

Playing with the Language

The folktales have language that is tempered to the tongue, with lots of repetitive phrases. Children like to play with language, and whenever they hear a delicious phrase, they will repeat it without invitation. Some of the tales that are especially fun are Arlene Mosel's *Tikki Tikki Tembo*, Galdone's *The Little Red Hen*, and Wanda Gág's *Millions of Cats*, a story in the folktale tradition. Ennis Rees's *Brer Rabbit and His Tricks* and *More of Brer Rabbit's Tricks* are also interesting.

Many folktales are familiar as songs and children enjoy singing them over and over. When these are printed in a book with exciting illustrations, the fun is increased. Rodney Peppe (1972), Galdone (1966), and Ed Emberley (Barbara Emberley, 1969) have each illustrated *Simon's Song*. John Langstaff's *Oh, A-Hunting We Will Go* and Pam Adams's *This Old Man* are two others which children will repeat often.

Creative Drama

Simple tales and strong character identity make improvisation easy and fun. A child needs nothing more than a red hat or scarf to become Red Riding Hood. A low table or a board placed across two chairs sets the stage for the three Billy Goats Gruff. Children are natural actors; encourage them to re-create the stories they have heard.

Puppetry

The simple plots and stereotypic characters of folktales make excellent source material for puppet shows. Simple stick puppets or those made with paper bags are adequate to represent the characters. Many of the traditional stories can be interpreted through puppetry, but those with only a few characters are easiest for small children to manipulate. A variation on the puppet stage can be made with a long strip of paper. By drawing the background scenery, each child can have an individual puppet stage merely by cutting a slit along the ground line and sliding the stick puppets through to move them along to meet the other characters and enact the story's events.

Flannel Board Stories

Cumulative tales are easily adapted to flannel boards. The characters can be represented with cutout figures which do not require a lot of detail and can be cut from flannel or paper (oaktag) backed with flannel or felt. As each new character is added, the figure can be placed on the board to fill the space and tell the story. Not only adults can make these cutouts; children enjoy making their own. Once the pieces are cut, children will use them again and again to tell the story. Some of the many stories adaptable for flannel board use include *One Fine Day* by Hogrogian, *The Wise Man on the Mountain* by Ellis Dillon, *There Was an Old Lady Who Swallowed a Fly* by Pam Adams, and *Why Mosquitoes Buzz in People's Ears* by Verna Aardema.

Games

Cumulative tales suggested under the plotting and flannel board sections are easily adapted to board games. The events in each story become signposts for children to advance a marker toward the final goal. Matching games can also be placed on a worksheet:

Which ones go together?

Little Red Riding Hood	Wolf
The Three Billy Goats Gruff	Fox
Jack and the Beanstalk	Giant
The Gingerbread Boy	Troll

Cooking

Cooking is a valuable learning experience for young children. Counting and measuring skills are developed as children create their own "stone soup" or "nail soup" and gingerbread boys. Black jelly beans can substitute for "24 blackbirds baked in a pie," and a "bitter butter batter" can be made. *The Funny Little Woman* by Mosel is a perfect story to read before making rice cakes; "Johnny Cake" can also be made after reading that story. Reading *Strega Nona* by Tomie de Paola can be followed by making a big pot of spaghetti.

Art Activities

The classroom should be well supplied with a wide variety of materials with which children can create their own interpretations of folklore tales and characters. These items should be easily accessible so that a drawing or construction activity is encouraged at any time. The children will help keep the art center stocked with egg cartons, yarn, string, buttons, styrofoam, toothpicks, magazines, uncooked macaroni and noodles, cardboard tubes, foil trays, and paper, fabric, and wood scraps.

Stuffed Animals

Doll characters can be made from stuffed paper bag forms, fabric stitched by hand or machine, or socks. Some commercial ones are available in which three or more characters are built into one doll and can be revealed by turning the doll upside down, removing a hat, or turning it around.

CHILDREN'S BOOK REFERENCES

Aardema, Verna. *Why Mosquitoes Buzz in People's Ears*. Illus. by Leo and Diane Dillon. Dial, 1975.

Adams, Pam. *There Was an Old Lady Who Swallowed a Fly*. Grosset, 1973.

_____. *This Old Man*. Grosset, 1974.

Alderson, Brian. *Cakes and Custard*. Illus. by Helen Oxenbury. Morrow, 1975.

Andersen, Hans Christian. *Hans Clodhopper*. Retold and illus. by Leon Shtainmets. Lippincott, 1975.

Anglund, Joan Walsh. *Nibble Nibble Mousekin: A Tale of Hansel and Gretel*. Harcourt, 1962.

Asbjørnsen, P. C. *The Squire's Bride*. Illus. by Marcia Sewall. Atheneum, 1976.

_____. *Three Billy Goats Gruff*. Illus. by Susan Blair. Holt, 1963. PB: Scholastic Book Services.

_____. *Three Billy Goats Gruff*. Illus. by Paul Galdone. Seabury, 1973.

Asbjørnsen, P. C., and Jorgen E. Moe. *Three Billy Goats Gruff*. Illus. by Marcia Brown. Harcourt, 1957.

Briggs, Raymond. *Jim and the Beanstalk*. Coward, 1970.

Brown, Marcia. *The Bun: A Tale from Russia*. Harcourt, 1972.

_____. *Stone Soup*. Scribner, 1947. PB.

de Paola, Tomie. *Strega Nona*. Prentice-Hall, 1975.

Dillon, Ellis. *The Wise Man on the Mountain*. Illus. by Gaynor Chapman. Atheneum, 1969.

Domanska, Janina. *The Turnip*. Macmillan, 1969. PB.

Emberley, Barbara. *Simon's Song*. Illus. by Ed Emberley. Prentice-Hall, 1969. PB.

Frasconi, Antonio. *The House That Jack Built: A Picture Book in Two Languages*. Harcourt, 1958.

Front, Sheila, adapter. *The Three Sillies*. Illus. by Charles Front. Addison-Wesley, 1975.

Gág, Wanda. *Millions of Cats*. Coward, 1928.

Galdone, Paul. *The Gingerbread Boy*. Seabury, 1975.

————. *Henny Penny*. Seabury, 1968.

————. *The History of Mother Twaddle and the Marvelous Achievements of Her Son Jack*. Seabury, 1974.

————. *The History of Simple Simon*. McGraw, 1966.

————. *The House That Jack Built*. McGraw, 1961.

————. *The Little Red Hen*. Seabury, 1973. PB: Scholastic Book Services.

————. *The Old Woman and Her Pig*. McGraw, 1960.

————. *The Three Bears*. Seabury, 1972. PB: Scholastic Book Services.

————. *The Three Little Pigs*. Seabury, 1970.

Grimm Brothers. *The Bremen Town Musicians*. Illus. by Paul Galdone. McGraw, 1968.

————. *The Elves and the Shoemaker*. Illus. by Katrin Brandt. Follett, 1967.

————. *The Frog Prince*. Illus. by Paul Galdone. McGraw, 1975.

————. "Goldilocks and the Three Bears" in *Old Tales*. Adapted by Joan Baratz and William Stewart. Education Study Center, 1970.

————. *Hans in Luck*. Illus. by Felix Hoffmann. Atheneum, 1975.

————. *Hansel and Gretel*. Trans. by Charles Scribner, Jr. Illus. by Adrienne Adams. Scribner, 1975.

————. *Hansel and Gretel*. Illus. by Arnold Lobel. Delacorte, 1971.

————. *King Grizzly Beard*. Trans. by Edgar Taylor. Illus. by Maurice Sendak. Farrar, 1973.

————. *Little Red Riding Hood*. Illus. by Bernadette. World Publishing, 1968.

————. *Little Red Riding Hood*. Illus. by Paul Galdone. McGraw, 1974.

————. *Rapunzel*. Illus. by Felix Hoffmann. Harcourt, 1961.

————. *Rapunzel*. Retold and illus. by Bernadette Watts. Crowell, 1974, 1975.

————. *Rumpelstiltskin*. Retold by Edith Tarcov. Illus. by Edward Gorey. Four Winds, 1973.

————. *Rumpelstiltskin*. Illus. by William Stobbs. Walck, 1970.

————. *The Shoemaker and the Elves*. Illus. by Adrienne Adams. Scribner, 1960.

————. *Snow White*. Trans. by Paul Heins. Illus. by Trina Schart Hyman. Little, 1974.

————. *Snow White and the Seven Dwarfs*. Trans. by Randall Jarrell. Illus. by Nancy Ekholm Burkert. Farrar, 1972.

————. *The Traveling Musicians*. Illus. by Hans Fischer. Harcourt, 1955.

Harper, Wilhelmina. *The Gunniwolf*. Illus. by William Wiesner. Dutton, 1967.

Hogrogian, Nonny. *One Fine Day*. Macmillan, 1971. PB.

Hutchinson, Veronica S. *Henny Penny.* Illus. by Leonard B. Lubin. Little, 1976.

Jacobs, Joseph. *Jack and the Beanstalk.* Illus. by Margery Gill. Walck, 1975.

———. *Johnny Cake.* Illus. by Emma L. Brock. Putnam, 1933.

———. *Tom Tit Tot.* Illus. by Evaline Ness. Scribner, 1965.

Jameson, Cynthia. *The Clay Pot Boy.* Illus. by Arnold Lobel. Coward, 1973. PB: Dell.

Kellogg, Steven. *There Was an Old Woman.* Parents, 1974.

Kent, Jack. *The Fat Cat.* Parents, 1974. PB: Scholastic Book Services.

Langstaff, John. *Oh, A-Hunting We Will Go.* Illus. by Nancy Winslow Parker. Atheneum, 1974.

Lobel, Anita. *King Rooster, Queen Hen.* Greenwillow, 1975.

McKee, David. *The Man Who Was Going to Mind the House.* Abelard-Schuman, 1972.

McLeish, Kenneth. *Chicken Licken.* Illus. by Jutta Ash. Bradbury Press, 1973.

Martin, Sarah C. *Old Mother Hubbard and Her Dog.* Trans. by Virginia Allen Jensen. Illus. by Ib Spang Olsen. Coward, 1975.

Mosel, Arlene. *The Funny Little Woman.* Illus. by Blair Lent. Dutton, 1972.

———. *Tikki Tikki Tembo.* Illus. by Blair Lent. Holt, 1968.

Mother Goose. *Brian Wildsmith's Mother Goose.* Illus. by Brian Wildsmith. Watts, 1965.

———. *Old Mother Hubbard and Her Dog.* Illus. by Evaline Ness. Holt, 1972. PB.

Peppe, Rodney. *Simple Simon.* Holt, 1972.

Perrault, Charles. *Cinderella.* Adapted by John Fowles. Illus. by Sheilah Beckett. Little, 1974.

———. *Cinderella.* Illus. by Marcia Brown. Scribner, 1954. PB.

———. *Cinderella.* Illus. by Errol Le Cain. Bradbury Press, 1972.

———. *Cinderella* (from the opera by Gioacchino Rossini). Illus. by Beni Montresor. Knopf, 1965. PB.

Rees, Ennis. *Brer Rabbit and His Tricks.* Illus. by Edward Gorey. Addison-Wesley, 1967.

———. *More of Brer Rabbit's Tricks.* Illus. by Edward Gorey. Addison-Wesley, 1968.

Sawyer, Ruth. *Journey Cake, Ho!* Illus. by Robert McCloskey. Viking, 1953. PB.

Schiller, Barbara. *The White Rat's Tale.* Illus. by Adrienne Adams. Holt, 1967. PB.

Stobbs, William. *Jack and the Beanstalk.* Delacorte, 1969.

Tolstoy, Alexei. *The Great Big Enormous Turnip.* Illus. by Helen Oxenbury. Watts, 1969.

Walker, Barbara. *Teeny Tiny and the Witch Woman.* Illus. by Michael Foreman. Pantheon, 1975.

Wiesner, William. *Turnabout.* Seabury, 1972.

Zemach, Harve. *Duffy and the Devil.* Illus. by Margot Zemach. Farrar, 1973.

———. *Nail Soup.* Illus. by Margot Zemach. Follett, 1964.

PROFESSIONAL REFERENCES

Bettelheim, Bruno. *The Uses of Enchantment: The Meaning and Importance of Fairy Tales.* New York: Alfred A. Knopf, 1976.

Chukovsky, Kornei. *From Two to Five.* Ed. and trans. by Miriam Morton. Berkeley, Calif.: University of California Press, 1963.

Favat, F. Andre. *Child and Tale: The Origins of Interest.* NCTE Research Report No. 19. Urbana, Ill.: National Council of Teachers of English, 1977.

Huck, Charlotte S. *Children's Literature in the Elementary School.* 3rd ed. New York: Holt, Rinehart and Winston, 1976.

Carolyn W. Carmichael

AVOIDING SEX
AND RACE STEREOTYPES
IN CHILDREN'S BOOKS

I n the last twenty-five years, we have become increasingly aware of discrimination against individuals based on characteristics determined at birth, above all, sexism and racism. Sexism can be defined as any doctrine or practice that stereotypes individuals on the basis of sex; early definitions of sexism were applied only to discrimination against females, but now there is an awareness that males suffer such prejudice as well. Racism can be defined as any doctrine or practice that assumes racial differences in character or intelligence or that asserts the superiority of one race over others. Social practices and codes that sanction certain behavior for one race or sex but not for others are racist or sexist, and such practices and codes are, regrettably, still part of our society despite our increased awareness of their perniciousness.

Racism and sexism continue to be transmitted to successive generations, in part through books for children. Overwhelming evidence of the presence of racism in children's books was uncovered by the research of the 1960s (Agree, 1973; Broderick, 1973; and Council on Interracial Books for Children, 1976). As for sexism, the research of the early 1970s (Gersoni-Stavn, 1974; Hillman, 1974; Stewig, 1973; and Weitzman, Eifler, Hokada, and Ross, 1972) showed its presence in children's books. All of the above studies document the fact that children were provided with role models that restricted their vision of what was possible for them to achieve.

Reinforcement of roles based on birth characteristics comes consistently throughout a child's life. Each year we have a class of entering kindergarten students who have firm attitudes and ideas about what "mommies and daddies" do and about roles which are ascribed to individuals solely on the basis of their racial or ethnic origin. In addition to the influences of overt behavior, there is subtle reinforcement of these roles through the books to which our children are exposed. Both the values and the contemporary events of a society are reflected in its literature; the same is true for nonprint media, including television, radio, and movies. Just as values and events have an impact on literature, literature has an impact on its audience. In the case of children's books, this can mean the communication and reinforcement of both productive and decidedly unproductive social attitudes.

If we look at the history of children's books, we can discern the prevailing values that were presented to children at different times. The goal of religious instruction, for instance, is apparent in the books of the Puritan age, as is moral didacticism in children's books of the Victorian period. But a historical perspective shows us that as social attitudes changed, children's books reflected the changes. We should be reassured then that sexism and racism will also disappear from children's books as they are eradicated from society. Because social change is a gradual process, the changes are absorbed into children's books slowly. Yet, although slow, the process is certain: the blatant sexism and racism apparent in books of the past will eventually disappear, becoming only a subject of historical study, not contemporary concern.

EXAMPLES OF NONSEXIST AND NONRACIST BOOKS

The books discussed in the following sections have been selected because they represent significant efforts at equalizing the treatment of sex and race in books for the young child. The books were *not* selected simply because their intentions are worthwhile, even if their execution leaves something to be desired. Rather, they were chosen for literary quality, a criterion that includes the embodiment of diversity in thoughts, feelings, and actions that stereotypes ignore or suppress.

Behavior

With text and illustrations, many current children's books concentrate on emotions and behavior that are experienced by all children, regardless of sex or race or ethnic origin.

In the book *Noisy Nora* by Rosemary Wells we find a hurt and angry mouse named Nora who feels resentment for having to wait for attention while her parents take time to care for her younger brother Jack. She expresses her resentment in various ways, none of which are acceptable to her parents. The audience of the book discovers the possible benefit of a direct expression of anger, i.e., a quickly resolved conflict. Kate expresses anger over the fact that her parents never seem to remember their promises in *Don't You Remember?* (Clifton, 1973). She not only jumps up and down shouting, "Dag, double dag!," but also physically expresses anger at her brother when he says he doesn't like girls.

Emotions are triggered by a variety of objects—not just people. Two books that utilize toys as the prime vehicle for stimulating emotions are *A Train for Jane* (Klein, 1974) and *William's Doll* (Zolotow, 1972). In *A Train for Jane*, Jane is implored by all concerned to want anything from beads, to a doll, to a box of chocolates for Christmas. Her only reply is "I want a train."

She rejoices on Christmas morning when she finds her deepest desire has been granted:

> But I have what I want,
> What's just right for me.
> A better toy train
> You never will see!

In *William's Doll* a very sensitive grandmother understands William's strong need for a doll. William's father does everything to squelch this desire and is outraged when the grandmother finally purchases a doll. In response, the grandmother says that William needs it so that "when he's a father/ like you,/ he'll know how to/ take care of his baby."

Moving outside of the family produces feelings in children which their books now faithfully depict. Betsy in *Betsy's First Day at Nursery School* (Wolde, 1976) sticks out her tongue at another girl as a gut-level reaction to treatment given her. *Benjie* (Lexau, 1964) is the story of a small black child who finds his usual withdrawal from people giving way to a new openness. It is his desire to find his grandmother's earring that forces him to approach and ask people if they have seen it. In both this book and the sequel, *Benjie on His Own*, the love of a grandmother is the motivating force behind a child's actions (see Fig. 28). Another example of love for a grandmother is given in Ruth Sonneborn's book *I Love Gram*.

Fig. 28. Benjie overcomes his shyness to help his grandmother in a story that focuses on an act of humanity rather than on racial stereotypes. *Illustration excerpted from Benjie, illustrated by Don Bolognese. Copyright © 1964 by Don Bolognese. Reprinted by permission of The Dial Press.*

Activities and Occupations

There are many books which emphasize the importance of not having sex prescribe an activity or occupation. Ilon Wikland's book *I Can Help Too!* is one example: a boy does domestic tasks that are usually thought of as being performed exclusively by girls, e.g., scrubbing a floor, washing dishes, and sewing. The fact that various activities and careers are pursued by members of both sexes is illustrated by Stan and Jan Berenstain in their book *He Bear, She Bear*, a fact emphasized by the refrain,

> We can do all these
> things,
> you see,
> whether we are he or
> she.

The range of adult female roles is being widened to better reflect what women actually do by such books as Norma Klein's *Girls Can Be Anything* and Gunilla Wolde's *Tommy Goes to the Doctor*. In the Klein book women are shown as pilots, politicians, and doctors. In Wolde's book Tommy is examined by a female doctor, and in another of her books, *Betsy and the Chicken Pox*, Betsy's baby brother is comforted by their father while their mother calls the doctor. When the woman doctor arrives, she's too busy to chat with Betsy. In Franz Brandenburg's *No School Today* the teacher is a man and the principal is a woman who rides to school on her bicycle, and in Charlotte Zolotow's *It's Not Fair* an adult character is both a loving grandmother and a busy lawyer. Nonfiction treatments of this topic are offered in the Lothrop series entitled What Can She Be?, which uses text and photographs to show the lives and careers of a female architect, lawyer, newscaster, and veterinarian. One of the newest releases in the series is *What Can She Be? A Musician* by Gloria and Esther Goldreich, with photographs by Richard Ipcar.

Miriam Cohen's *Will I Have a Friend?* blends characters from different races and ethnic backgrounds with a story about school activities and friendships. *Uptown* (Steptoe, 1970) relates the story of two black boys exploring Harlem, with each character describing what he sees, and *Train Ride* (Steptoe, 1971) describes how Charles and his friends take a subway ride to Times Square. Both books are written in an urban black idiom, making the stories even more true to life.

Families

Descriptions of families in which positive behavior is demonstrated are found in Arnold Adoff's *Black is brown is tan, Big Sister Tells Me That I'm Black*, and *Make a Circle Keep Us In*. In *Why Couldn't I Be an Only Kid Like You, Wigger?* complaints are expressed about living in a big family. The illustrations include boys wheeling carriages and folding laundry. Mommy monkey stereotypes Daddy monkey's expected despairing reaction to the news his baby ape is a girl, and is surprised when he reacts with delight, in Rosekrans Hoffman's book *Anna Banana*. Most children (and adults) will enjoy

Corinne Ramage's *The Joneses*, a wordless book in which Dad keeps house and Mom is employed as a submarine driver, and who, as parents of thirty-one dragons, manage just fine. In Sharon Bell Mathis's book *The Hundred Penny Box* a beautiful relationship is shown between a young black boy and his 100-year-old great aunt, whom he helps by keeping her special mementos secure in their box. *Michael* (Skorpen, 1975) also shows how a special act can draw family members together: a father, who at first seems stern and uncaring, turns out to be very thoughtful and sympathetic when his son rescues a baby rabbit. At Herbert's house (Lund, 1973) it's mother who helps Herbert solve his problems, e.g., putting up a tent, not his father, but in Genevieve Gray's *Send Wendell* a nurturant uncle and Wendell's affection for him help the boy to a sense of personal worth and the realization that he has to do other things besides running errands for everyone in the family. The frustrations of family life creep into Emily's day in *Emily and the Klunky Baby and the Next Door Dog* (Lexau, 1972), because she has to take care of her baby brother while her mother is doing the income taxes. This book reveals the emotions that can arise in a modern household where the divorced mother wants quiet and the older sibling does not want to be responsible for a "klunky baby brother," yet it presents a plausible resolution.

Recent books are taking a new look at aging as it applies to the family. Older people have not often appeared in children's books and even when they have, they were usually in the background. Now they are frequently important, lively characters. Barbara Williams' *Kevin's Grandma* shows that grandmothers are different these days: the boy who tells the story says that Kevin's grandmother rides a motorcycle, makes Kevin peanut butter soup, gives him judo lessons, and lets him hammer shingles on the roof. *Me and Neesie* (Greenfield, 1975) features some aggressive behavior on the part of dear old Aunt Bee, who beats the living daylights out of a child's imaginary friend. In *Mandy's Grandmother* (Skorpen, 1975) Mandy's dress and behavior do not quite fit her grandmother's ideas about little girls, but their working out a compromise is worth noting. That a grandparent can be an interesting person, as well as a loved one, is discovered by a young boy in *Grandmother's Pictures* (Cornish, 1974) when he and his grandmother look through her picture album.

Friendships

Diversity in the partners of a friendship is illustrated in the following group of books. Judith Viorst's *Rosie and Michael* concerns a friendship between a boy and a girl, something not usually seen in children's books, in which Rosie and Michael admit why each is fond of the other with no hang-ups regarding the existence of their friendship. In Judy Delton's *Two Good Friends* Bear and Duck, both males, are close friends who accept each other's differences, Duck being a superb housekeeper and Bear an excellent cook. The sharing of these abilities creates a relationship that becomes more meaningful to both of them. Delton's *Rabbit Finds a Way* (see Fig. 29) continues this friendship through disappointed expectations and an eventual sharing that leaves both parties pleased. Pura Belpré has developed the theme of

He was surprised to see
that he had already come to
Squirrel's house.
"Where are you going so fast?"
asked Squirrel. She was hammering
and sawing boards to make a
front porch for her house.
"I'm going to Bear's house."

Fig. 29. Squirrel hammers and saws to build the porch for her house instead of asking a
male to do it for her. (Original in color)
Taken from Rabbit Finds a Way *by Judy Delton, illustrated by Joe Lasker. Text © 1975 by Judy Delton.*
Illustrations © 1975 by Joe Lasker. Used by permission of Crown Publishers, Inc.

friendship in an unusual manner in her book *Santiago*. Santiago gains a great sense of pride when his classmates realize that his stories of his pet rooster are indeed true.

The recent harvest of books for young children gives clear evidence of the gradual changes apparent in society. Although traces of sexism and racism may persist in some books, there are many new books that portray, and thus encourage, a wide range of accepted behavior and realizable goals for both male and female children, whatever their racial or ethnic backgrounds might be.

CHILDREN'S BOOK REFERENCES

Adams, Florence. *Mushy Eggs*. Illus. by Marilyn Hirsh. Putnam, 1973.

Adoff, Arnold. *Big Sister Tells Me That I'm Black*. Illus. by Lorenzo Lynch. Holt, 1976.

———. *Black is brown is tan*. Illus. by Emily A. McCully. Harper, 1973.

———. *Make a Circle Keep Us In: Poems for a Good Day*. Pictures by Ronald Himler. Delacorte, 1975.

Allen, Jeffrey. *Mary Alice Operator Number 9*. Illus. by James Marshall. Little, 1975.

Bartoli, Jennifer. *Nonna*. Illus. by Joan E. Drescher. Harvey House, 1975.

Belpré, Pura. *Santiago*. Illus. by Symeon Shimin. McGraw, 1972.

Berenstain, Stan, and Jan Berenstain. *He Bear, She Bear*. Random, 1974.

Brandenburg, Franz. *A Secret for Grandmother's Birthday,* Illus. by Aliki. Greenwillow, 1975.

———. *I Wish I Was Sick, Too!* Illus. by Aliki. Macmillan, 1976.

———. *No School Today!* Illus. by Aliki. Macmillan, 1975.

Brenner, Barbara. *Cunningham's Rooster*. Illus. by Anne Rockwell. Parents, 1975.

Carlson, Natalie Savage. *Marie Louise's Heyday*. Illus. by Jose Aruego and Ariane Dewey. Scribner, 1975.

Chasek, Judith. *Have You Seen Wilhemina Krumpf?* Illus. by Sal Murdocca. Lothrop, 1973.

Chorao, Kay. *A Magic Eye for Ida*. Seabury, 1973.

Clifton, Lucille. *Don't You Remember?* Illus. by Evaline Ness. Dutton, 1973.

Cohen, Miriam. *Will I Have a Friend?* Illus. by Lillian Hoban. Macmillan, 1967. PB.

Cornish, Sam. *Grandmother's Pictures*. Illus. by Jeanne Johns. Bradbury Press, 1974. PB: Bookstore Press.

Delton, Judy. *Rabbit Finds a Way*. Illus. by Joe Lasker. Crown, 1975.

———. *Two Good Friends*. Illus. by Giulio Maestro. Crown, 1974.

de Paola, Tomie. *Watch Out for Chicken Feet in Your Soup*. Prentice-Hall, 1974.

Goldman, Susan. *Grandma Is Somebody Special*. A. Whitman, 1976.

Goldreich, Gloria, and Esther Goldreich. *What Can She Be? A Musician*. Photographs by Richard Ipcar. Lothrop, 1975.

Gray, Genevieve. *Send Wendell*. Illus. by Symeon Shimin. McGraw, 1974.

Greenfield, Eloise. *Me and Nessie*. Illus. by Moneta Barnett. Crowell, 1975.

Hazen, Barbara Shook. *Why Couldn't I Be an Only Kid Like You, Wigger?* Pictures by Leigh Grant. Atheneum, 1975.

Hoffman, Rosekrans. *Anna Banana*. Knopf, 1975.

Klein, Norma. *Girls Can Be Anything*. Dutton, 1973. PB.

―――. *A Train for Jane*. Illus. by Miriam Schottland. Feminist Press, 1974. PB.

Levy, Elizabeth. *Nice Little Girls*. Illus. by Mordicai Gerstein. Delacorte, 1974.

Lexau, Joan M. *Benjie*. Illus. by Don Bolognese. Dial, 1964.

―――. *Benjie on His Own*. Illus. by Don Bolognese. Dial, 1970.

―――. *Emily and the Klunky Baby and the Next Door Dog*. Illus. by Martha Alexander. Dial, 1972.

Lund, Doris Herold. *You Ought to See Herbert's House*. Illus. by Steven Kellogg. Watts, 1973.

Mathis, Sharon Bell. *The Hundred Penny Box*. Illus. by Leo and Diane Dillon. Viking, 1975.

Parker, Nancy Winslow. *Mrs. Wilson Wanders Off*. Dodd, 1976.

Ramage, Corinne. *The Joneses*. Lippincott, 1975.

Simon, Norma. *All Kinds of Families*. Illus. by Joe Lasker. A. Whitman, 1976.

Skorpen, Liesel Moak. *Mandy's Grandmother*. Pictures by Martha Alexander. Dial, 1975.

―――. *Michael*. Illus. by Joan Sandin. Harper, 1975.

Sonneborn, Ruth A. *I Love Gram*. Illus. by Leo Carty. Viking, 1971.

Steptoe, John. *Train Ride*. Harper, 1971.

―――. *Uptown*. Harper, 1970.

Terris, Susan. *No Boys Allowed*. Illus. by Richard Cuffari. Doubleday, 1976.

Tobias, Tobi. *The Quitting Deal*. Illus. by Trina Schart Hyman. Viking, 1975.

Viorst, Judith. *Rosie and Michael*. Illus. by Lorna Tomei. Atheneum, 1974.

Waber, Bernard. *Lyle Finds His Mother*. Houghton, 1974.

Wells, Rosemary. *Noisy Nora*. Dial, 1973.

Wikland, Ilon. *I Can Help Too!* Random, 1974.

Williams, Barbara. *Kevin's Grandma*. Illus. by Kay Chorao. Dutton, 1975.

Wolde, Gunilla. *Betsy and the Chicken Pox*. Random, 1976.

―――. *Betsy's First Day at Nursery School*. Random, 1976.

―――. *Tommy Goes to the Doctor*. Houghton, 1972.

Zolotow, Charlotte. *It's Not Fair*. Illus. by William Pène du Bois. Harper, 1976.

―――. *William's Doll*. Illus. by William Pène du Bois. Harper, 1972.

PROFESSIONAL REFERENCES

Agree, Rose H. "The Black American in Children's Books: A Critical Analysis of the Portrayal of the Afro-American as Delineated in the Contents of a Select Group of Children's Trade Books Published in America from 1950-1970." Ph.D. dissertation, New York University, 1973. University Microfilms no. 73-30,045.

Broderick, Dorothy M. *Image of the Black in Children's Fiction*. New York: R. R. Bowker, 1973.

Council on Interracial Books for Children. *Human and Anti-Human Values in Children's Books*. New York: Council on Interracial Books for Children, 1976.

Gersoni-Stavn, Diane. *Sexism and Youth*. New York: R. R. Bowker, 1974.

Hendler, Marjorie R. "An Analysis of Sex Role Attributes, Behaviors, and Occupations in Contemporary Children's Picture Books." Ph.D. dissertation, New York University, 1976.

Hillman, J. S. "An Analysis of Male and Female Roles in Two Periods of Children's Literature." *Journal of Educational Research* 68 (October 1974): 84-89.

Stewig, John Warren, and Margaret Higgs. "Girls Grow Up to Be Mommies: A Study of Sexism in Children's Literature." *School Library Journal* 19 (January 1973): 44-49.

Weitzman, Lenore, Deborah Eifler, Elizabeth Hokada, and Catherine Ross. "Sex Role Socialization in Picture Books for Pre-School Children." *American Journal of Sociology* 77 (May 1972): 1125-1150.

READING LITERATURE ALOUD

Ideally, long before children learn to read they will have many experiences with stories and poems read or told to them by loving and enthusiastic adults. Ideally, too, those experiences will continue during the time children are learning to be independent readers and beyond. If those experiences are pleasurable and if literature is made an important and natural part of their environment, it is likely that children will establish positive attitudes toward reading and literature that will remain with them throughout their lives. Reading aloud, then, is one of the most important activities of adults who work with and care for young children. It should be a daily activity, a respected aspect of any instructional program for young children (Huck, 1976, pp. 702-760).

This chapter attempts first to establish the values of reading aloud and then to provide some practical ideas for adult readers. It concludes with a brief list of selected titles for reading aloud.

VALUES OF READING ALOUD

Motivation for learning to read. Reading aloud can be the magnet that attracts children to books. The pleasure and entertainment derived from listening to well-chosen literature may not only lead prereaders to pore over the pictures (and text) of their favorite books, but may also make them anticipate joyfully the time when they can read for themselves. Anyone who works with young children has probably had the experience of watching a child "read" a favorite book. It may be that the text is so familiar the child knows it "by heart," or the child may be making up a story to go with the pictures. But in either case children will tell you they are reading. Whether one views that behavior as merely imitative of adult behavior or as evidence of a genuine desire to read, the point is that these children are beginning to see reading as a natural part of their world. It is something they, too, will do. It is probable also that these children look at reading as a pleasurable experience and at books as a source of delight. Thus, reading aloud is one of the first steps in the process of helping children learn to read.

Development of a taste for quality literature. Frequent exposure to a variety of good literature will help to initiate the development of that elusive goal, appreciation of literature. Nearly 2,000 new children's books are published each year, but only a relative few are of high quality. Reading aloud books of literary and artistic quality helps children develop a taste for them. Once children have learned to enjoy the rhythmic prose and pictures of Wanda Gág's *Millions of Cats* or to shudder when Maurice Sendak's marvelous wild things "roar their terrible roars" (*Where the Wild Things Are*; see Fig. 30), they will be less likely to settle for language that is stilted, pictures that are flat, and stories that are dull. Since the time when children can discover and read good literature on their own comes later in childhood, it is important that they be exposed early, through listening and viewing, to books of literary quality.

Fig. 30. The wild things roar their terrible roars as a greeting to Max. The language and drawings of this story invite children to join in with the storyteller. *Illustration from* Where the Wild Things Are *by Maurice Sendak. Copyright © 1963 by Maurice Sendak. Reprinted by permission of Harper & Row, Publishers, Inc., and The Bodley Head.*

Preparation for understanding written language. Writing is not exactly "talk written down." There are some differences between written and spoken language which a beginning reader must come to understand, yet a reader must also gain some sense of the relationship between oral language and written language. Beginning readers must gain some sense of what written language "sounds like," so that they will know what is likely to make sense in their own struggle with the printed page. Hearing many types of literature will extend the range of language that children understand. They will be able to understand language beyond that heard in their family and community. The more children can understand as listeners, the better prepared they are to cope, as readers, with variety in written materials. Words which are recognized in oral language are much easier to recognize in print than ones not recognized orally.

As readers, children will learn to use their intuitive knowledge of the way language works. For instance, they will expect to find familiar English word order in the sentences they read. Having heard and enjoyed many varieties of stories will help children reaffirm the language patterns they know best and also extend the ones they can recognize as possibilities.

Expansion of language. While children are becoming familiar with the "sound" of written language, they can also be expanding the language they already know and use. Vocabulary in good literature is not controlled, i.e., limited to a few words that are supposed to be common and familiar, so the opportunities for hearing and understanding and adopting new words are many. In addition, reading to young children provides many opportunities for hearing familiar words used in new contexts. Some books, such as Remy Charlip's *Fortunately* and Ruth Krauss's *A Very Special House*, invite language play and enable children to expand their language by deliberately experimenting with sounds and patterns.

Development of listening skills. Reading aloud implies that children are listening. Many children need help in understanding how to listen and what to listen for. Since listening is an important activity for learning, skill in listening, in understanding spoken language, is a valuable ability for a child to develop. While it is undesirable to turn the story hour into a listening skills lesson, it is important to recognize that reading aloud can be one way to help children become better listeners.

Acquaintance with books "too good to miss." For both older and younger children, there seems to be an optimum time for becoming acquainted with some literature. For prereaders this is especially true, since by the time they can read many picture books on their own, their interests will have matured beyond the stories. Actually, many picture books are meant to be shared aloud with young children who cannot yet read. Children who are just learning to read are often unable to handle books which they would find extremely interesting and comprehensible; and even children who have learned to read often cannot or will not read for themselves books they would enjoy listening to. It would be unfortunate indeed to allow children to miss out on some of the fine books created for them, because hearing such books read aloud whets their appetite for reading them.

Expansion of experiences. Reading aloud can be one way adults help children expand their experiential background. Even though such experiences are vicarious, they help children expand their understanding of this world. Reading aloud nonfiction or informational books can be invaluable in helping children grasp concepts, particularly about their physical environment. Harlow Rockwell's *My Dentist* (see Fig. 31) and *My Doctor* aid in understanding the role of such people in children's lives. Reading books about such social and psychological concerns as family relationships, relationships with other children, and the problems and adventures of childhood can broaden social concepts and help children gain greater insight into human

Fig. 31. Understanding the work of a dentist and the equipment found in a dental office is enriched by this informational book for young children. (Original in color)
Reprinted by permission of Greenwillow Books and Curtis Brown Ltd. from My Dentist *by Harlow Rockwell. Copyright © 1975 by Harlow Rockwell.*

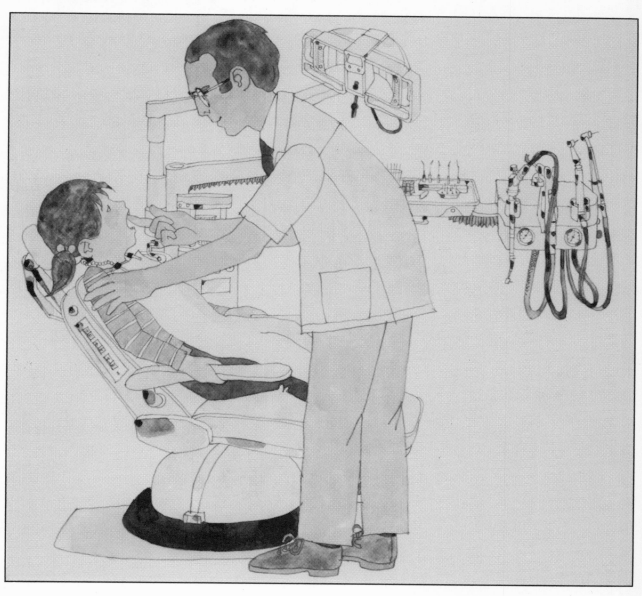

behavior. Reading Ann Herbert Scott's *Sam*, for instance, helps in understanding the universal feeling of being ignored (see Fig. 32).

Providing experience with a group. Reading aloud is a group activity, whether the group is a whole class, a family, or one child and one adult. During story time, young children can begin learning the value and necessity of sharing, taking turns, respecting the rights of others, and contributing to discussions. Since many school experiences are group activities, such knowledge, built into the pleasure of story time, can help prepare a child for successful participation in other school activities.

Providing a pleasurable experience. In listing the values of reading aloud, there is a natural tendency to justify the practice by emphasizing the utilitarian aspects—skills development, language development, concept development. But we need to remember that all of us need pleasurable experiences in

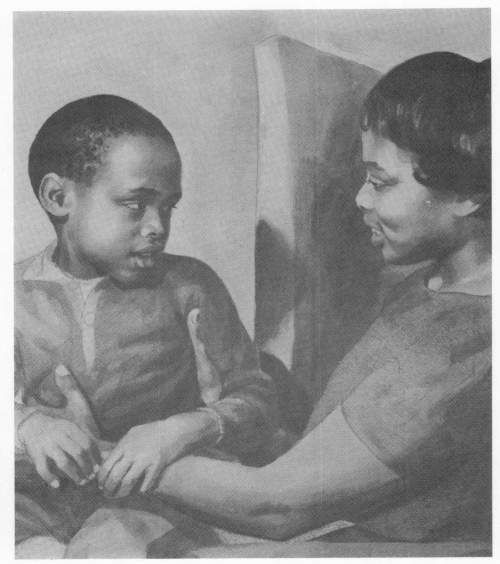

Fig. 32. It is common for young children to feel that everyone is too busy to pay attention to them. Sam finally gets his family's attention after many attempts. (Original in color) *From* Sam *by Ann Herbert Scott, with drawings by Symeon Shimin. Copyright © 1967 by Ann Herbert Scott and Symeon Shimin. Used with permission of McGraw-Hill Book Company.*

our lives. We need to do some things for no other reason than that they are fun and we enjoy doing them. Listening to and reading stories and poems can be one of those pleasant experiences. Literature, like beauty, is its own excuse for being, and we really need no other reason to read it aloud to young children.

SOME PRACTICAL SUGGESTIONS

When to Read Aloud

As an important aspect of an instructional program for young children, reading aloud ought to be included in the *daily* schedule. Often teachers have found it satisfactory to sandwich story time between particularly active times —after lunch, before playtime. The actual time is not important and can be flexible, but the point is to make story time a regularly scheduled part of the day. Many children may not have had the benefit of literally hundreds of bed-time stories. They especially need many opportunities during school hours to hear their favorites again and again.

Story time ought likewise to be a regular part of the family routine. Bedtime and naptime have long been a traditional story time, but after dinner might be just as satisfactory. Parents should keep in mind a statement quoted by Annis Duff (1944):"I wonder what a family does that doesn't read together? It's like not knowing each other's friends" (p. 23).

In addition to a regularly scheduled story hour, stories or poems can provide welcome breaks in routine between other activities. They can also make a dull, humdrum activity into an enjoyable experience. For instance, a good story can make the time go by quickly while waiting in the classroom, in the car, or in the doctor's office. A good story or saying rhymes together can also help make a long ride seem shorter. Putting on rain gear can be more fun when accompanied by a poem like Laura Richards' "The Umbrella Brigade" (in *Tirra Lirra*), Taro Yashima's *Umbrella*, or Rhoda Bacmeister's "Galoshes" (in Jean McKee Thompson's *Poems to Grow On*).

How to Choose Books for Reading Aloud

When choosing books to read aloud, it is good to remember that young children can benefit from exposure to a wide variety of children's books. Children will ask to hear old favorites repeated, and well they should. But they will also enjoy new and different ones. It is a good idea to consciously arrange to read from as many different kinds of books as possible—fantasy, folktales, poetry, realistic stories, funny stories, nonfiction, and so on (see Bernice E. Cullinan's chapter, "Books in the Life of the Young Child," for descriptions of children's book categories). Such choices can assure contact with many different writing styles and many different literary forms. This will also guard against saturation with just one kind of story.

Choose on the basis of children's interests. Reports show the reading interests of young children have varied somewhat over the years. However, some interests appear to be very stable. Animal stories and folktales seem to remain favorites with young children, as do stories about children like themselves and their everyday experiences. Children also seem to enjoy imaginative escapades and humorous stories, such as Judith Viorst's *Alexander and the Terrible, Horrible, No Good, Very Bad Day.*

In addition, it is possible to take advantage of the special interests that a group of children may have at a particular time. If there is a new turtle in the room, one might read *The Turtle Pond* by Berniece Freschet, an informational book about turtles, or one about their habits and their care. It may also be the time to read some turtle poems. Reading and listening interests of any particular group may vary from time to time and may be influenced by past experiences with stories and by the recommendations of other children and adults.

Assess your audience. Can your children sit still for twenty minutes or only ten? Is their experiential background such that they can relate to the story? Consider the possible problem involved in reading a "city" story to a farm child or vice versa. Do you need to prepare children for a story with a brief explanation? Is there enough information in the description of the setting, and are the characters vivid enough to overcome an unfamiliar setting? A story about a common experience, the arrival of a new baby, for example, can be understood no matter what the setting. But you may need to provide background if reading *White Snow, Bright Snow* (Tresselt, 1947) to children who have never seen snow.

Consider book format and quality. Picture books to be read aloud to a group of children must be large enough for the group to see. For groups, both the book and its illustrations must be large. Small books can be shared with one or two children at a time or can be projected on a screen with an opaque projector. Flannel boards and puppets are good to use with such books.

Fig. 33. Alexander's teacher refuses to recognize his genius when he draws an "invisible" castle. *Pictures copyright © 1972 by Ray Cruz. From* Alexander and the Terrible, Horrible, No Good, Very Bad Day *(by Judith Viorst). Used by permission of Atheneum Publishers and Angus and Robertson, Ltd.*

Other considerations, such as size of the type and the amount of text on a page, become more important as the child tries to read alone, but these might be considered as indications of possible difficulty.

Not all books for young children are of uniformly high quality. Adults who read to young children will develop their own criteria for deciding whether a book is a good one. Undoubtedly, though, one ought to consider first whether the story (if there is one) is interesting and whether it seems to "hang together" and is plausible and logical. Once the story line is set up, do the events seem to make sense? One might also consider whether the characters seem real, or at least believable, even when they are fantasy creatures. When stories are to be read aloud, language becomes especially important. Some writers are much better storytellers than others. Good storytellers use language that is tempered to the tongue; they use common words in uncommon ways, develop rhythm in their phrases, and paint clear pictures with words. It is much better to try out a story by reading it aloud to oneself before presenting it to children. Even though the story may be written for very young children, if it is well written, adults will find it enjoyable, too. In fact, the adult *must* like a book to share it well with children. Your attitude toward a story shows when you are sharing a book with children. Pick stories *you* like.

Many of the books chosen for young children will be picture books, so it is important to consider the quality of the illustrations. While it is not the purpose here to fully describe and explain criteria for judging illustrations, it might be useful to mention some crucial factors. In a picture book, the illustrations are as important as the text. They should illustrate the story but also add something of their own. Children seem to enjoy poring over the details in pictures. Color is enjoyed but so are good black and white drawings or photographs. One good strategy is to expose children to many illustrations done in a variety of styles and media and allow their tastes to develop. There are enough excellent illustrators being published today to avoid dull, flat, one-dimensional pictures. Picture books may be the child's first exposure to good art. We want to give them more than the clichés and stereotypes found in supermarket books.

How to Read Aloud

Plan before reading. Familiarize yourself with the story. Take time to read over the story ahead of time, looking for unfamiliar words or concepts, unusual language, repeated phrases. If possible, try a "dry run" of the story aloud. Such preparation frees the reader from such total dependence on the text during reading that he or she is unable to look away from the book. It also helps, of course, in planning a story time that runs smoothly.

Arrange the seating. Seat the children so they can all see the reader and the pictures. A semicircle or clustered group with the reader at its center can be effective. If the group is large enough for some children to be seated in front of others, the reader might want to sit on a chair that is slightly higher than those of the children (or children on the floor, reader on a low chair).

Introduce the story. The introduction need not be an elaborate one. A simple statement of what the book is about will probably suffice. It might help to relate a new story to some recent common experience, e.g., "Remember the story about Frederick? Well this one is about another mouse. I think you will like this one, too." It is often a good idea to set a listening purpose in the introduction, "Let's see if we can find out . . . ."

Pay attention to the way you sound. Readers need to be sure that their reading is understandable, because we are not always aware of our own lack of clarity in speaking. Clear but natural articulation is especially important when reading to young children. Volume and dramatic quality are important, too. Readers must, of course, be loud enough to be heard by the group but not loud enough to disturb those who may be working nearby. Readers who use their voices to convey mood and emotion or to portray different characters make a story much more interesting than those who read in a monotonous, never changing voice. Listening to a tape of your own oral reading is an excellent way of studying your delivery.

Define unfamiliar words. If a reader believes, or the children indicate, that they do not understand a key word in the story, simply interject a brief one- or two-word definition. Frequently, however, key words are explained in the story or are repeated numerous times, with their meaning becoming clear through the context. It is not a good idea to define every unfamiliar or new word in a story; children will not remember those that are meaningless to them, and the enjoyment of the story can be spoiled by excessive attention to vocabulary.

Anticipate and prevent disruptions. One good reason for prereading a story is that the familiarity thus gained frees the reader to maintain eye contact with the children during the reading. In addition to making the story time more personal, eye contact also enables the reader to gauge reactions and to spot potential trouble before it erupts. The simple precaution of holding the book so that the pictures can be seen by all and so that the children have sufficient time to view them also helps ensure order and attention. Naming the author and title at the end of the reading, rather than at the beginning, prevents such comments as "I heard it already."

Wait for children's responses. It is difficult for adults to be quiet for a moment to give children a chance to react or respond to a story or poem. We tend to want to rush in with a question—"Did you like that story?"—but such a question most often gets a yes and short circuits any real thinking. It is usually best to wait for the children's comments. Remember, too, that while some stories are excellent lead-ins to discussions, dramatizations, or other creative activities described in this and other chapters, every story need *not* be followed by discussion. Frequently, it is enough to have shared the story.

What to Read Aloud

In addition to supplying bibliographic information on books cited in this chapter, the children's book references that follow are meant to be a starter list to help anyone unfamiliar with children's books make selections for reading aloud. It is meant, too, to introduce a few author/illustrators who have done several books and whose work is usually commendable. The list, all picture books, contains some old favorites, as well as some more recent ones. It is not an attempt to represent all kinds of books available but just a few that sound good when read aloud, have pictures that are of high quality, and are interesting or fun to listen to.

CHILDREN'S BOOK REFERENCES

Realistic Stories — Everyday Experiences

Clifton, Lucille. *The Boy Who Didn't Believe in Spring.* Illus. by Brinton Turkle. Dutton, 1973.

Keats, Ezra Jack. *The Snowy Day.* Viking, 1962. PB.

McCloskey, Robert. *One Morning in Maine.* Viking, 1952. PB.

Scott, Ann Herbert. *Sam.* Illus. by Symeon Shimin. McGraw, 1967.

Steptoe, John. *Stevie.* Harper, 1969.

Tresselt, Alvin. *White Snow, Bright Snow.* Illus. by Roger Duvoisin. Lothrop, 1947.

Viorst, Judith. *Alexander and the Terrible, Horrible, No Good, Very Bad Day.* Illus. by Ray Cruz. Atheneum, 1972.

Yashima, Taro. *Umbrella.* Viking, 1958. PB.

Animals as People — Everyday Experiences

Hoban, Russell. *Bread and Jam for Frances.* Illus. by Lillian Hoban. Harper, 1964. PB: Scholastic Book Services.

Kraus, Robert. *Leo the Late Bloomer.* Illus. by Jose Aruego. Windmill, 1971. PB.

Lobel, Arnold. *Frog and Toad Are Friends.* Harper, 1970.

Marshall, James. *George and Martha.* Houghton, 1972. PB.

Animal Fantasies — Talking Animals

Carle, Eric. *The Very Hungry Caterpillar.* Collins-World, 1970.

Flack, Marjorie. *Ask Mr. Bear.* Macmillan, 1932. PB.

Lionni, Leo. *Frederick.* Pantheon, 1967.

————. *Inch by Inch.* Astor-Honor, 1960.

Steig, William. *Sylvester and the Magic Pebble.* Simon and Schuster, 1969. PB: Dutton.

Folk Stories and Stories in Folktale Style

Brown, Marcia. *The Three Billy Goats Gruff.* Harcourt, 1957. PB.

Gág, Wanda. *Millions of Cats.* Coward, 1928.

Galdone, Paul. *The Little Red Hen.* Seabury, 1973. PB: Scholastic Book Services.

Hogrogian, Nonny. *One Fine Day.* Macmillan, 1971. PB.

Ryan, Cheli. *Hildidid's Night.* Illus. by Arnold Lobel. Macmillan, 1971.

Slobodkina, Esphyr. *Caps for Sale.* Addison-Wesley, 1947.

Tolstoy, Alexei. *The Great Big Enormous Turnip.* Illus. by Helen Oxenbury. Watts, 1969.

Poetry

Bissett, Donald J., ed. *Poems and Verses to Begin On.* Chandler and Sharpe, 1967.

Clifton, Lucille. *Some of the Days of Everett Anderson.* Illus. by Evaline Ness. Holt, 1970. PB.

de Regniers, Beatrice Schenk. *Something Special.* Harcourt, 1958.

Fisher, Aileen. *In One Door and Out the Other: A Book of Poems.* Illus. by Lillian Hoban. Crowell, 1969.

Hopkins, Lee Bennett, ed. *The City Spreads Its Wings.* Illus. by Moneta Barnett. Watts, 1970.

Livingston, Myra Cohn. *Happy Birthday.* Illus. by Erik Blegvad. Harcourt, 1964.

Milne, A. A. *When We Were Very Young.* Illus. by E. H. Shepard. Dutton, 1924. PB: Dell.

Richards, Laura E. *Tirra Lirra.* Illus. by Marguerite Davis. Little, 1955.

Stevenson, Robert Louis. *A Child's Garden of Verses.* Illus. by Brian Wildsmith. Watts, 1966. PB.

Thompson, Jean McKee, compiler. *Poems to Grow On.* Illus. by Gobin Stair. Beacon, 1957.

Wright, Blanche Fisher. *The Real Mother Goose.* Rand McNally, 1916, 1965.

Rhyming Stories

Bemelmans, Ludwig. *Madeline.* Viking, 1939. PB.

de Regniers, Beatrice Schenk. *May I Bring A Friend?* Illus. by Beni Montresor. Atheneum, 1964. PB.

Emberley, Barbara. *Drummer Hoff.* Illus. by Ed Emberley. Prentice-Hall, 1967. PB.

Geisel, Theodor S. [Dr. Seuss]. *Horton Hatches the Egg.* Random, 1940.

Zemach, Harve. *The Judge: An Untrue Tale.* Illus. by Margot Zemach. Farrar, 1969.

Fun with Language

Adoff, Arnold. *Ma nDa la.* Illus. by Emily A. McCully. Harper, 1971.

Charlip, Remy. *Fortunately.* Parents, 1964.

Eichenberg, Fritz. *Ape in a Cape.* Harcourt, 1952. PB.

Gwynne, Fred. *The King Who Rained.* Windmill, 1970. PB.

Krauss, Ruth. *A Very Special House.* Illus. by Maurice Sendak. Harper, 1953.

Parish, Peggy. *Amelia Bedelia and the Surprise Shower.* Illus. by Fritz Siebel. Harper, 1966.

Rand, Ann. *Sparkle and Spin: A Book about Words.* Illus. by Paul Rand. Harcourt, 1957.

Children and Their Fantasies

Coombs, Patricia. *Lisa and the Grompet.* Lothrop, 1970.

McPhail, David. *The Bear's Toothache.* Atlantic Monthly Press/Little, 1972.

Sendak, Maurice. *Where the Wild Things Are.* Harper, 1963.

Informational

Freschet, Berniece. *The Turtle Pond.* Illus. by Donald Carrick. Scribner, 1971.

Rockwell, Harlow. *My Dentist.* Greenwillow, 1975.

————. *My Doctor.* Macmillan, 1973.

PROFESSIONAL REFERENCES

Cianciolo, Patricia Jean, ed. *Picture Books for Children.* Chicago: American Library Association, 1973.

Chan, Julie M. T. *Why Read Aloud to Children?* IRA Micromonograph Series. Newark, Del.: International Reading Association, 1974.

Duff, Annis. *Bequest of Wings: A Family's Pleasures with Books.* New York: Viking Press, 1944.

Huck, Charlotte S. *Children's Literature in the Elementary School.* 3rd ed. New York: Holt, Rinehart and Winston, 1976.

Larrick, Nancy. *A Parent's Guide to Children's Reading.* 4th rev. ed. New York: Doubleday, 1975.

Yeager, Allan. *Using Picture Books with Children: A Guide to Holt Owlet Books.* New York: Holt, Rinehart and Winston, 1973.

Sandra Stroner Sivulich

STRATEGIES FOR
PRESENTING LITERATURE

Educators should take a few lessons from the business world when discussing reading readiness and the importance of books. A good product needs to be advertised to the consumer. Thus, merely stating to children that reading is good for them will be as effective as telling them to go practice the piano or not to eat sweets because they're bad for them. We need to advertise and promote literature by using it effectively; since our "product" is the best, it will sell itself if properly made available to children.

Books will stand on their own. It is quite enough to tell a story or read a story aloud and end the activity with the closing of the book. As the movie *The Pleasure Is Mutual* shows, what happens in the minds and hearts of children after a story is presented can never be measured but might manifest itself months or years later. Lessons and morals should never be the purpose of presenting literature. If you quiz and drill at the end of each story session, the joy and beauty of that special time is destroyed. One would not pick apart a rose petal by petal to find what makes it beautiful. And so, too, one should not moralize and make didactic a fine picture book or story. However, books can be used as the springboard or motivator for other activities; if handled with integrity and skill, these activities can preserve the literary intent of the author and perhaps even magnify or intensify the story. The "extensions" of literature, or enrichment strategies, described here are merely beginnings of lists you can develop, adapt, and expand for your own situations. If, as Aristotle says, "all knowledge comes through the senses," these activities can prepare the way for knowledge by making books used in the classroom more concrete and visual.

Preparing and Presenting Stories

One of the major ways to present literature is through storytelling. However one defines storytelling, one thing is certain: it is one of the most satisfying and rewarding ways to share books. The art of storytelling and reading aloud are different ways to share, but both are as important in the classroom as the teacher and the children are.

Everyone is a storyteller and each person does it in a unique manner, but all should observe three *L*'s in storytelling: (1) like your story; (2) learn your story; and (3) live your story. The first *L* deals with the selection of the story and is perhaps most important. As in any communication, you must consider your audience—attention span, maturity, listening skills, interest, background. Always keeping them in mind, you begin to read and you read and then you read some more. Finally, you will find a folktale or story that you really like. If you don't find a piece of literature amusing or exciting or touching or something special, then do not try to tell it. But when you do find something that suits you and your audience, go on to the next *L*. Learning a story is not memorizing it word by word, but learning sequence by sequence or event by event. You visualize in storytelling, you do not memorize. The storyteller goes over the story so many times that a good deal of it is remembered naturally. After all, storytelling has come to us from the oral tradition in which tales were handed down by word of mouth in many different forms. So don't get too tense about getting the story precisely as it appears on the page. Retain the spirit and flavor of the original work. However, judicious use of poetic editing, such as consistently eliminating some of the many characters in *Henny Penny* (Galdone, 1968) or in any cumulative tale, is not tampering with the essentials of the story. In your learning process you of course practice all the principles of good speech, such as voice variation, varied pitch, effective pauses, eye contact, expression, and timing, along with learning the story line.

Having learned this story that you like and that is suited to your group, the next step is to "live" it. The most important part of this process is the desire or urgency to tell the story. Think of this part of storytelling as you would if someone told you a juicy bit of gossip and you can't wait to relate it to someone else. So, in a sense, you can think of storytelling as "literary gossip"! The storyteller has to "see" the story so clearly that he or she uses every possible means of communication to have the audience see and feel the same things the teller does. In short, the storyteller is the medium of the message.

Reading Aloud

If you are going to tell your story with a book, go through the same three *L*'s, but make sure your book has large enough pictures for all in your group to see. Hold the book upright and flat in front of you. Turn the pages from the top corner with your left hand, holding the book open in the center with your right thumb. The base of your right hand will give support to the bottom of the book. While learning to tell a story using the book, always practice with the book, preferably in front of a mirror. Another good technique is to paper clip the title page and whatever front pages the book may have—except when the front matter is relevant, as it is in *Sam* (Scott, 1967)—so that when you open the cover, you can turn directly to the story and not lose your audience's attention while you turn pages. Selection is just as important in reading aloud as it is in storytelling. You may also want to edit. At least two read throughs before the presentation are recommended to insure proper expression and emphasis.

Reading aloud is not as practiced or intimate as storytelling. However, even though you lose eye contact because you are looking at the words more than at the children, it should be done daily (Allen, 1974, pp. 15-18). To expose children every day to the well-ordered and beautifully crafted language found in books is more important than a flawless delivery. All curriculums stress reading and writing skills, yet perhaps the most important communication skill is listening and where do we routinely find time for that? But storytelling and reading aloud develop listeners, as well as appreciators, and, as Roach Van Allen (1974) points out, lay the groundwork for reading skills, since "a word heard orally is much more easily recognizable in print" (p. 10).

Setting Conditions for Storytelling.

Careful consideration of your audience *before* storytelling is important to the success of the story itself. First of all, the beginning: one must establish a listening atmosphere for effective sharing of books. Don't just plunge in and begin telling stories to fill in time before the lunch bell rings or in an attempt to silence a rowdy group. You will hate storytelling, and so will your children, if you treat it as unimportant. If you really feel it is vital to aesthetic development and reading readiness, you will help create a special mood for listening to this special event.

Ritual has always been an important factor in art forms and storytelling is no exception. American Indians would begin their tales around the camp-fire with "spirits above the ground, spirits below the ground, spirits gather round." African storytellers would begin, "A story, a story, let it come, let it go." And so we, too, must have a beginning, a clue to children that this is a time for listening, a special time. For young children the finger game "These are Grandmother's glasses" is useful:

> These are Grandmother's glasses. (Make pretend glasses with fingers)
>
> This is Grandmother's cap. (Put hand in a tent-like position on top of head)
>
> This is the way she folds her hands (Fold hands)
>
> And puts them in her lap. (Put hands in lap)

Follow this with some appropriate introduction, e.g., "Now, boys and girls, only I get to do this, but I'm going to take the magic story hour circle out of my pocket and go all around the room until everyone is in the magic story hour circle" (look at each child as you extend the very real imaginary circle over their heads). This magic wand effect draws the group together in a unity of silence, because they've all been pulled together for a magic time of stories. Of course, this is just one technique. Lighting a candle, as is done for story times in some schools, and blowing it out with a wish at the end of story time or saying a poem or singing a certain song is a good way to let the children know it is time to relax and listen.

Even before you get to the point of beginning, you must consider the physical setup of your audience. Transport their bodies as well as their spirits with your storytelling. Don't let them remain in the sandbox or with their finger paints for storytelling. Transfer them to an area rug or the listening area in your classroom. If a special area isn't available, place them somewhere that is different and away from the previous activity and where there are as few distractions as possible. And note whether there is a glare from the window you're in front of, whether you are blocking the washroom door, whether you are in front of the radiator, and the like.

Once you have the children in a tight knit group so that eye contact is easy and you don't have to shout your story, you can begin with the ritual and the prepared stories. Because you have considered your audience in your preparation, you are aware of their attention span and remember to include songs, finger games, and stretch activities along with your stories so that your story time is a well-balanced and fun time. No matter how well prepared your literature unit may be, you should not forget the attitudinal concepts of flexibility and spontaneity. Common sense and your rapport with the group should determine how rigidly you adhere to your plans. Always have a plan, but always be prepared to change. This philosophy makes it important to have a repertoire of many finger games, stories, and songs so that you can "pull one out of your pocket" if the group seems ready for it.

Never announce, "Today's story will be . . . ." As soon as the children know what story you are telling, they will comment, "Oh, I know that one, who wants to hear it again," or something similar. At the end of the story, you can give its name, but, in any case, begin in a straightforward manner and end the same way.

CONDUCTING ACTIVITIES FOLLOWING STORY PRESENTATION

Having communicated your story to the group in an artistic and satisfying manner, you can further this initial literary experience in many ways.

Duplicating the Story

One of the most obvious ways to extend the experience is to duplicate the story's activities. For example, after reading *The Listening Walk* by Paul Showers, take the class on a "sensitivity stroll." After reading *It Looked Like Spilt Milk* (Shaw, 1947), the class could become cloud watchers and make cloud pictures, which in turn could be compiled into the children's own version of the book. *The Backward Day* (Krauss, 1950) could really be enacted in your class: you could put a movie into reverse, the children could come to school dressed backwards, you could file out to recess all walking backwards, you could set the clock back and have the afternoon activities in the morning, bake a pineapple upside-down cake, and maybe talk about what it would be like to go backwards in time and who you would meet on our trip into history. Or your February classroom could be turned into a May room after reading *Really Spring* (Zion, 1956), or it could be turned into a greenhouse if your class became plant sitters like Tommy in *The Plant Sitter* (Zion, 1959).

Creative Dramatics

Another natural follow-up activity is creative drama or dramatic play. After you've stimulated the children with the story (fables and folklore work especially well here), it is very easy to guide them into laying out the story they've just heard. You could furnish, or they could make, masks of the little old lady, the little old man, and the cast of billions and trillions of cats from Wanda Gág's classic (1928) and have the children play this story out.

To dramatize a story, look for ones that have plot emphasis. A simple plot with dramatic conflict, distinct characters, and a good story line are the elements to look for. A few such stories to have fun with are *Three Billy Goats Gruff* (Stobbs, 1968), *The North Wind and the Sun* (La Fontaine, 1964), *Caps for Sale* (Slobodkina, 1947), *Stone Soup* (Marcia Brown, 1947), *Ask Mr. Bear* (Flack, 1958), "The Old Witch" (Hoke, 1966), *The Little Rabbit Who Wanted Red Wings* (Bailey, 1961), "Sody Sallyraytus" (Chase, 1948), *The Three Bears* (Galdone, 1972), and cumulative tales such as *The Fat Cat* (Kent, 1971) and *The Golden Goose* (Brooke, 1905).

Flannel Board Stories

Many stories lend themselves to flannel board presentation because of their sequential addition of characters or objects. Flannel board pieces can be made by adults or children and become a favorite activity for children's re-telling of the story as they manipulate the pieces. *The Man Who Didn't Wash His Dishes* (Krasilovsky, 1950) is a favorite flannel board story, since children can pile up all the dirty dishes, pots, pans, and ashtrays as the man neglects his household chores. When he brings in his truck, they can pile everything onto it for the eventual rain washing the dirty dishes get. *Little Blue and Little Yellow* (Lionni, 1959) is especially good for flannel boards and can be done with cellophane paper that blends blue and yellow into green. The old folktales which add characters in cumulative style work well for flannel boards. *The Cow in the House* (Watts, 1956), in which a man keeps bringing animals into his already crowded house and gradually removes them to show his wife they have plenty of room, is one such tale.

Pantomime

After reading *If All the Seas Were One Sea* (Domanska, 1971; see Fig. 34), it is fun to have the children pantomime out such ideas as, "If all the bugs were one bug, what a great bug that would be," having them pretend they're that great bug; or, "If all the ice cream cones were one cone, what a great cone that would be," with the children puffing out their cheeks and

Fig. 34. Pantomime can follow the reading of this favorite rhyme, *If All the Seas Were One Sea,* illustrated by Janina Domanska. (Original in color)
Copyright © Janina Domanska 1971. Reprinted by permission of Macmillan Publishing Co., Inc.

waddling around like a fat person after eating such a cone. After reading *Four Fur Feet* (M. W. Brown, 1961), you can discuss the fact that no one ever sees the animal in the book—only its feet. What if the child saw an animal that never existed? How would it sound? Would it growl or chirp or would it make sounds never before heard, like the animals that didn't get on Noah's ark in *The Lost Zoo* by Countee Cullen? If the children get down on all fours and pretend to be the animal, where would they go if they walked around the world on four fur feet? What would they see and who would see them? Perhaps the children could even draw a huge mural of what the animal would see on its journey or discuss the kinds of transportation needed to get around the world.

Cooking

Another activity that extends from books is cooking. Betty Coody's book *Using Literature with Young Children* deals with this subject quite adequately and so does Carol MacGregor's *Storybook Cookbook*. It's fun to make

Fig. 35. Mr. Higgins fills his house with clocks, which soon begin to take up most of his time. (Original in color)
From Clocks and More Clocks *by Pat Hutchins. Copyright © 1970 Pat Hutchins. Reprinted by permission of Macmillan Publishing Co., Inc., and The Bodley Head.*

jam sandwiches after reading *Bread and Jam for Frances* (Hoban, 1964) or to have a tea party after reading *And It Rained* (Raskin, 1969). This book can also be used when teaching how to tell time, as can *Clocks and More Clocks* (Hutchins, 1970; see Fig. 35). A delightful activity is making "happy day pancakes" by first forming the eyes and smile with batter and letting it bake a bit before putting the rest of the batter down. When you flip the pancake over, you have a smile face pancake. After reading *Journey Cake, Ho!* (Sawyer, 1953), you could wonder with the group where the pancake you just made would go if it jumped off the griddle. Books such as these could also lead into talks about nutrition and the world hunger problem. A discussion about what magic there is in technology, the sea, and synthetic foods could be started after hearing the stories *Strega Nona* (de Paola, 1975) and "Two of Everything" (Ritchie, 1949).

Puppetry

In puppetry you are using graphic and language arts in actually making the puppet and in preparing and doing the story with it. Make a Mr. Nobody puppet after reading the poem "Mr. Nobody" (Brewton, 1940) or monster puppets after doing *Where the Wild Things Are* (Sendak, 1963). When Max (*Wild Things*) says, "And let the wild rumpus start," the puppets can madly dance around to the background music of Stravinsky's *Rite of Spring*.

Discussion Follow Up

A class can be easily drawn into a discussion of color with books such as *Seeing Red* (Wolff, 1968) or *Little Blue and Little Yellow* (Lionni, 1959). You can dramatize *Pitidoe the Color Maker* (Dines, 1959) by using overhead and colored cellophane transparencies which serve as spotlights to turn the children different colors as someone narrates what happens when Pitidoe turns the world all purple or blue. Then a discussion can be initiated by asking, for example, what the world would be like without colors or, using Mary O'Neill's book *Take a Number*, by asking what the world would be like without numbers. This "negation" technique, very intriguing to children, can also be employed by putting words such as *treason, assassination*, and *cold war* "on trial" to see if they should be kept in our language. As with the preceding concepts, you can ask what the world would be like if these words did not exist.

An interdisciplinary approach leading from one activity to another can help integrate literature into your entire curriculum and school schedule. If you're at the point of spring clean-up, use *The Man Who Didn't Wash His Dishes* (Krasilovsky, 1950), or around Valentine's Day use *Play with Me* (Ets, 1955) or *May I Bring a Friend?* (de Regniers, 1964), both of which have strong themes of friendship. In a beginning science class, compare Curious George's curiosity (Rey, 1941) with scientific discovery; you can also plant seeds after reading *The Carrot Seed* (Krauss, 1945) or measure everything in your classroom after reading *Inch by Inch* (Lionni, 1962). After reading *May I Bring a Friend?*, one could certainly go into letter writing or how to introduce people. Numerous books lend themselves to field trips: from *Hercules* (Gramatky, 1940, 1971) to the fire station, from *Sugar Mouse Cake* (Zion, 1964) to the local bakery, and from *Quiet! There's a Canary in the Library* (Freeman, 1969) to, of course, the library.

If we agree with George Leonard's premise in *Education and Ecstasy* and take delight seriously, then expanding and developing the activities just described can surely make the educational process more joyful and meaningful for both the teacher and the child.

CHILDREN'S BOOK REFERENCES

Bailey, Carolyn Sherwin. *The Little Rabbit Who Wanted Red Wings*. Illus. by Dorothy Grider. Platt and Munk, 1961.

Brewton, John E. "Mr. Nobody" in *Gaily We Parade*. Macmillan, 1940.

Brooke, Leslie. *The Golden Goose*. Warne, 1905.

Brown, Marcia. *Stone Soup*. Scribner, 1947. PB.

Brown, Margaret Wise. *Four Fur Feet*. Illus. by Remy Charlip. Addison-Wesley, 1961.

Chase, Richard, ed. "Sody Sallyraytus" in *Grandfather Tales*. Illus. by Berkeley Williams, Jr. Houghton, 1948.

Cullen, Countee. *The Lost Zoo*. Illus. by Joseph Low. Follett, 1969.

de Paola, Tomie. *Strega Nona*. Prentice-Hall, 1975.

de Regniers, Beatrice Schenk. *May I Bring a Friend?* Illus. by Beni Montresor. Atheneum, 1964. PB.

Dines, Glen. *Pitidoe the Color Maker*. Macmillan, 1959.

Domanska, Janina. *If All the Seas Were One Sea*. Macmillan, 1971.

Ets, Marie Hall. *Play with Me*. Viking, 1955. PB.

Flack, Marjorie. *Ask Mr. Bear*. Macmillan, 1958. PB.

Freeman, Don. *Quiet! There's a Canary in the Library*. Golden Gate, 1969.

Gág, Wanda. *Millions of Cats*. Coward, 1928.

Galdone, Paul. *Henny Penny*. Seabury, 1968.

————. *The Three Bears*. Seabury, 1972. PB.

Gramatky, Hardie. *Hercules*. Putnam, 1940, 1971.

Hoban, Russell. *Bread and Jam for Frances*. Illus. by Lillian Hoban. Harper, 1964. PB: Scholastic Book Services.

Hoke, Helen. "The Old Witch" in *Witches, Witches, Witches*. Illus. by W. R. Lohse. Watts, 1966.

Hutchins, Pat. *Clocks and More Clocks*. Macmillan, 1970. PB.

————. *The Surprise Party*. Macmillan, 1969. PB.

Kent, Jack. *The Fat Cat: A Danish Folktale.* Parents, 1971. PB: Scholastic Book Services.

Krasilovsky, Phyllis. *The Man Who Didn't Wash His Dishes.* Illus. by Barbara Cooney. Doubleday, 1950.

Krauss, Ruth. *The Carrot Seed.* Illus. by Crockett Johnson. Harper, 1945. PB: Scholastic Book Services.

————. *The Backward Day.* Illus. by Marc Simont. Harper, 1950.

La Fontaine, Jean de. *The North Wind and the Sun.* Illus. by Brian Wildsmith. Watts, 1964.

Lionni, Leo. *Inch by Inch.* Astor-Honor, 1962.

————. *Little Blue and Little Yellow.* Astor-Honor, 1959.

MacGregor, Carol. *The Storybook Cookbook.* Illus. by Ray Cruz. Doubleday, 1967.

O'Neill, Mary. *Take a Number.* Illus. by Al Nagy. Doubleday, 1968.

Raskin, Ellen. *And It Rained.* Atheneum, 1969.

Rey, Hans Augusto. *Curious George.* Houghton, 1941. PB.

Ritchie, Alice. "Two of Everything" in *The Treasure of Li-Po.* Illus. by T. Ritchie. Harcourt, 1949.

Sawyer, Ruth. *Journey Cake, Ho!* Illus. by Robert McCloskey. Viking, 1953. PB.

Scott, Ann Herbert. *Sam.* Illus. by Symeon Shimin. McGraw, 1967.

Sendak, Maurice. *Where the Wild Things Are.* Harper, 1963.

Shaw, Charles. *It Looked Like Spilt Milk.* Harper, 1947.

Showers, Paul. *The Listening Walk.* Illus. by Aliki. Crowell, 1961.

Silverstein, Shel. *The Giving Tree.* Harper, 1964.

Slobodkina, Esphyr. *Caps for Sale.* Addison-Wesley, 1947.

Stobbs, William. *Three Billy Goats Gruff.* McGraw, 1968.

Udry, Janice May. *A Tree Is Nice.* Illus. by Marc Simont. Harper, 1956.

Watts, Mabel. *The Cow in the House.* Illus. by Katherine Evans. Follett, 1956.

Wolff, Robert J. *Seeing Red.* Scribner, 1968.

Zion, Eugene. *The Plant Sitter.* Illus. by Margaret Bloy Graham. Harper, 1959. PB: Scholastic Book Services.

————. *Really Spring.* Illus. by Margaret Bloy Graham. Harper, 1956.

————. *Sugar Mouse Cake.* Illus. by Margaret Bloy Graham. Scribner, 1964.

PROFESSIONAL REFERENCES

Allen, Roach Van, and Claryce Allen. *Language Experiences in Reading, Teacher's Resource Book.* Level 1. Chicago: Encyclopaedia Britannica Press, 1974.

Carlson, Ruth K. *Literature for Children: Enrichment Ideas.* 2nd ed. Children's Literature Series. Dubuque, Iowa: William C. Brown, 1976.

Coody, Betty. *Using Literature with Young Children.* Dubuque, Iowa: William C. Brown, 1973.

Leonard, George B. *Education and Ecstasy.* New York: Delacorte, 1968.

Play It! Sing It! Gary, Ind.: Gary Public Library Children's Department, n.d.

Sawyer, Ruth. *The Way of the Storyteller.* New York: Viking Press, 1942.

Shedlock, Marie L. *The Art of the Storyteller.* New York: Dover, 1952.

Stroner, Sandra. "Media Programming for Children." *School Library Journal* 18 (November 1971): 25-27.

Joan Glazer

AUDIO-VISUAL MATERIALS

Audio-visual media are expanding in both type and amount. More companies are producing more material and, indeed, a greater variety of material. This chapter focuses on the basic audio-visual materials that may be used to provide literary experiences for young children, that is, films, filmstrips, film loops, slides, transparencies, study prints, and recordings, both tape and disc. Certain materials, such as flannel boards and puppets, are not included because they are discussed in other chapters of this book; others, such as the Xedia program of children's books on microfiche, are not included because they are more appropriate for use with older children.

When selecting and ordering A-V materials, teachers should note the type of equipment necessary for their use. Frequently one story may be purchased in several formats. Selecting media which are compatible with the equipment on hand may eliminate later frustration.

Criteria for Selecting Audio-Visual Materials

Criteria for selection of A-V materials fall into four general areas: literary qualifications, purpose, audience, and product quality.

For determining literary merit, the same standards one uses to evaluate the literary quality of a book apply to A-V media based upon books. Indeed, much of the quality of book-related A-V materials depends upon the quality of the original source. A poorly written book will not be improved by being read aloud on tape, nor will photography make weak illustrations better. Some A-V material which is technically excellent is nonetheless a poor choice for use with children because the text or illustrations are trite and unimaginative.

A-V media for young children produce a valid *literary* experience when they serve the following purposes: stimulate interest, enjoyment, and understanding of literature; enhance the development of children's imaginations; add to their knowledge of self and others; and increase their aesthetic appreciation. Not all media will meet all four purposes, but much will.

To provide a new interpretation of nursery rhymes which the children already know, the teacher may play parts of *Mother Goose* as read by Cyril Ritchard, Celeste Holm, and Boris Karloff (Caedmon Records). Pupils may be encouraged to talk about the record or to play again the parts they like. In each case, poems are being shared and enjoyed, thus laying the foundation for lasting literary interest.

To encourage children to think imaginatively, the teacher may show a filmstrip of *Gilberto and the Wind* (Weston Woods), letting them add sound effects during the showing. Afterwards, the children may be asked to describe how the wind feels to them or to move as though blown by a strong wind, an angry wind, or a gentle breeze. They should be allowed to express as many ideas as they can.

To help children grow in their knowledge of self and others, the teacher may use *So Much to Experience*, Set 1 in the Children's Literature Series (McGraw) designed by Patricia Cianciolo. After showing the sound filmstrips, the teacher might use some of the questions and activities in the teacher's guide, perhaps electing to use only a part of this media program. A teacher should not feel compelled to use a total series if parts of it are not appropriate for the children or for his or her purposes.

If the teacher wishes to help children develop an appreciation for various styles of art, filmstrips such as *Where Does the Butterfly Go When It Rains?* (Weston Woods) may be shown. The teacher may not discuss the pictures at all, simply exposing pupils to them in this form which allows all the children a clear view.

Whatever the purpose, audience considerations are crucial to the choice of A-V material. The teacher must keep in mind the developmental characteristics of young children. This means matching the length and complexity of the film or record with the attention span and maturity of the pupils.

Many teachers, particularly those who know children's books, can, from catalog information alone, determine the literary merit and appropriateness of a specific filmstrip or record. However, like technical quality, appropriateness can be fully assessed only by previewing the product. In previewing, consider the following questions. Does the story lend itself more readily to a recording, with narration an important part of the presentation, or does potentially confusing dialogue dictate pictures as well as sound? If there is sound, are the words easily understood? Does the sound track contribute to the story, either through musical background or sound effects? If environmental sounds are recreated, are they authentic? If the story requires a speaker of a particular dialect, is the dialect presented accurately and effectively? If pictures are created for a story, is the setting authentic? Do the technical procedures in filming, whether animation or iconography, add to the story? If live action is used, is the acting convincing? Finally, does the product have aesthetic integrity and wholeness in itself, whether or not it deviates from the original story?

Audio-visual material complements, rather than substitutes for, the books on which it is based. The teacher will want to require high quality in both in order to encourage the development of literary taste and enjoyment in young children.

Strategies for Using Audio-Visual Materials

Providing literary experiences with A-V materials has much in common with doing so by using books. Just as books serve an educational function, so too do the A-V materials based on books. Neither are simply devices for keeping children occupied or for filling those last twenty minutes on Friday afternoon. Rather both can and should contribute to young children's language learning, to the growth of their imaginations, and the development of their ability to empathize with other people. They are educational materials and should be used as such. Discussions and activities which are appropriate following the reading of a book are quite often equally as appropriate following the viewing and hearing of the same story in A-V form.

A-V materials do offer several unique opportunities, however. Transparencies are ideal for presenting cumulative tales, because the additive quality of such stories can be clearly expressed with overlays. For example, the teacher might select a book such as *Mr. Gumpy's Outing* by John Burningham. The first transparency could be of Mr. Gumpy, the next of his boat, aligned so that Mr. Gumpy appears to be in it. As the children, the rabbit, the cat, and all the other characters request permission to come along and are invited by Mr. Gumpy to join the group, a series of transparencies can be placed over the existing ones so that each character appears to be in the boat. When the animals misbehave and the boat finally tips, the teacher can show this by sliding the transparencies at all different angles. One further transparency, showing all the characters dried off and having tea at Mr. Gumpy's home, would complete the story. The teacher may want to tell the story several times during the year, perhaps having the children help with the telling and eventually having them tell the entire story themselves.

Filmstrips are another medium which allows the children to tell the story, to supply their own version of the text. The teacher should select a filmstrip in which the pictures convey the story rather explicitly. An example is

Rosie's Walk (Weston Woods). Children can relate what is happening in each frame as it shows on the screen. If the teacher later decides to read the actual text or to show the filmstrip with the sound portion, he or she will want to introduce it by saying, "Here is how the author of the story told what happened." The teacher should avoid using terminology which would suggest that the author's way was the "right" way and that the children's language was "wrong" or ineffective.

Sound recordings can be used to encourage pupils to visualize stories for themselves. The teacher may use stories which have been recorded to accompany a filmstip, as well as those which are in record form only. Children can listen with their eyes closed, later telling how they think the giant looked or showing how Petunia walked around the barnyard. Both filmstrips and recordings can augment language growth and the development of the imagination.

Many films and records accompanying filmstrips enhance a story by the addition of appropriate music. The music for the "rumpus" in the filmstrip *Where the Wild Things Are* (Weston Woods) connotes the rhythm and abandonment of the creatures as they swing among the trees. It brings an added dimension, one that children can explore, either through movement or discussion or perhaps through the creation of a new "score" for the book. Children can use simple percussion instruments, developing rhythms of their own, talking about the mood of their music. It provides an opportunity for the teacher to help the pupils develop listening skills and to discuss personal reactions to the story and to the music.

Some films, such as *The Erie Canal* (Weston Woods) and *Hush Little Baby* (Weston Woods), are invitations for children to sing along. The books from which these films are made use the lyrics of the songs as text, then develop the ideas fully in the illustrations. Children are presented with an authentic representation of life along the Erie Canal in the one and with colorful pictures depicting colonial life in America in the other. Both merit several viewings. There is much to observe, and as the songs become more familiar, the teacher will find more children singing with the film.

The film *Really Rosie*, which was originally shown on television, is now available from Weston Woods and the sound track is available separately as a recording (Ode Records). The film combines characters from Maurice Sendak's *Nutshell Library* (*One Was Johnny, Alligators All Around, Pierre,* and *Chicken Soup with Rice*) with his *The Sign on Rosie's Door*. The music which accompanies it was composed and is sung by Carole King. The combination of Sendak's poetry and King's music is entrancing. Children can be encouraged to select a favorite, to act out parts of the film, to look at the books upon which the film is based, to compare the film with the books, or to look at illustrations in the book (see Fig. 37) while listening to the recording. Children can be developing critical thinking skills by comparing differing presentations of the same story, while at the same time enjoying the presentation of good literature.

Teachers should capitalize on other special opportunities offered by A-V media. Study prints from *A Child's World of Poetry*, Group 1 (Society for Visual Education) provide large, colorful pictures which correlate with poems printed on the back of the pictures. This allows the children to focus attention on a picture while they listen to the poem, either from the record or the

Fig. 37. Characters from several of Sendak's earlier books appear in *Really Rosie* and the film versions of it.
Illustrations by Maurice Sendak. Copyright © 1975 by Maurice Sendak. Reprinted by permission of Harper & Row, Publishers, Inc.

teacher's reading. "Suggestions for Utilization" are printed with each poem. A teacher may want to develop new questions for discussion so that they are geared to a particular group of children. If working with preschool youngsters, "Raining" by Rhoda W. Bacmeister from the "It's Raining! It's Raining!" print might be selected. As children look at the picture of two children in the rain, the teacher might ask such questions as "Do you like to be outside when it rains?" "How do you think these children feel about being in the rain?" "How does rain sound when it hits your umbrella?" "How does it sound when it hits the leaves on a tree?" He or she would then introduce the poem with "Here's what one poet said about rain." After reading the poem, ask, "How did the rain sound to her?" While you read the poem once more, have the children listen for the sounds of rain as described by the poet and report any new findings. The teacher will find that young children's enjoyment of literature will be better enhanced by frequent short experiences with literature than by a few lengthy ones. Thus, the teacher should provide many experiences of ten to fifteen minutes duration.

Teachers will want to make the sharing of literature through A-V media a meaningful experience for pupils. They will make certain that the children can all see and hear what is being presented; they will set the stage for listening by giving a purpose for careful listening (or viewing) and by setting an example themselves; they will allow time for children to respond to what has been experienced. They will involve pupils sometimes by having them respond during the presentation. Recordings of stories, such as *Henny Penny*, read by Boris Karloff (Caedmon Records), lend themselves readily to pantomime during the story as well as to dramatization following it. Teachers may show a story more than once or make it available to those children who wish to see or hear it again. One of the most basic values of A-V material is that it allows pupils to hear favorite stories or poems repeatedly, often independent of the teacher. Occasionally teachers will plan activities based on the media presented. And finally, they will want to have copies of some of the books on which the audio-visual materials have been based. They will use A-V material for its unique qualities, for the new interpretation of stories and poems which it provides, for its artistic merit, and for the enjoyment it can bring to young children.

Locating Audio-Visual Materials

The opportunity for learning inherent in book-related audio-visual materials is so great that the teacher of young children will want to know exactly what materials can be obtained and will want to become skillful in their use. The annotated bibliography at the end of this chapter is designed to help the teacher become aware of available A-V materials. The books listed give basic information about the content of the material and about purchase and rental fees. Listed also are several journals which regularly review new media. In addition to perusing books and catalogs, it is often helpful to contact state departments of education. Usually they have an audio-visual department which will lend materials, either for direct use with a group of children or for previewing purposes.

SOURCES FOR LOCATING MEDIA

Books

Bielowski, Joseph G. *Guide to Educational Technology: Early Childhood Education.* Westport, Conn.: Technomic Publishing, 1973.

> Lists companies which provide equipment, materials, or services in technology and whose markets include the preschool level. Addresses and telephone numbers are given, as are the type of media produced by each company. Can be used for finding companies which produce a specific type of media and for obtaining the address of companies for purchasing media.

Greene, Ellin, and Madalynne Schoenfeld, eds. *A Multimedia Approach to Children's Literature.* Chicago: American Library Association, 1972.

> Brief annotations for approximately 425 books, 175 16mm films, 175 filmstrips, and 300 recordings, both tapes and discs. Selection was based upon "firsthand evaluation and use with children," with children's responses being a primary factor for determining inclusion. Thus, this is a recommended list of materials. Entries are listed in alphabetical order by title, with the book first, followed by one or more examples of the story in nonprint form. Authors, films, filmstrips, media presented by authors and illustrators, records, and subjects are all separately indexed at the back of the book. A directory of distributors is included and each entry indicates purchase and rental price. The selection procedure, the organizational pattern, and the information included make this book extremely useful.

McDaniel, Roderick, ed. *Resources for Learning: A Core Media Collection for Elementary Schools.* New York: Bowker, 1971.

> Brief annotations for approximately 4,000 audio-visual materials, indexed by subject, by title and author, and by subject heading. Selections were based on positive recommendations by one or more reviews in media journals or books. Full information is given and a producer/distributor directory included. However, because the selections were based on reviews rather than on specific policy, the book does not provide the balanced "core media collection" the title suggests. Another inadequacy is that not all items which appear elsewhere in the book appear under subject headings. For example, there is no subject heading for *camels*, yet in the title/author section there are three entries for *The Camel Who Took a Walk*—one sound filmstrip, one Super 8 sound filmstrip, and one 16mm film. Nonetheless, this is a useful book, particularly for elementary school library or media centers, and is reasonably priced.

Markham, Lois, ed. *New Educational Materials*. New York: Citation Press, 1970.

A compilation of reviews which have been published in *Scholastic Teacher*. Publishers and producers submit their new products for review; the reviewer classroom tests the materials and in the review suggests grade level, possible classroom uses, and a rating. The materials are listed first as "Pre-K through Grade Six" or "Grades Seven through Twelve" and then listed by subject area. Literature-related media are under the general heading "Language Arts."

Mills, Josephine M. "Multimedia for Children's Literature, Parts I and II." Offprint from *Instructor* 81 (November 1971): 50-57 (Part I) and 81 (April 1972): 105-111 (Part II). Dansville, N.Y.: The Instructor Publications, 1972.

A "selected list of children's literature in nonbook form" that includes approximately 400 entries, listed in alphabetical order by the book title of the original source. Although the criteria for selection are not stated, one assumes that literary and production quality were basic considerations. The entries are not annotated, but all other information about form, playing time, and purchase and rental is given. For the teacher who knows children's books, this is an excellent guide to other forms of a story.

Neal, J. A., and Elaine T. Hall, eds. *Audiovisual Market Place—A Multimedia Guide, 1975-76*. New York: Xerox, 1976.

Lists the names of companies producing and/or distributing audiovisual materials; under each company are listed the address and telephone number, key personnel, the type of media produced, and grade levels and subject areas covered. Listings are in alphabetical order by company name, followed by listings of producers/distributors categorized by type of media and by subject matter of the media.

Rufsvold, Margaret I., and Carolyn Guss. *Guides to Educational Media*. 3rd ed. Chicago: American Library Association, 1971.

Lists media catalogs available and describes the scope, arrangement, entries, and special features of each. It also describes professional organizations and periodicals in the field of educational media.

Wall, C. Edward, ed. *Media Review Digest*. Vol. 6. Ann Arbor, Mich.: Pierian Press, 1976.

Formerly titled *The Multi-Media Reviews Index*, this work is published annually, with supplements appearing in four issues of *Audiovisual Instruction*. Included are brief descriptions of the material being reviewed, where the material has been reviewed, quotations from journal reviews, and a general rating based upon the evaluations of reviewers. Contributors stress that these ratings are not endorsed by them or by the publisher and that they should not be used as the primary basis for purchasing. Thus, the book may be best used as a source for finding more extensive reviews for specific materials.

Periodicals

Audiovisual Instruction. Association for Educational Communications and
Technology (1201 Sixteenth St., N.W., Washington, D.C. 20036).

Describes new media in a regular feature titled "Have You Seen
These?" The materials are selected on the basis of newness only and
are not necessarily recommended. A second section titled "New Products" describes new A-V machines and hardware. Includes all grade
levels, but seems to stress secondary. Nonetheless, an occasional
skimming of several issues may provide ideas for both selection and
use of A-V materials.

Early Years (11 Hale Lane, Box 1223, Darien, Conn. 06820).

For teachers of preschool through grade three, *Early Years* heads
its "Materials Testing Service" column with the following explanation:

All programs and materials reported in this column were screened for
Early Years under actual classroom conditions and were found to meet the
needs of the classroom teacher and her pupils.

Materials, the test sites, conditions, and results are described. Both
the strengths and weaknesses of the product are explained, with
suggestions for classroom use completing the review. Usually two or
three of the products in each issue are A-V media.

Instructor. The Instructor Publications, Inc. (7 Bank St., Dansville, N.Y.
14437).

For teachers of preschool through grade six, *Instructor* devotes one
part of its "Reviews" section to instructional media. Fairly lengthy
descriptions, evaluative comments, results of classroom use in some
cases, and suggestions for classroom use are given. The reader is provided with enough detail to make decisions about whether the product
is worth a personal review.

Language Arts. National Council of Teachers of English (1111 Kenyon Rd.,
Urbana, Ill. 61801).

"Staying on Top," a bimonthly column, includes reviews of non-
print instructional materials; emphasis is on language arts from early
childhood through the middle school. Reviews describe and briefly
evaluate materials and give price and ordering information.

Learning. Education Today Company (530 University Ave., Palo Alto,
Calif. 94301).

For teachers of preschool through grade six. Includes a variety of
subheadings in the regular feature "Thumbs Up," which reviews
"high-quality, low-cost learning materials." A-V media are reviewed
under the subheading "Sights and Sounds." Detailed descriptions,
evaluations, and occasionally the responses of children, as well as
price and ordering information, are given.

Previews: News and Reviews of Non-Print Media. R. R. Bowker and Company (1800 Avenue of the Americas, New York, N.Y. 10036).

An audio-visual magazine published since 1972 by Bowker that provides reviews of new media. Previously the reviews were included in the *School Library Journal* as a regular feature. Each issue has "Recordings," "Screenings," "Audiovisual Guide," and "Checklist" sections, all of which provide a brief description of the new products, an analysis of their strengths and weaknesses, and recommendations for their use.

School Library Journal. R. R. Bowker and Company (1800 Avenue of the Americas, New York, N.Y. 10036).

The entire April and November issues are devoted to reviews and articles on audio-visual materials.

Teacher. Macmillan Professional Magazines, Inc. (22 West Putnam Ave., Greenwich, Conn. 06830).

For teachers of preschool through grade six. Includes two regular sections which review A-V media. One, "New AV Materials," reviews new films, records, and filmstrips, with evaluations and suggestions for use; the other, "Book Bonanza," discusses books and book-related media, both new and "time-tested," and also gives suggestions for classroom use.

MEDIA REFERENCES

A Child's World of Poetry. Group 1. Chicago: Society for Visual Education. Study prints and records.

The Erie Canal (Peter Spier). Weston, Conn.: Weston Woods Studios. Film, filmstrip, record, and cassette.

Gilberto and the Wind (Marie Hall Ets). Weston, Conn.: Weston Woods Studios. Filmstrip, record, and cassette.

Henny Penny. Read by Boris Karloff. New York: Caedmon Records. Record.

Hush Little Baby (Aliki). Weston, Conn.: Weston Woods Studios. Film, filmstrip, record, and cassette.

Millions of Cats (Wanda Gág). Weston, Conn.: Weston Woods Studios. Filmstrip, record, and cassette.

Mother Goose. Read by Cyril Ritchard, Celeste Holm, and Boris Karloff. New York: Caedmon Records. Record and cassette.

Mr. Gumpy's Outing. John Burningham. New York: Holt, Rinehart and Winston, 1971. Book.

Petunia (Roger Duvoisin). Weston, Conn.: Weston Woods Studios. Filmstrip, record, and cassette.

Really Rosie. Pictures, story, and lyrics by Maurice Sendak. Music by Carole King. Weston, Conn.: Weston Woods Studios. Film.

Really Rosie. Carole King. Hollywood, Calif.: Ode Records. Record.

Rosie's Walk (Pat Hutchins). Weston, Conn.: Weston Woods Studios. Filmstrip, record, and cassette.

So Much to Experience. Children's Literature Series. Set 1. New York: McGraw-Hill. Six filmstrips, cassettes, records, and teacher's manual.

The Tomten (Astrid Lindgren, illus. by Harald Wiberg). Weston, Conn.: Weston Woods Studios. Filmstrip, record, and cassette.

Where Does the Butterfly Go When It Rains? (May Garelick, illus. by Leonard Weisgard). Weston, Conn.: Weston Woods Studios. Filmstrip, record, and cassette.

Where the Wild Things Are (Maurice Sendak). Weston, Conn.: Weston Woods Studios. Filmstrip, record, and cassette.

Jessie A. Roderick

RESPONSES TO LITERATURE

Young children are anxious to tell us how they feel, what they are curious about, and what they like and dislike. But we need to listen to them and to watch them if we are to receive their messages. The child who calls out, "Come see my rocket," or, "I like this book. I want to take it home," uses a very direct way of telling us something. Children can also try to tell us something by their actions. Sometimes they will come and tug at our clothing. At times a loud bang will get our attention, and at other times just a glance will indicate they want to share something with us or want us to come and see what they are doing. The purpose of this chapter is to encourage adults who work with young children to become more aware of how children respond to experiences with books both verbally and nonverbally. It is important to try to view children's responses to books from their perspective—how they see the world. Too often we are tempted to superimpose our own feelings and our view of the world on the child's behavior.

WHY STUDY CHILDREN'S RESPONSES?

Adults who help provide good literary experiences for young children need to be concerned about how children respond to these experiences. Older children can be asked to write about their reactions to literature, or they can be questioned about them in an interview, but young children often do not possess the necessary writing skills nor are they always ready to answer questions about how they liked a story, poem, or film. Because of this, we have little organized and public knowledge about the young child's reactions to books and other media. This lack of knowledge points up the need to develop specific ways of becoming more aware of what children think and feel about literature.

Another reason for seeking this information is the guidance it can give us as we look for ways to help individual children from different backgrounds experience literature to its fullest. When we have specific information about individual children's verbal and nonverbal responses to literature, our plans for these children can be tailor-made to reflect the individuality of each child. The child who responds quietly by inching ever so slowly closer and closer to the storyteller or who rocks back and forth to the sound of the words is giving some clues as to how he or she is responding at that moment to a particular story. Persons who are aware of these clues and who put them into perspective over many observations can get to know children in more depth. The more knowledge we can gain about children through close attention to the subtle and not so subtle cues they give, the better able we are to plan for them.

A final reason for finding ways of becoming more aware of young children's responses to literature is what we learn in the process. What questions and new areas for exploration are uncovered when careful attention is given to what children say and do in response to books? How does the knowledge gained by obtaining specific information about these responses influence or change how we view children or the literary experiences that seem to be appropriate for them? Does knowing how to obtain information about children's responses to literature and how to use this information enrich the experience for the youngsters? How do we know? These are but a few of the questions which might be raised as we devise ways to learn about children's responses to literature and to use the information gained. Just as children are encouraged to ask questions, we, too, must constantly raise questions about our own efforts.

OBSERVING AND DESCRIBING

Among the many ways we can alert ourselves to how children are responding to literature, one of the most important is observing, describing, and recording what children do and say during and after a literary experience. However, in order to accurately obtain and use this information, we need to carefully examine the setting in which children are exposed to literature. We also need to acquaint ourselves with the various aspects or types of verbal and nonverbal behaviors.

The Setting

When we observe and listen to children respond to the telling of a story or the showing of a filmstrip or record and slide presentation, we are observing their interacting with a part of their surroundings. Consequently, any observations we make of this interaction must take into account the child's surroundings at that time. Which persons were with the child during the story? Was the group large or small? Were there distractions such as persons interrupting the story or outside noises that made it difficult to hear at times? Was the place where the children were listening to the story an inviting one with comfortable chairs or cushions? Which books, records, or pictures were available for children to examine on their own or share with a friend? Answers to these and other questions provide a picture of the setting in which the child participated in a literary experience.

If we are to place our observations of children in the larger context of the conditions surrounding them, it might also be helpful to know such things as whether the children felt free to join and leave story time when they wished. Were they asked to join the group and to remain with it until the story was finished? If there were follow-up activities, were they planned by an adult, by both adult and children, or were they spontaneous? For example, if a few children make a number game such as the one illustrated in *Moja Means One*

Fig. 38. Counting games are a natural follow-up activity for *Moja Means One*. (Original in color) *Illustration from* Moja Means One, *illustrated by Tom Feelings. Copyright © 1971 by Tom Feelings. Reprinted by permission of The Dial Press.*

(Feelings, 1971; see Fig. 38), did the teacher suggest this follow-up activity or did the idea come from the children? If the person doing the observing is also responsible for the activity, he or she knows the answers to these questions; all that needs to be done when examining the records of observations is to recall what was planned for and what happened. If the observer did not plan the activity, he or she can talk to the person who did.

It might also be helpful to record how the literary experience was presented or provided for. Did an adult or older child read a story from a book or was the story told with the aid of posters or flannel figures? Did the adult invite the children to participate? Were aids such as projectors and recorders used? Were children asked for suggestions for follow-up activities? Were they asked if they wanted a second telling of the story or showing of the film? Answers to these and other questions can help us see how the behavior of the person guiding the experiences can influence children's responses to them.

Being able to carefully describe the different aspects of the setting in which the child experiences literature is one of the prerequisites to obtaining and utilizing specific information about children's responses to literature. Another prerequisite is an understanding of verbal and nonverbal aspects of behavior.

Verbal Behavior

We are quite aware that children talk or engage in verbal communication. Verbal utterances are readily heard even if a child is not in view of another person. However, adults sometimes need to be cautioned not to tune out talkative youngsters too readily or to forget that some youngsters need to be encouraged to express themselves by talking. Even though we are aware of verbal communication in that we hear youngsters and generally respond to what they say, there are some ways of looking at talk that might help us listen to and record what the child says. We can group a child's verbal communication according to the function or purpose it serves. Is it a question, an interjection, an elaboration upon an idea, or the repetition of a phrase or group of words? In the latter, a child might join in the repeating of phrases in a story such as *Drummer Hoff* (Emberley, 1967).

It is often helpful to note to whom or to what the child appears to be responding. Are the child's comments in response to what another person says or does during a literary experience or are they in response to a part of a story or what a character does or says? To whom does the child address comments while he or she is responding to literature? These questions and others provide some guidelines for examining that aspect of a child's talk which involves other persons or the content of books.

How often a child speaks and how much is said can be noted as he or she responds to a story. We can also look at *when* a child responds. Does the child comment during the experience, after it, or at both times? Does this vary with different kinds of stories? Does the child ask to take the book home or to make something suggested by the book? The timing of verbal responses is an individual matter when the climate encourages a child to respond as he or she sees fit. Knowledge of the child's timing can be helpful in planning experiences that give the child time to think or time to respond.

What children talk about in response to literature is also important. Do they talk about what is happening or what might happen in a story? Do they add to the story? Do they relate what is happening in the story to themselves? Do they comment on things that have happened to them? Do they comment on the interests or responses of others in the group?

Nonverbal Behavior

Since children's nonverbal behavior also gives clues to how they are responding to literature, we need to be as aware of their actions as we are of their words. Young children often tell us much more about themselves through their actions than they do through their words, particularly in a setting where adults expect children to be quiet and pay close attention. Unfortunately, in such instances the nonverbal behaviors children exhibit often suggest discomfort or dissatisfaction with their not being able to express their feelings and reactions aloud. But sometimes children who are in a so-called quiet situation or quiet time communicate much to us nonverbally about their response to a literary experience. Of course a quiet time is not the only situation in which children communicate nonverbally; they also do this while they are talking.

If we recognize the fact that children use nonverbal behavior to tell us much about themselves, then we must become more aware of these behaviors and be able to record them. Grouping together similar kinds of nonverbal behaviors is one way of doing this. Nonverbal behaviors may be grouped in terms of larger body movements, such as moving the whole body from one place to another, or other movements, such as jumping or clapping hands, in which the body is not necessarily moved from one place to another. Often children move their whole body in response to a book like *Sometimes I Dance Mountains* (Baylor, 1973). A second grouping of smaller body movements includes gestures and facial expressions. Among these are pointing at an object or person, motioning for someone to come closer, shaking a head yes or no, smiling, frowning, and the like. The facial expressions of children whose families have just been joined by a new baby can be noted during the reading of a book such as *She Come Bringing Me That Little Baby Girl* (Greenfield, 1974).

In observing nonverbal communicative behaviors, it is helpful to note to whom or to what a child responds nonverbally, the manner in which the child responds, and the timing of the responses. Notice, for example, whether the child imitates actions described and illustrated in a story; comes close to the person reading the story and helps turn the page; motions for other children to come see or hear the story; laughs, squints, or opens his or her eyes wide while hearing or seeing different parts of a story. Another aspect of nonverbal communication worthy of note is how a person uses space. During a literary experience we can observe whether a child gets close to other listeners or sits separated from them. Does the child like to be close to the source of the story? Does a kindergarten or nursery school child like to be held on the adult's lap while *The Knee Baby* (Jarrell, 1973) is being read? Does the child appear more satisfied and better able to concentrate when not crowded?

The nonverbal aspects of a child's response to literature require special consideration and attention for several reasons. Not only do nonverbal behaviors often go unnoticed, but they often occur simultaneously. For example, a person can move from one place to another, motion to another person, and smile all at the same time. Although such a pattern might provide several clues to a child's response to literature, it does make the observation and recording of behavior more difficult. Verbal behavior also presents some problems in recording, but a person is only capable of producing one verbal statement at a time.

Another special consideration in observing nonverbal responses of children is related to the content, or message, which appears to be conveyed. When we observe youngsters we often have to infer from what we see. That is, although nonverbal behaviors can tell us much about a child if properly interpreted, they do not often "speak" as clearly as verbal ones. When a child says, "I want you to come and help me read this book," the message is quite clear. However, if a child just motions for you to come over, you may not be sure at the moment why he or she wants you to come. For this reason we need to be alert to the variety of nonverbal behaviors exhibited and where and when they are exhibited. It is also important for observers to try to note as many behaviors as possible before making judgments about what they might mean. Before leaving this point, it should be noted that some nonverbal behaviors do "speak" clearly and leave very little question as to what a child is trying to convey, e.g., hands on hips and a firm stomp of the foot.

Alerting the reader to these special considerations in observing youngsters' nonverbal responses to literature is not meant to discourage focusing on them. On the contrary, awareness of these considerations should help us make the best use of our observations. Persons who are aware of these special considerations are also more apt to appreciate the value of nonverbal expression as a more spontaneous indication of true feelings. The nonverbal aspects of communication can also support and reinforce what children say, as well as negate or contradict what they say. For instance, a child who says a book such as *The Tyrannosaurus Game* (Kroll, 1976) is funny but who did not laugh at the humorous parts when the book was read *might* make us wonder whether the child really caught the humor in the story. The agreement or lack of agreement between a person's verbal and nonverbal behavior is another aspect to consider when observing and listening to children as they respond to literature.

TECHNIQUES FOR DESCRIBING RESPONSES

So far, the need for becoming more aware of children's responses to literature and some prerequisites for obtaining specific information about these responses have been discussed. In this section some sample guidelines and observation instruments for describing children's responses to literature are presented.* These instruments were derived from written observations of three, four, and five year olds' responses during a group literary experience. The following is a description of the procedures used in developing these instruments.

1. Children in three different age groupings were observed as they engaged in a literary experience (for the most part, they listened to a story being told by an adult).

2. The observer focused on the nonverbal and verbal behaviors of the group as a whole. As communicative behaviors were observed, they were described in diary fashion on a sheet of paper. The observer also made notes about the setting in which the storytelling took place.

3. After all groups had been observed and behaviors recorded, the written observations were examined and behaviors were grouped. Nonverbal and verbal behaviors were analyzed separately, but the observations from all three age groupings were treated as one set of behaviors (although there were some differences among the age groups, they were not considered in developing these guidelines).

4. After behavior groupings had been established, they were labeled "Responds to Story," "Comments to Adult," and the like, with specific examples cited under each. These groupings and examples became the nucleus for the observation guidelines.

5. Spaces for describing the setting and for marking which behaviors were observed were added to the groupings, or categories, to form the guidelines.

6. These guidelines were then used to observe youngsters engaged in literary experiences.

Please note that the guidelines presented in this chapter (pp. 149, 150, and 151) are not intended to be research tools in the sense that reliability and validity have been established for them. They are offered in the hope that persons who are concerned about high quality literary experiences for children will become interested in the responses children make to books and that the guidelines will generate more specific knowledge about these responses.

Suggestions for Using the Observation Guidelines

The guidelines have been developed for use either *during* a literary experience or *following* one. Each of these instruments is designed to help the observer focus on verbal and nonverbal behaviors. Although nonverbal and verbal behaviors often occur at the same time, they are separated on the forms for the convenience of the observer. The reader will also note that the examples of verbal and nonverbal behaviors are those which were discussed earlier in this chapter. In each grouping of behaviors there is space for the

---

*The material from which these instruments were derived was obtained through the kind help of Susan Akman, Cindy Roach, Marion Leiserson, and Lynne Sherald, teachers in the Center for Young Children, University of Maryland.

Guidelines for Observing a Child *During* a Literary Experience

The Setting: Date _____ Time _____ Place _____

Child Observed _____ Kind of Literary Experience _____

_____

(storytelling, film, etc.)

Other Persons Present _____

General Comments *(e.g., Are children free to enter and leave group as they wish?)*

_____

_____

Verbal Behaviors	*Check (✔) box opposite behavior each time it occurs*					
Responds to Story						
Asks questions about character, plot, etc.						
Predicts what might happen next						
Repeats words, sounds, phrases in story						
Relates what is happening in story to own experiences						
Other						
Comments to Adult						
About the story (character, setting, plot, etc.)						
About another child's response or behavior						
About own behavior (e.g., as child imitates action in book)						
Other						
Comments to Other Child or Children in Group						
About the story (character, setting, plot, etc.)						
About another child's behavior						
About own behavior						
Other						

General Comments That Do Not Appear to Be Related to Story or Persons in Group (e.g., "I can't see.")

observer to add other behaviors noticed while working with children. These guidelines should not be considered complete; persons using them are urged to revise and add or delete items as they see fit.

It is helpful to get information about the setting each time an observation is made. The first section of the guidelines for observing a child during a literary experience contains suggestions for describing the setting. It is assumed that similar information will be obtained when observing youngsters after a literary experience.

In using these guidelines, it is suggested that the observer place a check (✔) in the box to the right of the description of the behavior observed or statement heard. When the observation has been completed, the checks on the guideline will tell which behaviors occurred and how often. The format for recording may be revised to obtain other kinds of information, such as the sequence in which the behaviors occurred.

It is important to note that the guidelines as they appear do not have to be used in their entirety. An observer may want to focus on a child's verbal responses to a story. In that case, only the first grouping of verbal behaviors on the guideline for observing a child during a literary experience will be used. Or, if an observer wanted to compare a child's verbal responses during a story with those after a story, he or she would use the "Responds to Story" category under "Verbal Behaviors" on the form for observing a child during a literary experience and the "Verbal Comments" grouping on the guideline for

Nonverbal Behaviors *(During Story)*

Responds to Story	*Check (✔) box opposite behavior each time it occurs*						
Larger Body Movements							
Walks to person holding book, or stands looking at book							
Imitates action in story when action involves larger body movements							
Other							
Smaller Body Movements and Facial Expressions							
Points to illustrations							
Smiles, laughs							
Opens eyes wide							
Other							

General Nonverbal Behaviors That Do Not Appear to Be Directed at Another Person or in Response to Story (e.g., shifting position to get more comfortable)

after an experience. The observer should feel free to combine categories or use them singly as individual purposes dictate. Also, these guidelines are designed to observe a single child, but they can be revised to catch the responses of more than one child.

An observer may want to watch a child respond to different literary experiences over a period of time. For example, how does a child respond when *The Five Chinese Brothers* (Bishop, 1938) is read and when it is told using a flannel board? An observer may also want to observe different children as they respond to the same literary experience. For instance, we might note how closely children attend to the turning of pages in a book such as *Everybody Needs a Rock* (Baylor, 1974) where consecutive step-by-step rules for finding a rock are given on successive pages.

In addition to noting children's spontaneous responses to literature, we can solicit responses in a variety of ways. We can plan literature activities

---

Guidelines for Observing a Child *After* a Literary Experience

Child Observed _____

    Experience or Experiences Responded to
    (i.e., title of book, filmstrip, etc.)   _____

    _____

Verbal Comments	*Check (✔) box opposite behavior each time it occurs*					
Are you going to read that book again?						
May I take the book home with me?						
I didn't like the film we saw this morning.						
My mommy bought me that book.						
Let's make a garden like the one in the book.						
Others						

Nonverbal Behaviors						
Takes book from table or book rack.						
Leafs through book with a friend.						
Draws picture like one in the book.						
Gives book to a friend.						
Makes a macaroni necklace as in book.						
Does creative movements like those in book.						
Tries tricks shown in book or film.						
Others						

that invite children to become actively involved, and we can engage children in conversations about books by asking them questions related to the books or other literature materials. For example, we might include in a dress-up area of the classroom a group of books which might encourage children to engage in dramatic play. Books such as *Under Christopher's Hat* (Callahan, 1972) and *I Like Old Clothes* (Hoberman, 1976) could be presented, and we could observe children's responses to these materials. When we discuss with a child books such as *Nothing Ever Happens on My Block* (Raskin, 1966) or *Puzzles* (Wildsmith, 1970), we can get some idea of his or her ability to note inconsistencies between illustrations and texts and also the ability to pick out details in configurations. After having met and talked with a child from another part of the country or the world or after having listened to other students tell about their hobbies or work, children could be asked to recommend books they think their guests might enjoy. We might also ask a child who has selected a book he or she likes to find another most like it and tell why it was chosen. For example, if *Owliver* (Kraus, 1974) is a favorite of a child, we might ask him or her to find another book that is most like it.

EXAMINING AND USING RECORDS OF RESPONSES

Once children's responses have been recorded, the next step is to carefully examine the records to see what they might suggest for future planning of literary experiences, as well as for future observing and recording. How this is done and the extent to which we do it are determined by our individual situations. The following suggestions for examining and applying the information gained are offered as starting points. Hopefully, readers will begin to develop their own procedures.

The guidelines for observing that have been presented in this chapter might be used to gain some idea of how much a child responds to literature, whether he or she uses more nonverbal than verbal expressions as a response, and whether the responses change over time or with different literary experiences. It also would be possible to determine whether a child usually reacts to similar elements in a story and whether a child uses a limited number of communicative behaviors to express reactions. If several observations of one child are made, it would be possible to compare responses in different settings. For instance, do a child's responses to *In the Night Kitchen* (Sendak, 1970) differ when he or she hears the story told in a large group and when the child and a friend read the book together? If the responses are different, how do they differ? An observer could also gain some evidence as to how aware the child is of others in the setting: how does he or she respond to other's comments about the story and what does he or she say to others?

Specific information about children's responses to literature can help us plan better for individual children. As a result of becoming more aware of a child's verbal and nonverbal responses, we might know better what the child is interested in, likes or dislikes, doesn't understand, and would like to know more about. Careful observation of children also helps to reveal what they bring to a literary experience and what they take from it. How do they respond to humor, to sadness, to excitement in books?

In addition to helping us improve the quality of literary experiences, information about children's responses to literature can guide us in revising procedures for becoming more aware of these responses. As observational guidelines are used, the need to revise them becomes apparent. New forms may need to be developed, and with new forms come new questions— questions which can extend our horizons and those of the children. The appreciation of literature by young children should have no bounds. Studying the ways young children respond to literature and incorporating that knowledge into classroom practice make possible a more intimate matching of books and children, thus improving the chances that each encounter children have with literature will lead them to a deeper appreciation of it.

CHILDREN'S BOOK REFERENCES

Baylor, Byrd. *Everybody Needs a Rock*. Illus. by Peter Parnall. Scribner, 1974.

————. *Sometimes I Dance Mountains*. Illus. by Ken Longtemps. Photographs by Bill Sears. Scribner, 1973.

Bishop, Claire Hucket. *The Five Chinese Brothers*. Illus. by Kurt Wiese. Coward, 1938.

Callahan, Dorothy. *Under Christopher's Hat*. Scribner, 1972.

Emberley, Barbara. *Drummer Hoff*. Illus. by Ed Emberley. Prentice-Hall, 1967. PB.

Feelings, Muriel. *Moja Means One: A Swahili Counting Book*. Illus. by Tom Feelings. Dial, 1971.

Greenfield, Eloise. *She Come Bringing Me That Little Baby Girl*. Illus. by John Steptoe. Lippincott, 1974.

Hoberman, Mary Ann. *I Like Old Clothes*. Illus. by Jacqueline Chwast. Knopf, 1976.

Jarrell, Mary. *The Knee Baby*. Illus. by Symeon Shimin. Farrar, 1973.

Kraus, Robert. *Owliver*. Illus. by Jose Aruego and Ariane Dewey. Windmill/Dutton, 1974.

Kroll, Steven. *The Tyrannosaurus Game*. Illus. by Tomie de Paola. Holiday House, 1976.

Raskin, Ellen. *Nothing Ever Happens on My Block*. Atheneum, 1966. PB: Scholastic Book Services.

Sendak, Maurice. *In the Night Kitchen*. Harper, 1970.

Wildsmith, Brian. *Brian Wildsmith's Puzzles*. Watts, 1970.

PROFESSIONAL REFERENCES

Coller, Alan R. *Systems for the Observation of Classroom Behavior in Early Childhood Education*. Urbana, Ill.: ERIC Clearinghouse on Early Childhood Education, 1972.

Goodlad, John I., and M. Frances Klein. *Looking Behind the Classroom Door.* 2nd ed. Worthington, Ohio: Charles A. Jones Publishing, 1974.
    A general overview of observing in schools.

Hennings, Dorothy Grant. *Smiles, Nods, and Pauses: Activities to Enrich Children's Communication Skills.* New York: Citation Press, 1974.

Huck, Charlotte S. *Children's Literature in the Elementary School.* 3rd ed. New York: Holt, Rinehart and Winston, 1976.

Lindberg, Lucile, and Rita Swedlow. *Early Childhood Education: A Guide for Observation and Participation.* Boston: Allyn and Bacon, 1976.
    Chapter 16 deals specifically with books and stories.

Lundsteen, Sara W. *Children Learn to Communicate.* Englewood Cliffs, N. J.: Prentice-Hall, 1976.
    Observation of children's responses is highlighted throughout this language arts text.

Purves, Alan C., and Richard Beach. *Literature and the Reader: Research in Response to Literature, Reading Interests, and the Teaching of Literature.* Urbana, Ill.: National Council of Teachers of English, 1972.

Roderick, Jessie A., Diane M. Lee, and Louise M. Berman. *Observation: Basis for Planning, Implementing, and Evaluating.* Occasional Paper 16. College Park, Md.: University of Maryland, Center for Young Children, 1975.
    Contains a variety of observational guidelines developed in the Center for Young Children.

Ross, Ramon R. *Storyteller.* Columbus, Ohio: Charles E. Merrill, 1972.
    Chapter 2, "People to People," has suggestions for observing a person telling a story.

Thompson, James. *Beyond Words: Nonverbal Communication in the Classroom.* New York: Citation Press, 1973.

White, Mary Lou. *Children's Literature: Criticism and Response.* Columbus, Ohio: Charles E. Merrill, 1976.
    Chapter 5, "Helping Children Respond to Literature," as well as the other chapters, contains practical suggestions and activities.

The idea for identifying a basic collection of good books for young children was presented early in the discussion of the Committee on Literary Experiences for Preschool Children. We wanted to share with others the specific books that we had used to bring a light to children's eyes and that warmed children's hearts and our own. We wanted to tell others about certain books that were perennial favorites with children from many different backgrounds. As we each submitted our lists, certain authors' names reappeared. One person would like Ezra Jack Keats's *The Snowy Day* best, whereas another would like *Whistle for Willie* best. Finally, we decided to list outstanding authors and each of their books that we have found to be most popular with young children. There are a few authors for whom only one book is listed, but the appeal of that one book was such that it is included here.

The list of authors cited here can serve as a basic guide for selecting books for young children. Their work has consistently reflected both quality and appeal for children. It is highly probable that other work by these people will reflect a similar quality and appeal.

Some books on the list are particularly appropriate for certain activities. We do not think of reading Wanda Gág's *Millions of Cats* without asking children to join in on the refrain. We have indicated possible activities for specific books. You will think of many other ways to enhance children's appreciation of good books. Your primary task is to get children and books together.

Aldis, Dorothy. *All Together: A Child's Treasury of Verse.* Illus. by Marjorie Flack, Margaret Frieman, and Helen Jameson. Putnam, 1952.

A collection of 144 poems for young children. If you read aloud from it often, children will want to read it alone.
See also: *Favorite Poems of Dorothy Aldis.* Putnam, 1970.

Adams, Adrienne, illus. *Hansel and Gretel.* Trans. by Charles Scribner, Jr. Scribner, 1975.

Both the retelling and the illustrations are especially good in this edition of a favorite tale. Read aloud, dramatize, make a gingerbread house.
See also: *The Shoemaker and the Elves.* Scribner, 1960. PB.

Alderson, Brian. *Cakes and Custard.* Illus. by Helen Oxenbury. Morrow, 1975.

A new collection of well-illustrated Mother Goose. For reading aloud and reading alone.

Alexander, Martha. *Bobo's Dream.* Dial, 1970. PB: Scholastic Book Services.

A wordless book that young children can read alone. Tape record children's versions of the story.
See also: *I'll Protect You from the Jungle Beasts.* Dial, 1973.
       Nobody Asked Me If I Wanted a Baby Sister. Dial, 1971.
       Out, Out, Out. Dial, 1968.

Anno, Mitsumasa. *Anno's Alphabet: An Adventure in Imagination.* Crowell, 1975.

Letters of the alphabet look as if they were made of wood, with each represented by a large, clear, but unusual object on a facing page. The borders of the pages contain many other objects representing each letter, but they require careful searching.

Bemelmans, Ludwig. *Madeline.* Viking, 1939. PB.

Madeline is the smallest of the twelve little girls, in two straight lines, who live in Miss Clavel's boarding school. Her surprise appendectomy makes her the envy of the other girls. An old favorite with rhyming text and Bemelmans' expressionistic and child-like water color illustrations. Read aloud.
See also: *Madeline and the Bad Hat.* Viking, 1956. PB.
       Madeline in London. Viking, 1961. PB.
       Madeline's Rescue. Viking, 1953. PB.

Bodecker, N. M. *It's Raining Said John Twaining.* Atheneum, 1973.

Danish nursery rhymes translated and illustrated by Bodecker. Children will join in after hearing them a few times.

Brown, Marcia. *The Three Billy Goats Gruff.* Harcourt, 1957. PB.

The traditional tale of the three goats who had to outdo the troll to get to the good grass on the hillside. Brown's crayon and gouache illustrations seem just right for a Norwegian countryside. Lends itself to dramatization.

See also: *All Butterflies.* Scribner, 1974.

The Bun: A Tale from Russia. Harcourt, 1972.

How, Hippo. Scribner, 1969. PB.

Once a Mouse. Scribner, 1961.

Stone Soup. Scribner, 1947. PB.

Brown, Margaret Wise. *Four Fur Feet.* Illus. by Remy Charlip. Addison-Wesley, 1961.

All that is shown of the animal in this story is its four fur feet. As it walks around the world, the reader must turn the book in order that the feet stay at the top of the page (and on the top of the earth). Repetition of the refrain is good for choral speaking.

See also: *Goodnight Moon.* Illus. by Clement Hurd. Harper, 1947.

The Important Book. Illus. by Leonard Weisgard. Harper, 1949.

Nibble, Nibble. Illus. by Leonard Weisgard. Addison-Wesley, 1959.

The Runaway Bunny. Illus. by Clement Hurd. Harper, 1942, 1972.

Buckley, Helen E. *Grandfather and I.* Illus. by Paul Galdone. Lothrop, 1959.

A young boy and his grandfather like to take walks together because neither is in a hurry. The feeling of love for and enjoyment of each other permeates the story. Read aloud. Discussion.

See also: *Grandmother and I.* Illus. by Paul Galdone. Lothrop, 1961.

Michael Is Brave. Illus. by Emily A. McCully. Lothrop, 1971.

My Sister and I. Illus. by Paul Galdone. Lothrop, 1963.

Burningham, John. *Mr. Gumpy's Outing.* Holt, 1971.

Mr. Gumpy agrees to take two children and a variety of animals for a ride in his boat but warns each not to do certain things. All do just what they were not to do, the boat tips, they all get wet, and Mr. Gumpy good naturedly invites them all to his home for tea. Repetitive plot is good for a flannel board story.

See also: *Mr. Gumpy's Motorcar.* Macmillan, 1975.

Seasons. Bobbs-Merrill, 1970.

John Burningham's ABC. Bobbs-Merrill, 1967.

Burton, Virginia Lee. *Mike Mulligan and His Steam Shovel.* Houghton, 1939.

Mike Mulligan and his steam shovel Mary Ann find a new job after modern engines replace steam shovels. Read aloud. Create alternate endings.

See also: *Katy and the Big Snow.* Houghton, 1943. PB.

The Little House. Houghton, 1942.

Carle, Eric. *The Very Hungry Caterpillar.* Collins-World, 1970.

A caterpillar eats its way through the days of the week and through the pages of the book. The vivid use of color and bold design plus the holes left by the hungry caterpillar invite children's participation.

See also: *Do You Want to Be My Friend?* Crowell, 1971.

1, 2, 3 to the Zoo. Collins-World, 1968.

Clifton, Lucille. *Some of the Days of Everett Anderson.* Illus. by Evaline Ness. Holt, 1970. PB.

A book of poems about a week in the life of active six-year-old Everett Anderson, who is "black and runs and loves to hop." Read aloud. Discussion.

See also: *The Boy Who Didn't Believe in Spring.* Illus. by Brinton Turkle. Dutton, 1973.

My Brother Fine with Me. Illus. by Moneta Barnett. Holt, 1975.

Cohen, Miriam. *Will I Have a Friend?* Illus. by Lillian Hoban. Macmillan, 1967. PB.

A preschooler's concern for finding a friend during his first day in school. Situations appear true to what actually happens in many pre-school programs. Read aloud. Discussion.

See also: *Best Friends.* Illus. by Lillian Hoban. Macmillan, 1971. PB.

de Angeli, Marguerite. *Book of Nursery and Mother Goose Rhymes.* Double-day, 1953.

Hundreds of favorite verses in a beautifully illustrated book. Read aloud. Choral speaking. Dramatize. Browsing.

de Paola, Tomie. *Strega Nona.* Prentice-Hall, 1975.

Strega Nona's magic chant is overheard and misused, which creates a disaster. Read aloud. Cook spaghetti. Dramatize.

See also: *Charlie Needs a Cloak.* Prentice-Hall, 1974.

The Cloud Book. Holiday House, 1975.

Watch Out for Chicken Feet in Your Soup. Prentice-Hall, 1974.

de Regniers, Beatrice Schenk. *May I Bring a Friend?* Illus. by Beni Montresor. Atheneum, 1964. PB.

A boy is invited to have tea with the king and queen, and each time he goes, he takes a different animal friend, most of whom perform funny antics. Illustrations resemble stage settings and are arranged so the readers can anticipate which friend comes next. Rhymed text is good for choral speaking.

See also: *A Little House of Your Own.* Illus. by Irene Haas. Harcourt, 1955.

Poems Children Will Sit Still For. Citation, 1969. PB: Scholastic Book Services.

Domanska, Janina. *The Turnip.* Macmillan, 1969. PB.

A great deal of help is needed to harvest a turnip. Surprisingly, a tiny bird makes the difference. Compare with other versions of the same tale.

See also: *Din, Dan, Don, It's Christmas.* Greenwillow, 1975.

I Saw a Ship a-Sailing. Macmillan, 1972.

If All the Seas Were One Sea. Macmillan, 1971.

Spring Is. Greenwillow, 1976.

What Do You See? Macmillan, 1974.

Duvoisin, Roger. *Petunia.* Knopf, 1950. PB.

> Petunia learns that it takes more than carrying a book around to make one wise. Read aloud.

See also: *Petunia, I Love You.* Knopf, 1965.
> *Petunia's Treasure.* Knopf, 1975.
> *Veronica.* Knopf, 1961. PB.

Emberley, Barbara. *Drummer Hoff.* Illus. by Ed Emberley. Prentice-Hall, 1967. PB.

> Written in repetitive verse; tells of the firing of a cannon and the events leading up to it. This book is excellent for young readers and listeners and for joining in on the refrain.

See also: *Simon's Song.* Illus. by Ed Emberley. Prentice-Hall, 1969. PB.

Emberley, Ed. *London Bridge Is Falling Down.* Little, 1967.

> The familiar nursery song is presented with lively illustrations that will invite children to sing along.

Ets, Marie Hall. *Play with Me.* Viking, 1955. PB.

> The animals run away when the little girl tries to catch them, but they come back when she sits quietly. Dramatize.

See also: *Gilberto and the Wind.* Viking, 1963. PB.
> *In the Forest.* Viking, 1974. PB.
> *Talking without Words.* Viking, 1968.

Feelings, Muriel. *Moja Means One: A Swahili Counting Book.* Illus. by Tom Feelings. Dial, 1971.

> The numbers from one to ten in Swahili (and English, of course). Designed to acquaint children with life in a West African country. Develops concepts of numbers.

See also: *Jambo Means Hello: A Swahili Alphabet Book.* Illus. by Tom Feelings. Dial, 1974.

Fisher, Aileen. *Cricket in a Thicket.* Illus. by Feodor Rojankovsky. Scribner, 1963. PB.

> A collection of nature poems for young children. Read aloud, read alone, and read together.

See also: *Feathered Ones and Furry.* Illus. by Eric Carle. Crowell, 1971.
> *Going Barefoot.* Illus. by Adrienne Adams. Crowell, 1960.
> *I Like Weather.* Illus. by Janina Domanska. Crowell, 1963.
> *In One Door and Out the Other: A Book of Poems.* Illus. by Lillian Hoban. Crowell, 1969.
> *In the Middle of the Night.* Illus. by Adrienne Adams. Crowell, 1965.
> *In the Woods, in the Meadow, in the Sky.* Illus. by Margot Tomes. Scribner, 1965.
> *Listen Rabbit.* Illus. by Symeon Shimin. Crowell, 1964.

> *The Ways of Animals.* Bowmar, 1973. Ten books, ten film-
> strips, cassettes or records, and teacher's guide.
> *Where Does Everyone Go?* Illus. by Adrienne Adams.
> Crowell, 1961.

Flack, Marjorie. *Ask Mr. Bear.* Macmillan, 1932, 1958. PB.

> Danny asks the advice of a succession of animals as he tries to
> decide on a birthday present for his mother. Finally Mr. Bear provides
> an acceptable answer—a big birthday bear hug. The surprise ending
> and the repetitive plot make this a good one for the flannel board.
> See also: *The Story about Ping.* Illus. by Kurt Wiese. Viking, 1933.
> PB.

Freeman, Don. *Dandelion.* Viking, 1964. PB.

> Dandelion, a lion with a most expressive face, is invited to a come-
> as-you-are party, but rather than following this suggestion, he gets a
> haircut, buys new clothes, and is subsequently not recognized by the
> hostess. A rainstorm restores his usual looks, and Dandelion learns to
> be himself. Read aloud. Discussion.
> See also: *Corduroy.* Viking, 1968. PB.
>   *Mop Top.* Viking, 1955. PB.
>   *Quiet! There's a Canary in the Library.* Golden Gate, 1969.

Gág, Wanda. *Millions of Cats.* Coward, 1928.

> A lonely little old man goes off to find a cat for himself and his
> lonely wife. He returns with "hundreds of cats, thousands of cats,
> millions and billions and trillions of cats." A terrible fight eliminates
> all but one. Told in the style of a folktale, the repetition of the refrain
> invites participation.
> See also: *Nothing at All.* Coward, 1928.

Galdone, Paul. *The Frog Prince.* McGraw, 1975.

> Galdone has illustrated many of the favorite old tales. Many can be
> dramatized, compared with other versions of the tales, and done on
> the flannel board. All should be read aloud often.
> See also: *The Gingerbread Boy.* Seabury, 1975.
>   *Henny Penny.* Seabury, 1968.
>   *The House That Jack Built.* McGraw, 1961.
>   *The Little Red Hen.* Seabury, 1973. PB: Scholastic Book
>   Services.
>   *Little Red Riding Hood.* McGraw, 1974.
>   *The Old Woman and Her Pig.* McGraw, 1960.
>   *The Three Bears.* Seabury, 1972. PB: Scholastic Book
>   Services.
>   *The Three Billy Goats Gruff.* Seabury, 1973.
>   *The Three Little Pigs.* Seabury, 1970.

Geisel, Theodor S. [Dr. Seuss]. *Horton Hatches the Egg.* Random, 1940.

> Horton, the elephant who is 100 percent faithful, sits on the egg of
> lazy Maizy as promised, and despite many trials and tribulations, he
> successfully hatches an elephant bird. Read aloud. Children will pick
> up the repetitive refrain.

See also: *And to Think That I Saw It on Mulberry Street.* Vanguard, 1937.

Five Hundred Hats of Bartholomew Cubbins. Vanguard, 1938.

Horton Hears a Who. Random, 1954.

Ginsburg, Mirra. *Mushroom in the Rain.* Illus. by Jose Aruego and Ariane Dewey. Macmillan, 1974.

The mushroom grows to provide shelter for all the animals who want to get in out of the rain. Compare with Tresselt's *The Mitten.*
See also: *The Chick and the Duckling.* Illus. by Jose Aruego and Ariane Aruego. Macmillan, 1972.

Goodall, John S. *Naughty Nancy.* Atheneum, 1975.

Nancy was supposed to be the flower girl in her sister's wedding, but she finds more interesting things to do. A wordless book good for storytelling. Tape record children's versions of the story.
See also: *Jacko.* Harcourt, 1971.

The Adventures of Paddy Pork. Harcourt, 1968.
The Midnight Adventures of Kelly, Dot and Esmeralda. Atheneum, 1972.
Paddy's Evening Out. Atheneum, 1973.
Shrewbettina's Birthday. Harcourt, 1971.

Greenfield, Eloise. *She Come Bringing Me That Little Baby Girl.* Illus. by John Steptoe. Lippincott, 1974.

Sibling rivalry is portrayed anew as a boy dislikes the attention paid to his new sister. Finding out that his mother was once a baby girl helps the boy overcome the resentment. Natural black dialect is used to express a universal feeling. Read aloud. Discussion.

Hill, Elizabeth Starr. *Evan's Corner.* Illus. by Nancy Grossman. Holt, 1967. PB.

A young boy's need to establish a place of his own in a crowded apartment. Plan your own private place. Compare with de Regniers' *A Little House of Your Own.*

Hoban, Russell. *A Birthday for Frances.* Illus. by Lillian Hoban. Harper, 1968.

Frances suffers pangs of jealousy when the family prepares to celebrate her little sister's birthday; spending two whole allowances for a gift is almost more than she can bear. Read aloud. Discussion.
See also: *A Baby Sister for Frances.* Illus. by Lillian Hoban. Harper, 1964.

A Bargain for Frances. Illus. by Lillian Hoban. Harper, 1970.
Bedtime for Frances. Illus. by Garth Williams. Harper, 1960.
Best Friends for Frances. Illus. by Lillian Hoban. Harper, 1969.
Bread and Jam for Frances. Illus. by Lillian Hoban. Harper, 1964. PB: Scholastic Book Services.

Hoban, Tana. *Look Again.* Macmillan, 1971.

Plain white frames invite the viewer to predict what lies on the next page and to view again the one just passed.

See also: *Big Ones, Little Ones.* Greenwillow, 1976.

Circles, Triangles and Squares. Macmillan, 1974.

Count and See. Macmillan, 1972. PB.

Dig, Drill, Dump, Fill. Greenwillow, 1975.

Over, Under, and Through and Other Spatial Concepts. Macmillan, 1973.

Push Pull, Empty Full: A Book of Opposites. Macmillan, 1972. PB.

Shapes and Things. Macmillan, 1970.

Where Is It? Macmillan, 1974.

Hogrogian, Nonny. *One Fine Day.* Macmillan, 1971. PB.

The fox gets his tail chopped off for drinking the old woman's milk. He travels far before he can find anyone to cooperate in helping him get his tail back. Plot the action. Make a mural. Dramatize.

See also: *Rooster Brother.* Macmillan, 1974.

Hutchins, Pat. *Rosie's Walk.* Macmillan, 1968. PB.

Rosie's life is charmed, for every time the fox tries to catch her some fortunate accident prevents him. Rosie saunters happily along with a twinkle in her eye that suggests she planned all the "accidents." Plot the action. Dramatize.

See also: *Changes, Changes.* Macmillan, 1971. PB.

Clocks and More Clocks. Macmillan, 1970. PB.

Don't Forget the Bacon. Greenwillow, 1976.

Goodnight Owl. Macmillan, 1972. PB.

The Surprise Party. Macmillan, 1969. PB.

Titch. Macmillan, 1971. PB.

Jeffers, Susan. *Three Jovial Huntsmen: A Mother Goose Rhyme.* Bradbury, 1973.

The three hunters do not see all the animals hidden in the forest but children will find them. Read aloud. Read alone.

See also: *All the Pretty Horses.* Macmillan, 1974.

Johnson, Crockett. *Harold and the Purple Crayon.* Harper, 1955.

Harold solves his problems by drawing himself a make-believe world with his purple crayon. Storytelling. Roller movie.

See also: *A Picture for Harold's Room.* Harper, 1960. PB: Scholastic Book Services.

Keats, Ezra Jack. *The Snowy Day.* Viking, 1962. PB.

Peter is a black child having fun in the snow, experimenting with making tracks, angels, and snowmen. He discovers the snowball he saved has melted.

See also: *Goggles.* Macmillan, 1970. PB.

Hi, Cat. Macmillan, 1970. PB.

Louie. Greenwillow, 1975.

Pet Show. Macmillan, 1972. PB.
Peter's Chair. Harper, 1967.
Whistle for Willie. Viking, 1964. PB.

Kellogg, Steven. *There Was an Old Woman.* Parents, 1974.

A humorous version of a favorite song. This cumulative tale can be told with a flannel board. Sing along.

Kent, Jack. *The Blah.* Parents, 1970.

A story for kids who think that nobody pays any attention to them. Billy doesn't think anybody has time for him; in fact, he thinks he must be a Blah. So Billy creates a whole army of Blahs and has great fun.
See also: *The Egg Book.* Macmillan, 1975.
          The Fat Cat: A Danish Folktale. Parents, 1971. PB: Scholastic Book Services.

Kraus, Robert. *Whose Mouse Are You?* Illus. by Jose Aruego. Macmillan, 1970. PB.

A simple rhyming story in which a mouse answers questions about his missing family. Children give his answers after the first reading.
See also: *Herman the Helper.* Illus. by Jose Aruego and Ariane Dewey. Windmill, 1974.
          Leo the Late Bloomer. Illus. by Jose Aruego. Windmill, 1971. PB.
          Milton the Early Riser. Illus. by Jose Aruego and Ariane Dewey. Windmill, 1972.
          Three Friends. Illus. by Jose Aruego and Ariane Dewey. Windmill, 1975.

Krauss, Ruth. *The Carrot Seed.* Illus. by Crockett Johnson. Harper, 1945. PB: Scholastic Book Services.

A simple story of a child planting a seed which no one else believes will come up. The surprising climax restores faith. Songs, repetition, flannel board story, dramatization follow the reading.
See also: *The Backward Day.* Illus. by Marc Simont. Harper, 1950.
          A Hole Is to Dig. Illus. by Maurice Sendak. Harper, 1952.
          A Very Special House. Illus. by Maurice Sendak. Harper, 1953.

Kuskin, Karla. *The Rose on My Cake.* Harper, 1964.

Whimsical poetry with simple line drawings. Read aloud. Choral speaking.
See also: *Just Like Everyone Else.* Harper, 1959.

Langstaff, John. *Over in the Meadow.* Illus. by Feodor Rojankovsky. Harcourt, 1957. PB.

Number concepts are presented in verse and song. Read and sing along.
See also: *Frog Went a' Courtin.* Illus. by Feodor Rojankovsky. Harcourt, 1955. PB.
          Oh, A-Hunting We Will Go. Illus. by Nancy Winslow Parker. Atheneum, 1974.

Lexau, Joan M. *Emily and the Klunky Baby and the Next Door Dog.* Illus. by Martha Alexander. Dial, 1972.

Emily's parents are divorced and her mother is too busy to play with her. She runs away from home with her klunky baby brother hoping to find their daddy. Discussion. Read aloud.

See also: *Benjie.* Illus. by Don Bolognese. Dial, 1964.

Benjie on His Own. Illus. by Don Bolognese. Dial, 1970.

Me Day. Illus. by Robert Weaver. Dial, 1971.

Lindgren, Astrid. *The Tomten.* Illus. by Harald Wiberg. Coward, 1961.

The Tomten is a troll who wanders around the farm, seen only by animals, never by people. In the cold of winter he reassures the animals that spring will come, repeating the same refrain. Choral speaking.

See also: *The Tomten and the Fox.* Illus. by Harald Wiberg. Coward, 1966.

Lionni, Leo. *Swimmy.* Pantheon, 1963.

Swimmy helps the other little fish by showing them how to swim together to escape from the big fish. Mobiles, murals. Creative dramatics.

See also: *Alexander and the Wind Up Mouse.* Pantheon, 1969. PB.

Fish Is Fish. Pantheon, 1970. PB.

Frederick. Pantheon, 1967.

Little Blue and Little Yellow. Astor-Honor, 1959.

Pezzetino. Pantheon, 1975.

Lobel, Arnold. *Frog and Toad Together.* Harper, 1972.

An easy-to-read story with lots of humor and characterization.

See also: *Frog and Toad Are Friends.* Harper, 1970.

Hansel and Gretel. Delacorte, 1971.

Mouse Tales. Harper, 1972.

Owl at Home. Harper, 1975.

McCloskey, Robert. *Make Way for Ducklings.* Viking, 1941. PB.

A mother and father mallard must find a new home in the city for their family of ducklings. On the way to their island in the Charles River, the ducks stop traffic with the aid of a friendly policeman. Read aloud.

See also: *Blueberries for Sal.* Viking, 1948. PB.

One Morning in Maine. Viking, 1952. PB.

McCord, David. *Every Time I Climb a Tree.* Illus. by Marc Simont. Little, 1967.

Twenty-five poems in picture book format, including "The Pickety Fence," "Pad and Pencil," and "This Is My Rock."

See also: *Star in the Pail.* Illus. by Marc Simont. Little, 1975.

Marshall, James. *George and Martha.* Houghton, 1972. PB.

A series of stories about two great hippopotamus chums. Create new stories about George and Martha.

See also: *George and Martha Encore.* Houghton, 1973.
   The Guest. Houghton, 1975.
   Yummers. Houghton, 1973.

Massie, Diane. *Dazzle.* Parents, 1969.

A magnificent peacock who proclaims himself lord of the jungle is challenged by the lion. Creative dramatics.
See also: *Walter Was a Frog.* Scribner, 1970.

Matthiesen, Thomas. *ABC: An Alphabet Book.* Platt and Munk, 1968.

An alphabet book illustrated with simple color photographs of common everyday objects.
See also: *Things to See: A Child's World of Familiar Objects.* Platt and Munk, 1966.

Mayer, Mercer. *Frog, Where Are You?* Dial, 1969.

One of several wordless books about Frog. Create new stories.
See also: *A Boy, a Dog, and a Frog.* Dial, 1967.
   Frog Goes to Dinner. Dial, 1974.
   One Frog Too Many (with Marianna Mayer). Dial, 1975.

Milne, A. A. *When We Were Very Young.* Illus. by E. H. Shepard. Dutton, 1924. PB: Dell.

A collection of poems written for the author's son. Favorites for memorization.
See also: *Now We Are Six.* Dutton, 1927. PB: Dell.

Minarik, Else Holmelund. *Little Bear.* Illus. by Maurice Sendak. Harper, 1957.

A collection of four stories: Little Bear plays in the snow, makes "birthday soup," pretends to go to the moon, and finally talks with his mother at bedtime.
See also: *Father Bear Comes Home.* Illus. by Maurice Sendak. Harper, 1959.
   A Kiss for Little Bear. Illus. by Maurice Sendak. Harper, 1968.
   Little Bear's Friend. Illus. by Maurice Sendak. Harper, 1960.
   Little Bear's Visit. Illus. by Maurice Sendak. Harper, 1961.

Mosel, Arlene. *Tikki Tikki Tembo.* Illus. by Blair Lent. Holt, 1968.

Tikki Tikki Tembo's long name nearly costs him his life in this tale which explains why Chinese names are now so short. Choral speaking. Creative dramatics.
See also: *The Funny Little Woman.* Illus. by Blair Lent. Dutton, 1972.

Munari, Bruno. *Bruno Munari's ABC.* Collins-World, 1960.

Imaginative interpretation of the letters of the alphabet in large, clear pictures. Find the tiny fly which creeps onto pages that are not his own.
See also: *Animals for Sale.* World Publishing, 1957.
   The Birthday Present. World Publishing, 1959.

Bruno Munari's Zoo. Collins-World, 1963.
The Circus in the Mist. Collins-World, 1975.
The Elephant's Wish. World Publishing, 1959.
Tic, Tac, and Toc. Collins-World, 1970.
Who's There? Open the Door. World Publishing, 1957.

Ness, Evaline. *Sam, Bangs and Moonshine*. Holt, 1966. PB.

Sam (Samantha) has a cat named Bangs who talks to her. *Moonshine* is the word for all the fibs Sam tells herself. One day her Moonshine tale causes real trouble. Read aloud. Discussion.

See also: *Amelia Mixed the Mustard*. Scribner, 1975.
Do You Have the Time, Lydia? Dutton, 1971. PB.
Exactly Alike. Scribner, 1964.
Old Mother Hubbard and Her Dog. Holt, 1972. PB.
Tom Tit Tot (by Joseph Jacobs). Scribner, 1965.
Yeck, Eck. Dutton, 1974.

Peet, Bill. *The Wump World*. Houghton, 1970.

The planet of the Wumps is invaded by the Pollutions who destroy the quiet, peaceful world and then move on. Children will understand the message and will engage in a lively discussion about ecology.

See also: *The Ant and the Elephant*. Houghton, 1972.
Chester the Worldly Pig. Houghton, 1965.
The Gnats of Knotty Pine. Houghton, 1975.
Hubert's Hair Raising Adventure. Houghton, 1959.
The Pinkish, Purplish, Bluish Egg. Houghton, 1963.
The Whingdingdilly. Houghton, 1970.

Pieńkowski, Jan. *Shapes*. Harvey House, 1975.

Circles, squares, and triangles appear in simple line drawings of familiar objects. Three year olds can read it alone.

See also: *Numbers*. Harvey House, 1975.

Piper, Watty. *The Little Engine That Could*. Illus. by George and Doris Hauman. Platt and Munk, 1930, 1954.

The classic story of the little engine that carried the trainload of toys across the mountain top because it thought it could, it thought it could. Children repeat the refrain readily.

Potter, Beatrix. *The Tale of Peter Rabbit*. Warne, 1902. PB: Scholastic Book Services.

The classic tale of disobedient Peter Rabbit and his frightening adventure in Mr. MacGregor's garden, ending with Peter properly chastised, but secure and safe. Read this and the other Potter titles aloud.

See also: *The Sly Old Cat*. Warne, 1906, 1972.
The Tale of Benjamin Bunny. Warne, 1904. PB: Dover.
The Tale of Jemima Puddleduck. Warne, 1908, 1936.
The Tale of Jeremy Fisher. Warne, 1906. PB: Dover.
The Tale of Mrs. Tiggy Winkle. Warne, 1905. PB: Dover.
The Tale of Tom Kitten. Warne, 1907.

Prelutsky, Jack. *The Pack Rat's Day.* Illus. by Margaret Bloy Graham. Macmillan, 1974.

Prelutsky's poems give the essence of the animal he describes from the inside out. Choral speaking. Memorization.

See also: *Circus.* Illus. by Arnold Lobel. Macmillan, 1974.

A Gopher in the Garden. Illus. by Robert Leydenfrost. Macmillan, 1967.

Toucans Two. Illus. by Jose Aruego. Macmillan, 1970.

Preston, Edna Mitchell. *Pop Corn and Ma Goodness.* Illus. by Robert Andrew Parker. Viking, 1969. PB.

The story of Pop Corn and Ma Goodness, their meeting, marriage, hardships, and good times, written in nonsensical verse and illustrated with simple watercolor paintings which enhance the rural atmosphere of the book. Read aloud.

See also: *Squawk to the Moon, Little Goose.* Illus. by Barbara Cooney. Viking, 1974.

The Temper Tantrum Book. Illus. by Rainey Bennett. Viking, 1969. PB.

Quackenbush, Robert. *Clementine.* Lippincott, 1974.

Favorite old songs are illustrated with zest and humorous appeal. Good for sing-alongs since the music is included.

See also: *Go Tell Aunt Rhody.* Lippincott, 1973.

The Man on the Flying Trapeze. Lippincott, 1975.

Old MacDonald Had a Farm. Lippincott, 1972.

Pop Goes the Weasel and Yankee Doodle. Lippincott, 1976.

She'll Be Comin' 'Round the Mountain. Lippincott, 1973.

Skip to My Lou. Lippincott, 1975.

There'll Be a Hot Time in the Old Town Tonight. Lippincott, 1974.

Raskin, Ellen. *Nothing Ever Happens on My Block.* Atheneum, 1966. PB: Scholastic Book Services.

All the while a child complains that nothing ever happens on his block, the wildest things *are* happening. A fire, a robbery, and a wild chase occur although he never notices a thing.

See also: *Spectacles.* Atheneum, 1968. PB.

Who, Said Sue, Said Whoo? Atheneum, 1973.

Reiss, John J. *Numbers.* Bradbury Press, 1971.

Bold pictures with lavish use of bright colors show the numbers one to twenty and, by tens, thirty to one hundred. Young children will want to look through it repeatedly.

See also: *Colors.* Bradbury Press, 1969.

Rey, Hans Augusto. *Curious George.* Houghton, 1941. PB.

The first of many books about a monkey whose curiosity gets him into trouble. Storytelling. Create new Curious George stories.

See also: *Curious George Gets a Medal.* Houghton, 1957. PB.

Curious George Rides a Bike. Houghton, 1952. PB.

Curious George Goes to the Hospital (with Margaret Rey). Houghton, 1966.

Rockwell, Anne. *The Three Bears and 15 Other Stories.* Crowell, 1975.

Sixteen old favorites are presented here with simple illustrations. Read aloud. Compare with different versions of the same tales. Dramatize. Flannel board.

See also: *Big Boss.* Macmillan, 1975.
   Games (and How to Play Them). Crowell, 1973.
   Toad. Illus. by Harlow Rockwell. Doubleday, 1972.
   The Toolbox. Illus. by Harlow Rockwell. Macmillan, 1971. PB.

Rockwell, Harlow. *My Doctor.* Macmillan, 1973.

Large and clear illustrations show a doctor's procedures and equipment. Large print and ample white space add to the visual clarity. Browse. Discussion.

See also: *I Did It.* Macmillan, 1974.
   Machines (with Anne Rockwell). Macmillan, 1972.
   My Dentist. Greenwillow, 1975.
   Printmaking. Doubleday, 1974.

Scott, Ann Herbert. *Sam.* Illus. by Symeon Shimin. McGraw, 1967.

Sam becomes upset when nothing he wants to do or tries to do is appreciated by the members of his family. He feels rejected until the family realizes how unhappy he is and begins to make him feel needed and important. Dramatize.

See also: *On Mother's Lap.* Illus. by Glo Coalson. McGraw, 1972.

Segal, Lore. *Tell Me a Mitzi.* Illus. by Harriet Pincus. Farrar, 1970.

Three stories which border on fantasy are the result of Mitzi's plea to her mother to "tell me a Mitzi" about all the things Mitzi would like to do. Create new Mitzi stories.

See also: *All the Way Home.* Illus. by James Marshall. Farrar, 1973.
   The Juniper Tree and Other Tales from Grimm (Grimm Brothers). 2 vols. Trans. by Lore Segal and Randall Jarrell. Illus. by Maurice Sendak. Farrar, 1973. PB.

Sendak, Maurice. *Where the Wild Things Are.* Harper, 1963.

Max wears his wolf suit, gets into mischief, is sent to bed supperless, and sails in his dreams to where the wild things are. After a wild rumpus with the wild things, he returns to his very own room where his hot supper is waiting. Repetition, dramatization, puppetry are natural follow-up activities.

See also: *In the Night Kitchen.* Harper, 1970.
   Pierre and *Chicken Soup with Rice* in *The Nutshell Library.* Harper, 1962.
   Really Rosie. Music by Carole King. Harper, 1975. PB.

Shulevitz, Uri. *Rain, Rain, Rivers.* Farrar, 1969.

Rain is described in a variety of settings, with the child who is actually experiencing the rain living in a city. Expressive, poetic text leads to repetition.

See also: *Dawn.* Farrar, 1974.

The Fool of the World and the Flying Ship. Retold by Arthur Ransome. Farrar, 1968.

One Monday Morning. Scribner, 1967. PB.

Slobodkina, Esphyr. *Caps for Sale.* Addison-Wesley, 1947.

A peddler loses his caps to some mischievous monkeys. After much unsuccessful shouting and foot stomping, he inadvertently discovers how to get his caps back. Dramatize. Puppetry. Flannel board.

Spier, Peter. *Fast-Slow, High-Low: A Book of Opposites.* Doubleday, 1972.

A book of opposites which presents concepts such as size, speed, spatial relations, quantity, texture, and temperature through comparisons.

See also: *Crash, Bang, Boom.* Doubleday, 1972.

The Erie Canal. Doubleday, 1970. PB.

The Fox Went Out on a Chilly Night. Doubleday, 1961. PB.

Gobble, Growl, Grunt. Doubleday, 1971.

Hurrah. We're Outward Bound. Doubleday, 1968.

London Bridge Is Falling Down. Doubleday, 1967. PB.

The Star Spangled Banner. Doubleday, 1973.

To Market, to Market. Doubleday, 1967. PB.

Steig, William. *Amos and Boris.* Farrar, 1971.

A friendship between Amos the mouse and Boris the whale. Compare with *The Lion and the Rat.*

See also: *Sylvester and the Magic Pebble.* Windmill, 1969. PB.

Steptoe, John. *Stevie.* Harper, 1969.

Robert resents the intrusion of little Stevie when Stevie becomes a boarder in his home for a while but misses him when he is gone. Natural dialect catches the language style of some blacks.

Stobbs, William. *Rumpelstiltskin.* Walck, 1970.

A vividly illustrated edition to compare with other versions of the Rumpelstiltskin story.

See also: *Jack and the Beanstalk.* Delacorte, 1969.

Johnny Cake. Viking, 1973. PB.

Little Red Riding Hood. Walck, 1972.

Tolstoy, Alexei. *The Great Big Enormous Turnip.* Illus. by Helen Oxenbury. Watts, 1969.

Children can recognize the slight variations between this and other turnip stories. Compare with *The Turnip* by Janina Domanska. Flannel board.

Tresselt, Alvin. *Hide and Seek Fog.* Illus. by Roger Duvoisin. Lothrop, 1965.

A mood is created through the description of the fog and its effect on the lives of people in a little fishing village. Read aloud. Make fog pictures.

See also: *The Beaver Pond.* Illus. by Roger Duvoisin. Lothrop, 1970.

The Dead Tree. Illus. by Charles Robinson. Parents, 1972.

It's Time Now. Illus. by Roger Duvoisin. Harper, 1969.

The Mitten. Illus. by Yaroslava. Lothrop, 1964.

Wake Up City. Illus. by Roger Duvoisin. Lothrop, 1957.

Wake Up Farm. Illus. by Roger Duvoisin. Lothrop, 1955.

White Snow, Bright Snow. Illus. by Roger Duvoisin. Lothrop, 1947.

The World in the Candy Egg. Illus. by Roger Duvoisin. Lothrop, 1967.

Turkle, Brinton. *Thy Friend, Obadiah.* Viking, 1969. PB.

Much to Obadiah's displeasure, a sea gull decides to follow him around. Then suddenly it disappears and Obadiah finds himself looking for the bird. He finds the sea gull and discovers a rusty fishhook stuck in the bird's beak. After Obadiah removes the hook, the bird again follows him around, but this time Obadiah enjoys his friend. Read aloud. Discussion.

See also: *The Adventures of Obadiah.* Viking, 1972. PB.

Obadiah the Bold. Viking, 1965. PB.

The Sky Dog. Viking, 1969. PB.

Udry, Janice May. *Let's Be Enemies.* Illus. by Maurice Sendak. Harper, 1961. PB: Scholastic Book Services.

The trials of friendship and the ready forgiveness of young children are aptly portrayed. Compare with *The Quarreling Book* by Charlotte Zolotow and *I'm Not Oscar's Friend Anymore* by Marjorie Weinman Sharmat (illus. by Tony DeLuna; Dutton, 1975).

See also: *Mary Jo's Grandmother.* Illus. by Eleanor Mill. A. Whitman, 1970.

The Moon Jumpers. Illus. by Maurice Sendak. Harper, 1959.

A Tree Is Nice. Illus. by Marc Simont. Harper, 1956.

What Mary Jo Shared. Illus. by Eleanor Mill. A. Whitman, 1966. PB: Scholastic Book Services.

What Mary Jo Wanted. Illus. by Eleanor Mill. A. Whitman, 1968.

Ungerer, Tomi. *Crictor.* Harper, 1958. PB: Scholastic Book Services.

A pet boa constrictor is used as a slide and a jump rope and captures a burglar in a hilariously absurd story. Art activities. Stuffed animals. Dioramas.

See also: *Zeralda's Ogre.* Harper, 1967.

Viorst, Judith. *Alexander and the Terrible, Horrible, No Good, Very Bad Day.* Illus. by Ray Cruz. Atheneum, 1972.

The terrible situations a young boy experiences on one of those days when nothing goes as it should. Create your own story of a bad day.

See also: *I'll Fix Anthony.* Illus. by Arnold Lobel. Harper, 1969.
The Tenth Good Thing about Barney. Illus. by Erik Blegvad. Atheneum, 1971. PB.

Waber, Bernard. *Ira Sleeps Over.* Houghton, 1975. PB.

Ira has no misgivings about spending his first night sleeping at a friend's house—until his sister plants the seeds of doubt. Read aloud. Discussion. Dramatize.

See also: *A Firefly Named Torchy.* Houghton, 1970.
The House on East 88th Street. Houghton, 1962. PB.
Lyle, Lyle Crocodile. Houghton, 1965. PB.
"You Look Ridiculous" Said the Rhinoceros to the Hippopotamus. Houghton, 1966.

Watson, Clyde. *Father Fox's Pennyrhymes.* Illus. by Wendy Watson. Crowell, 1971. PB: Scholastic Book Services.

Father Fox sings happy nursery rhymes with bouncy, rhythmic, and often nonsensical word play. Repetition is a natural outcome of hearing the verses.

Ward, Lynd. *The Biggest Bear.* Houghton, 1952. PB.

Johnny Orchard finds a bear cub in the forest and takes him home to care for him, never realizing that as the bear grows in size, so will the bear's appetite and his own problems. Read aloud.

See also: *The Silver Pony.* Houghton, 1973.

Watts, Bernadette. *Rapunzel.* Crowell, 1974, 1975.

This beautiful oversized interpretation of *Rapunzel* is good to compare with that of other artists.

See also: *Little Red Riding Hood.* World Publishing, 1968. PB: Scholastic Book Services.

Wezel, Peter. *The Good Bird.* Harper, 1964.

The good bird befriends a goldfish trapped in a bowl. Large crayon-like drawings tell the story without words. Tape record children's versions of the story.

See also: *The Naughty Bird.* Follett, 1967.

Wildsmith, Brian. *Brian Wildsmith's Mother Goose.* Watts, 1965.

A colorful collection of Mother Goose rhymes in Wildsmith's unique style. Read aloud. Repetition.

See also: *Birds.* Watts, 1967.
Brian Wildsmith's ABC's. Watts, 1963.
Brian Wildsmith's 1, 2, 3's. Watts, 1965.
Brian Wildsmith's Puzzles. Watts, 1970.
A Child's Garden of Verses (by Robert Louis Stevenson). Watts, 1966.
Circus. Watts, 1970.
The Lazy Bear. Watts, 1975.

The Lion and the Rat (by Jean de La Fontaine). Watts, 1964.
Python's Party. Watts, 1975.
Wild Animals. Watts, 1967.

Williams, Garth. *The Rabbits' Wedding.* Harper, 1958.

Soft, furry rabbits run and play together throughout the forest. The other animals dance around them in a wedding circle. Read aloud. Enjoy.
See also: *Baby's First Book.* Western, 1955.

Yashima, Taro. *Umbrella.* Viking, 1958. PB.

Momo is anxious to use the new umbrella she received as a present on her third birthday. The sounds of the rain invite a chorus of children's voices.
See also: *Crow Boy.* Viking, 1955. PB.
        Momo's Kitten. Viking, 1961. PB.
        Plenty to Watch. Viking, 1954.
        Seashore Story. Viking, 1967.
        Youngest One. Viking, 1962.

Zemach, Harve. *Duffy and the Devil.* Illus. by Margot Zemach. Farrar, 1973.

This Cornish version of *Rumpelstiltskin* can be compared with the German and English versions of the same story.
See also: *The Judge: An Untrue Tale.* Illus. by Margot Zemach. Farrar, 1969.
        Nail Soup. Illus. by Margot Zemach. Follett, 1964.
        A Penny a Look: An Old Story. Illus. by Margot Zemach. Farrar, 1971.
        The Speckled Hen: A Russian Nursery Rhyme. Illus. by Margot Zemach. Holt, 1966. PB.

Zion, Eugene. *Harry the Dirty Dog.* Illus. by Margaret Bloy Graham. Harper, 1956.

Harry, a white dog with black spots, hates baths so much that when he hears the tub filling, he runs away from home. He tours the town and gets so dirty that he becomes a black dog with white spots. Thus, when Harry returns home his family doesn't recognize him until he has a bath. Compare with Don Freeman's *Dandelion.*
See also: *Dear Garbage Man.* Illus. by Margaret Bloy Graham. Harper, 1957.
        Harry by the Sea. Illus. by Margaret Bloy Graham. Harper, 1965.
        The Plant Sitter. Illus. by Margaret Bloy Graham. Harper, 1959. PB: Scholastic Book Services.

Zolotow, Charlotte. *William's Doll.* Illus. by William Pène du Bois. Harper, 1972.

William wants a doll in spite of being called a creep and a sissy and in spite of his worried father's gifts of a basketball and a train set. Grandmother takes him shopping and explains to his father why it is important for William to have a doll.

See also: *A Father Like That.* Illus. by Ben Shecter. Harper, 1971.

The Hating Book. Illus. by Ben Shecter. Harper, 1969.

If It Weren't for You. Illus. by Ben Shecter. Harper, 1966.

Mr. Rabbit and the Lovely Present. Illus. by Maurice Sendak. Harper, 1962.

My Friend John. Illus. by Ben Shecter. Harper, 1968.

My Grandson Lew. Illus. by William Pène du Bois. Harper, 1974.

When I Have a Son. Illus. by Hilary Knight. Harper, 1967.

When the Wind Stops. Illus. by Howard Knotts. Harper, 1975.

AUTHORS AND ILLUSTRATORS

TITLES